Henry Sturcke
On Second Thought

On Second Thought

From a Sect Called Worldwide to a Wider World Community

Henry Sturcke

Photo on front cover by Henry Sturcke
Author photo by Edel Sturcke

ISBN 978-3-952-52272-1 (hardcover)
ISBN 978-3-952-52273-8 (paperback)
ISBN 978-3-952-52274-5 (ebook)

For who can know himself, and the multitude of subtle influences which act upon him? and who can recollect, at the distance of twenty-five years, all that he once knew about his thoughts and his deeds, and that, during a portion of his life, when even at the time his observation, whether of himself or of the external world, was less than before or after, by very reason of the perplexity and dismay which weighed upon him,—when, although it would be most unthankful to seem to imply that he had not all-sufficient light amid his darkness, yet a darkness it emphatically was?

John Henry Cardinal Newman
Apologia pro vita sua

Prelude

The Reformed Church in Effretikon, which lies twelve miles northeast of Zurich, just before Winterthur, meets in a modern building set on a hill; its imposing free-standing bell tower can be seen for miles around. On a Sunday morning in October 2002 every one of the nearly three hundred seats in the nave was filled, and a group of fifteen candidates gathered in a meeting room of the adjacent church hall to prepare for the formal procession with which that day's ordination service would open. I was one of them, although I had been ordained twenty-five years earlier. And I had my guitar, for the group asked me to lead the procession, during which we would repeatedly sing "Siyahamba," a modern Zulu hymn, until we reached the seats reserved for us in front. It was one of the many songs that had accompanied us during the thirteen months that prepared us for this day.

Repetition can be an effective tool in music. But ordination, a sacred ritual, is something not normally repeated. So, what was I doing there?

When I was a high school sophomore, stunned like the rest of the world on the weekend of John F. Kennedy's assassination, I immersed myself in a stack of back issues of the *Plain Truth*, a monthly magazine published by the Worldwide Church of God, a high-demand religious group living in expectation of the imminent end of the age and the return of Jesus Christ, interspersing my reading with repeated plays of Bob Dylan's *Freewheelin'*, whose songs, especially "A Hard Rain's A-Gonna Fall" expressively captured the mood of the moment. I spent the rest of my high school years vibrating to these two influences. At times the message of each reinforced that of the other, at other times, they clashed.

This oscillation continued when I entered Boston University and seemingly reached resolution when I was baptized and became a member of Worldwide. Or perhaps not: four months later, I was at the Woodstock music festival, as I recount in *Fooled into Thinking: Dylan, the Sixties, and the End of the World*.

Like ordination, baptism is a sacred rite that only needs to be performed once, but Worldwide taught that only adult baptism by immersion, after repentance and a profession of faith, was valid.

I traveled to Southern California after graduating from Boston University and earned a second college degree (why must I do everything twice?) at Worldwide's educational arm, Ambassador College. When my three years there drew to a close, my life was far from settled. I yearned to contribute to the proclamation efforts of Worldwide, but was torn between helping with its media efforts and entering the ministry to help care for one of the church's local congregations. Bafflingly, the administration seemed equally unsure. On the day ministerial candidates were told they would be sent to the field for training, ten classmates summoned before me were told they'd be going. I arrived to learn there were eleven assignments and I might be sent. Two summoned after me were told the same thing.

In the end, I received what I felt was the plum assignment that year: to go to Brussels and assist the magazine's correspondent there. While in Europe, I met and married my wife, Edel, after she graduated from Ambassador's English campus. Soon we were transferred to Washington, D.C. where I became the *Plain Truth* correspondent there. Before a year elapsed, however, that job was eliminated and we lost our first child (as told in *Those Elusive True Values: Journey to the Center of the Armstrong World*).

This book begins as that *annus horibilis* 1976 drew to a close, when an unexpected opportunity to continue serving Worldwide materialized.

Like the first two books, this book does not attempt to offer a comprehensive history of the Worldwide Church of God. The journey taken by Worldwide has been often told, notably by two of those most responsible for the revolution in the church's teachings that occurred in the years covered in this book. They are Joseph Tkach (*Transformed by Truth*, Multnomah, 1997), and J. Michael Feazell (*The Liberation of the Worldwide Church of God*, Zondervan, 2001). An excellent account from a scholarly perspective is *Fragmentation of a Sect*, by David V. Barret, Oxford University Press, 2013.

Instead, I will recount my personal journey, yet include enough of the overall story to place my struggles and decisions in context.

Chapter One

Back-to-back phone calls in late December 1976 solved one dilemma and created another. The first was from the editor of the European Community's monthly magazine, the second was from Worldwide's area coordinator for eastern Canada, Carn Catherwood.

The dilemma solved was that of when to pull the plug on my effort to find work in journalism and return to my hometown in New Jersey and work in my dad's delicatessen. To do that, I would never have had to leave home to study ten years earlier. Although my dad would have welcomed the prospect of having a successor for the business into which he'd poured so much hard work, I had been aware since childhood of the undertone of his regret in not having used the scholarship he'd earned to study. For me to go to university, even if not to study one of the natural sciences—as he would have—was for him the vicarious fulfilment of a dream.

The new dilemma was that Edel and I went in less than an hour from having no prospects to a choice of two. One meant we could remain in the D. C. area, and I could continue my journalism career. The other would allow us to continue our service to the church to which we felt firmly committed. That's what we opted for.

I notified Carn of our decision, thus initiating the process for our migration to Canada. There would be paperwork, which was beginning to seem routine since this was the third international move in less than five years. We gave notice on our apartment and booked a moving company for early February. After that, we would stay with my parents until our immigrant visas were approved.

Three weeks after Carn's first call, he called again, on a Thursday morning, to ask us to fly to Montreal that weekend. Wayne Cole, Canadian director, would be in town for a church visit; it would be good, Carn said, for us to be there.

I'm not a suspicious person, so, I didn't ask myself why it would be good to be there until halfway through the Sabbath service (Worldwide observed the seventh day, Saturday), when Cole began expounding the Biblical qualifications and requirements of a minister. I had witnessed ordination ceremonies in Worldwide, so, I knew where this was going. The next minutes, as I was summoned forward and had hands laid on me, were a strange mixture of a hyper-consciousness, stunned numbness, and intense excitement.

Typically, an ordination followed at least a year of assisting an experienced pastor as a trainee. I understood that one reason for an exception in my situation was that the case for government approval of my application would be stronger if I were already ordained. Yet I also knew that it wasn't just a formality performed for that procedure. I'm sure Larry Salyer, Washington pastor, had been consulted and had vouched for me. Both he and an associate pastor in D.C., Randal Dick (who had been one of my best friends in college), had taken me to accompany them on pastoral visits, and I had often spoken in services. Combined with the six months I had spent helping the local pastor in New England before going to Ambassador, that was nearly equivalent to the training an assistant received, although mine had been informal.

We traveled twice more to Canada while waiting for our visas. The first of these was to Toronto in mid-February, where Garner Ted Armstrong, son of Worldwide founder Herbert Armstrong, held a two-night evangelistic campaign, followed by a three-day conference for the ministry from Canada's eastern half, of which I was now a part, even though I hadn't yet begun to work. A month later, we returned to Montreal to find an apartment.

Meanwhile, our base of operations was my childhood home. Edel and I moved into the room I had shared with my brother. In addition to my parents and my sister, there was one more person in the household. My maternal grandmother was terminally ill, and my parents had brought her from Florida to care for her. They placed a hospital bed in the family room, which she rarely left. We were there to share my mom's tears after she gathered her courage to inject her mother with morphine for the first time. And Edel was sitting with Grandma the morning she passed away.

It was poignant to be with her in her last weeks. I hadn't known either of my grandfathers, but the temper of my two grandmothers, as well as my maternal great-grandmother in Georgia, had flowed into me. Now the last of these three indomitable women was gone. Grandma had been the first in our family to subscribe to the *Plain Truth*. She had given me the Oxford wide-margin Bible (with Scofield annotations) I had studied and marked in my years in Pasadena, and that still served as my primary Bible. Now she had lived long enough to know I would enter the ministry.

During the week my parents spent in Florida for Grandma's funeral and emptying her house to prepare it for sale, I managed the delicatessen.

Meanwhile, there was no word on when the visa would come through. We'd gone to the Canadian consulate in Manhattan for an interview, then waited as the spring holy days approached. In addition to the weekly Sabbath, Worldwide observed the Lord's Supper once a year, commemorating its institution on the night Jesus was betrayed, one day before Jewish observance of Passover, yet called it by the same name. It also observed the annual festivals outlined in Leviticus 23 instead of Christmas and Easter.

Despite the uncertainty of whether my visa would be granted in time, Carn scheduled me to spend the weekend in Sherbrooke, ninety miles east of Montreal, where I would conduct the Passover Friday evening, April 1, then give sermons the following two days, the weekly Sabbath and the First Day of Unleavened Bread. Sherbrooke had two congregations, one English-speaking, the other French; Sam Kneller pastored both. My presence would mean he could speak to the French-speaking congregation.

I had become accustomed to this kind of planning in the eight years since entering Worldwide. It was called "stepping out on faith." Nor was I overly surprised on Friday morning, April 1, to learn that we could pick up our visas. We packed, my parents drove us to the consulate in Manhattan, and from there to LaGuardia airport to take the last available seats on a flight to Montreal.

Carn met us at Dorval airport with the keys to a leased fleet car, pointed east, and said, "Sherbrooke is that way." There was hardly a moment to savor becoming landed immigrants in a new country, which would have been enough excitement for any day.

By the time we returned to our motel after the Passover ceremony, I had a splitting headache. We half-unpacked, then collapsed into bed. When we woke the following morning, I wanted to review my sermon notes before going to the hall but couldn't find my Samsonite slimline briefcase. I panicked, ransacked the room—no sign of it. Finally, I went outside to where our car was parked in front of our door. The briefcase was standing next to the right rear tire, no doubt where I had set it down the night before to open the car trunk to remove our suitcases.

After services on the Sabbath, we and others had dinner in the home of members of the congregation. Worldwide divided the Biblical instructions for the Passover over two evenings, calling the second, in the antiquated terminology of the King James Version, the Night to Be Much Observed (see Exod. 12:42). After the service the next day, Edel and I had a simple meal in the home of Sam and Marilyn Kneller (she had been a classmate in Pasadena), and their two children. It was good to unwind with them, but we didn't stay long, since we had to return to Montreal. As they had during our short trip in mid-March, Carn and Joyce Catherwood welcomed us into their home in Pierrefonds, a suburb just west of the city, which allowed him to fill me in on much of what I would need to know in my new assignment. Carn and Joyce were two of the most wise and empathetic people we ever had the privilege of working with.

The time with them was a good way to transition to working with the Montreal English church pastor, Bill Rabey. Bill and his wife Linda were roughly the same age as Edel and I. Bill was from the Montreal area; he was one of the few ministers to serve in his home town. He had the reticence I came to feel was typically Canadian, yet he was a sharp observer and an energetic, caring pastor. I'm grateful for the way he put up with my ebullient nature, which he may have felt was all-too typical for someone from the lower forty-eight. They lived south of the St. Lawrence; consequently, we rarely saw each other during the week. Much of the necessary communication between us was by telephone.

The apartment we found was not far from the Catherwoods' home. It was on the fourth floor, and we had an open view to the west, from which a constant wind blew, and to Laval in the north, across the Rivière des Prairies (a branch of the mighty Saint Lawrence). We painted each room a different color (it was the Seventies, so, one was green, a second blue, and a third creamy yellow-beige) and set to work making it our own while waiting for our belongings to be delivered. To keep our spirits up as we worked, we had our portable cassette player and a few tapes.

For me, Montreal resonated as the city where Jackie Robinson had broken into organized baseball in 1946 with the Montreal Royals, the top farm team of the Brooklyn Dodgers. Eight years before our move, in 1969, the Montreal Expos began competing in the National League, the first major league franchise located outside of the United States (even though the inter-league championship at the end of each season had always been called the "World" Series). In every one of those seasons, they had posted losing records. Now they had built a nucleus of young players and looked like contenders. 1977 also marked the year the Olympic Stadium became their home field, replacing their temporary quarters at Jarry Park. Opening day coincided with the move to our new apartment, so, I listened to the game on the radio while setting up bookshelves in the spare bedroom I would use as my office.

Further exploration of the radio revealed the excellence of the CBC, the Canadian Broadcasting Corporation. Among the delights, a weekly program hosted by Sylvia Tyson, half of the duo Ian and Sylvia whose repertoire my high school sweetheart and I had raided for much of our song list when we performed. I wasn't surprised to find a strong folk music community in Canada in both languages. Canada had produced many of my favorite singer-songwriters, such as Joni Mitchell and Neil Young, in addition to poet and novelist-turned troubadour Leonard Cohen. I speculated that the sensory deprivation of long Canadian winters may have stimulated their imaginations (Bob Dylan, growing up not far south of the border, would have experienced similar winters). Now I discovered a thriving French-language music scene, which drew both on local folk music and France's *chansonniers*. I took a chance on one LP by a group named Beau Dommage and taught myself some of their songs.

As we took up our work of visiting church members and "prospects" (those who'd seen the telecast and read World-wide's literature and asked for a visit), we slowly found our way around Montreal with its main arteries—rue Saint-Denis, rue Ontario, boulevard Saint-Laurent—and the side streets lined with rows of apartment houses fronted with outdoor iron staircases. We ate out rarely, but one favorite was Dunn's on Metcalfe, where we feasted on smoked meat (a Montreal variant of pastrami, but spicier and preserved without brine).

Montreal is vibrant and cosmopolitan, the world's second-most populous Francophone city, after Paris. The influence of French culture meant that it was a fashionable city. But in addition to the French, there were strong admixtures of Iroquois and other native tribes who'd been there before Champlain arrived, as well as many Irish and Italians. Further waves of immigration from Portugal, Germany, Eastern Europe, South America, and the Caribbean made for a rich mix in our congregation's makeup. There was a well-established Jewish community, some of whose offspring—Mordecai Richler, Leonard Cohen—had enriched Canadian literature. It also contributed some of the young people in our congregation. And there were traditional English as well, some of them descendants of loyalists who had fled north across the border during the American War for Independence. Moving to Montreal also meant getting reacquainted with an old friend from the Boston congregation. She was the widow of a Baptist minister, and had been part of my carpool each week to services. Now retired as an executive secretary from one of the leading State Street banks, she had returned to her native Canada.

As the short, glorious spring turned to summer, I played on the soccer team our congregation fielded in the amateur city league. I'm not a gifted athlete, but had been on the junior varsity team in high school and for two years manager of the varsity squad and practiced with the team throughout the week. So, I wasn't a complete novice now, eleven years later. I especially enjoyed taking the field in Jarry Park, where Jackie Robinson and other future Dodger stars had played. One of our games, though, took place on one of the new playing fields built for the recent Olympics. A sliding tackle there gave me an intimate acquaintance with Astro-Turf, which left the worst scrape I've ever had.

We would boast of few victories that season. Our nadir was a game we lost 19–0. As we shook hands with our opponents after the game, the referee announced he would enter the score as 20–0. We protested, but he explained his reasoning: when our friends saw the score in the newspaper, they would assume it was a misprint for 2–0.

Another highlight of the summer was a bilingual coed teen camp at Canoe Lake in the Algonquin Provincial Park, west of Ottawa. To substitute for adequate sleep, I recharged each day at first light by getting out of the tent I shared with Edel to paddle a canoe out to the middle of the lake, then drift while I watched the loons fetching their breakfast.

The camp was conducted under the auspices of World-wide's new youth program, Youth Opportunities United (Y.O.U.). I had begun in Montreal just as Worldwide, concerned over the number of youths who stopped attending once they became adults, launched it. Each congregation had a chapter; to coordinate the program, each area coordinator selected an area youth coordinator, and Carn chose me. The appointment left me bemused; I had never felt much in common with other teenagers when I was a teen. It's strange I felt that way: I was on sports teams, enjoyed weekend campouts as an explorer scout, and made music at every opportunity. But I never felt part of the in-crowd and didn't feel I could be a motivational leader for teens. But Carn was firm.

My duties involved trips once or twice a year to Vancouver or Edmonton for national meetings. Many of my counterparts in other provinces studied at Ambassador when I had. While most of them had attended one of the other Ambassador campuses, Bricket Wood or Big Sandy, we had a similar take on things and got along well. One of them, Larry Greider, area youth coordinator in the Toronto region, became a good friend during my years in Canada. He coordinated the Feast of Tabernacles in Ottawa that fall as well, giving us an additional opportunity to work together.

No sooner had the Feast ended than the first snow fell, and we experienced our first Canadian winter. At times, the temperature dropped to thirty below, and the locals, knowing that we weren't used to that, warned us to be careful breathing. Air taken in at that temperature could freeze the lining of our lungs. We should take heed when we began driving each day: cold air has less volume than warm; the tires flattened while the car was parked and held that shape, creating a flop-flop sound until they had warmed.

We also received advice on stocking our car with blankets, food, and other supplies in case we got stuck in a blizzard far from any town. We learned the hard way about white-outs; a gust during a snowstorm could reduce visibility to nothing in an instant. The first time I experienced it, I landed in a ditch.

Neither the amount of snow nor the freezing temperatures daunted me, but the duration did. Winter spanned half the year, from October to April. Cabin fever crept in and wrapped itself in our sweaters, mittens, scarves, and boots. Strategies for combating it included any form of outdoor activity, even if no more than shoveling snow from one pile to another. As the sap in the maples began to run late one winter, I became acquainted with an important form of Canadian culture, a sugaring-off party in a hut in the woods. We poured the freshly boiled syrup over everything, not only pancakes but eggs and sausages as well, accompanied by hot coffee.

When Carn brought me to Canada, he had assured me my work would be in English, but before the summer was out, he was no longer area coordinator in Montreal. Instead, he would move to Europe to supervise the French-speaking congregations there and in the French West Indies. Previously, Dibar Apartian had done that from Pasadena (as well as the French-speaking congregations in Africa), in addition to editing the church's literature in French and recording radio broadcasts. Most other regional directors lived in the area they oversaw (the regional director of Spanish-language efforts was the other exception). Apartian's excuse was access to recording facilities, as well as the argument about which of the three areas he oversaw should he live in? But skillful courtier that he was, the proximity to the center of power was doubtless an additional factor.

As part of the shuffle, Sam and Marilyn Kneller left the Eastern Townships for Paris to succeed the pastor there, who would retire but continue to translate church publications. The two congregations in Sherbrooke would once again be attached to the Montreal French and English congregations, as they had been before the Knellers had moved there.

Carn's replacement as area coordinator would be Colin Wilkins, an Englishman who until then had pastored French-language congregations in Quebec City and Trois-Rivières, which would now be cared for by my classmate Bob, who'd been associate pastor in Paris. Colin was immediately confronted with a manpower shortage, however. On top of the two-for-one swap with Europe, another minister had to be removed for disciplinary reasons. That soon had consequences for my situation.

Worldwide followed a practice of prayer and anointing for illness, based on its understanding of a passage in the

Epistle of James. One of the French-speaking members fell ill one night and couldn't reach any of the French-speaking ministers. He phoned me, and I went and prayed for him. The next time I saw Colin, I felt I should report what I had done since it was outside my congregation. He asked some questions: I had understood what the member had told me? Yes. I had prayed for him in French? Yes. Before long, Colin poached me to give occasional sermonettes in the French congregation. Soon after, he reassigned me to the Montreal French congregation; a significant part of my visiting load would be in the Eastern Townships. Perhaps Carn would have found it necessary to do the same had he still been there. And given my commitment to Worldwide, I was willing to do whatever was needed, even if it were not my preference.

A few months later, as a blizzard abated before daylight on a March morning, I carefully drove Edel to the hospital, and she delivered a son. After losing our firstborn at birth two years earlier, this was a joyous event for us, although accompanied by the customary adjustments every couple experiences when it becomes a family.

As spring turned to summer, Edel's father was diagnosed with cancer, a tumor at the base of his spine. We hurried over to Hamburg so that he could see his only grandchild. No one knew at the time that he would live another thirty years, but the visit gave his spirits, and those of Edel's mother, a needed boost.

While we were in Germany, Colin decided that the congregations in Sherbrooke should be cared for locally, and we were to move there. Soon after returning to Canada, we found a small house in Sherbrooke in good condition on a good street. The money I had inherited from my recently deceased grandmother covered the down payment, and before the summer was out, we moved.

The move to Sherbrooke simplified our lives. For the past months, I often drove there on Thursday or Friday to visit members and prospects for a day or two before conducting services. On other weekends, Edel and I just drove there for the Sabbath. The main road to Sherbrooke was a portion of the Trans-Canada-Highway, which for long stretches runs directly east to west. So, when I started out early Saturday morning to hold services, I had the sun in my eyes for the better part of the two-hour drive, then again when I reversed direction and returned to Montreal after the second service in the afternoon.

With the pastorate in Sherbrooke came the responsibility of coordinating the French-language Feast of Tabernacles site for North America, which involved negotiating housing, working with the university to use an auditorium for services, and other duties.

In the summer of 1978, barely thirty years old, with a wife, an infant son, and a house, I was pastor of two small congregations in Sherbrooke, one English-speaking and one French. Each week I had to prepare a sermon in French, deliver it in the morning, have a lunch break, then deliver it again in English in the afternoon.

My aim in taking three years of French in addition to German in high school had been to boost my chances of working as a foreign correspondent, a dream fulfilled when I went to Brussels in 1973. That immersed me in a French (and Flemish) environment. My passive understanding of French (spoken and, to some extent, written) increased—and was a factor in the church placing me in Montreal. But to suddenly give sermons in that language was deep-end immersion, and not only was I forced to swim, but the congregants were too. I loved the French language, although not everyone exposed to my savage attempts to make myself understood might have gotten that impression. When my time in Canada ended, some admitted that they had no idea what I was talking about in the first few sermons. Since the sermon usually took up seventy-five minutes of a two-hour Worldwide service, that was a long time to leave listeners confused—apart from the stress on me. One of the members volunteered to read my manuscript in advance and offer corrections and suggestions, which I greatly appreciated. However, it meant having the sermon prepared by Thursday rather than using Friday to prepare.

It was unusual for Worldwide to appoint someone to pastor congregations who hadn't been raised to the status of preaching elder (Worldwide had a system of ranking ministers: local elder, preaching elder, pastor, and evangelist). It was understandable in my case, however, that the step wasn't yet taken; I had only been ordained a local elder a year-and-a-half before, and that step had been rushed to aid my immigration proceedings.

I still had a lot to learn when I took up my first pastorate, which alone would have sufficed to make the transition stressful. It took place, though, against the backdrop of turmoil in Worldwide's top echelons.

The previous August, Herbert Armstrong had suffered congestive heart failure—the same day, Elvis Presley, exactly half his age, died from the same affliction (we had been at Canoe Lake and only heard of Elvis's death, not Armstrong's near-death). Like many who come close to dying, the elder Armstrong felt his life had been spared for a purpose. After nine months convalescing in a home he'd bought in Tucson, he became restless and eager to reassert his authority.

He became obsessed with a need to get the church "back on the track," as he put it. There had been a widespread feeling that the church was drifting. Some long-time evangelists put it down to creeping liberalism, graphically depicted by the sideburns of the men edging down and the hemlines of the women edging up. They had Herbert Armstrong's ear. Another individual stood even closer to Herbert Armstrong, Stanley R. Rader, an accountant and attorney who had made himself indispensable to Armstrong.

This made Rader unpopular with many in the church, particularly with Herbert Armstrong's son, Garner Ted. Ted Armstrong had nominally been given full executive power over the church and college four years earlier, in 1974, in addition to his work as the public face of the church as a pioneering televangelist. However, his record as an executive in those years was mixed. While an outside observer might have attributed this to overextension, Ted Armstrong blamed, in addition to the traditionalists who now had his father's ear, Stan Rader, who, he felt, thwarted him and was ultimately behind his father's countermanding of measures Ted Armstrong had previously run past him.

On the other hand, Rader and the traditionalists remembered the moral failings of the younger Armstrong that had led to his banishment in 1972, unleashing two years of turmoil from which the church had not yet fully recovered. Growing public awareness of the church usually centered on Ted Armstrong, a charismatic figure. Lengthy articles appearing in outlets such as *Penthouse* meant that the shadier aspects of Worldwide's history would not soon go away.

In May 1978, Garner Ted Armstrong was stripped of his executive duties, then removed from the airwaves a month later; we were told he was on a leave of absence until the end of the year. The official explanation was that he had exceeded the authority delegated to him. Years later, I heard the deeper reason: Ted Armstrong had learned his father's darkest secret, recounted to him by the victim, his sister. In the course of a heated discussion in Herbert Armstrong's Tucson home, he blurted out what he knew and added, "I could destroy you." For Herbert Armstrong, who could not separate the good of Worldwide from his personal survival, this was the last straw.

Ted Armstrong did not go quietly. In media interviews, he detailed the tangle of interlocking corporations Rader had created to handle the church's affairs, enriching himself in the process. In addition, Ted Armstrong complained of being cut off from his father.

The younger Armstrong moved to Texas, incorporated a new church, and made plans to return to broadcasting. Given his prominence, it was uncertain at the time whether the majority of the church and its ministry would go with him or stay with Worldwide.

In months to come, he sought to replicate Worldwide's operations, with a telecast and free literature. I saw some of his first booklets and was immediately dismayed that he had carried over the worst external aspects of his father's writing style: italics, all capitals, exclamation points.

One of his first booklets covered the notion of the true gospel. Contrary to what Herbert Armstrong maintained, Ted Armstrong said it centered on "Christ, and him crucified" (see 1 Cor. 2:2). Still, he retained Worldwide's expectation of the kingdom of God established soon on earth (which, for the senior Armstrong, was the central message of the gospel). Above all, he criticized Worldwide's attitude in delivering the gospel. Worldwide saw its responsibility limited to proclaiming this "witness" as a warning, accompanied by an expectation that few would heed. Only God could call; we could not convert anyone. This led, in Ted Armstrong's mind, to an attitude that said, "Here it is, I don't care what you do with it." Instead, he stressed we should care whether people respond or not, for their sake.

From the time he was a teenager, Ted Armstrong was one of the church's best critics. He was good at pointing out hypocrisy and wrong attitudes that sprang from taking the church's teachings to an extreme. But in the end, he accepted the same teachings.

I wrestled with the matter and looked for the appropriate biblical model to guide me. Was Ted Armstrong a type of

David, unjustly accused by Saul, or was he Absalom, the son of David who rebelled against his father? In the end, I and most others stayed in Worldwide, but with lingering questions and mistrust and unease over the role of Stan Rader, who still seemed like an outsider.

1978 was a momentous year in Christianity in general, which also affected how I and others processed the turmoil in Worldwide. It was the year of three popes. The Roman Catholic Church held the world's attention as it did what it does best: the ceremonies associated with papal funerals and elections. It got Herbert Armstrong's attention. He wrote at length on the prophetic possibilities in this turn of events. When, during Worldwide's observation of the Feast of Tabernacles, the white smoke went up outside the conclave and an upper story window of the Vatican opened, the man who stepped out, Karol Wojtyla, seemed with his commanding presence and rich voice to be a likely candidate indeed to fulfill what Armstrong expected. The new pope might well be a figure who could promote European unity. Coming as he did from behind the Iron Curtain, he might even play a role in extending united Europe to the east.

The memory of that had hardly faded when, a month later, in November, more than nine hundred followers of a charismatic pastor, Jim Jones, committed mass suicide in the wilds of Guyana, to which they had moved after coming under increased public scrutiny in the Bay Area, where their People's Temple had been located. Their flight to the wilderness paralleled our expectation of being taken to a place of safety to be spared the great tribulation before Christ's return. I was shaken and suffered insomnia. This became the backdrop for anxious conversations with congregants and colleagues about the happenings in Worldwide.

When the inner turmoil became too great, I sought refuge in a nature preserve located a few blocks from our home in Sherbrooke. I discovered a boulder, undoubtedly left behind by a receding glacier at the end of the last ice age. I sat on it and felt calmer. I imagined all the time that had elapsed since it was deposited there, the empires that had come and gone, the plagues that had raged and passed. My next thought was that this rock was there long before Stan Rader was born and that it would be there long after Stan Rader was gone.

I often returned to that rock and made a decision on one of those trips. When it came time to flee to the place of safety, if Stan Rader were to be in authority there, then I would not be going. I wouldn't take my wife nor our infant son there. I didn't say a word about that at the time to my wife—I only revealed it to her shortly before writing this book.

The new year, 1979, only brought an intensification of Worldwide's crisis. The viewing stands on the grounds of the Ambassador College campus that lined the Rose Parade route hadn't been fully disassembled when armed deputies came to the Hall of Administration and news spread that the church had been placed in receivership.

The action had been initiated by a small number of church members, one of them an acquaintance since he was a member of the congregation nearest my parents' home. They alleged massive fraud and misuse of church funds. Their hope was that this action would lead to Stan Rader's dismissal, after which Herbert Armstrong would recall his son, Ted. The immediate effect was the opposite. Rader's hold seemed tighter than ever, and Herbert Armstrong's eventual successor was catapulted to prominence.

Rader mounted a spirited defense. He rallied religious figures and legal scholars who argued that this action was an egregious violation of church and state separation. His efforts were supported by an elder as yet little known outside the Pasadena area, Joe Tkach. I knew him because his son, also named Joe, was a classmate. The Tkach family had been brought to Pasadena a few years before I arrived. The Sixties were a time of rapid expansion for Worldwide, and the need for additional pastors outstripped the capacity of Ambassador College to produce them. As a result, some elders who served in local congregations were brought for a year of college training, after which they would be sent out as pastors. In most cases, this is what happened, although a few, among them Joe Tkach, remained in the headquarters area.

Now Tkach became instrumental in a second line of defense against the receivership by organizing a nearly continuous series of prayer and hymn-singing sessions in the large open foyer of the Hall of Administration. Because of church and state separation, the court-appointed receiver couldn't enter the building while worship meetings were going on.

Ministers and employees who opposed this aggressive response either resigned or were fired and disfellowshipped, most prominently, Wayne Cole, the man who hired me twice, first—as director of publishing—to go to Brussels, and then—as regional director in Canada—to the ministry. In spring 1978, he had been called back to Pasadena as personal assistant to Herbert Armstrong and coordinator of the ministerial management team (the rebranding of the responsibility he'd had before moving to Canada). He was seen as the one senior minister who had the trust of both Armstrongs. After Ted Armstrong's banishment, some hoped that he could mediate between the two. Some even envisioned a scenario in which he became chief executive of the church, with the aging Herbert Armstrong as pastor-general emeritus and Ted Armstrong restored as the church's public face on television.

Now, those on the confrontation course portrayed Cole as someone who would open the doors wide to the State of California and let the receiver walk over the church. Men we had looked up to were now branded as traitors.

When this erupted, we had already booked airplane tickets to fly to a ministerial conference in Pasadena. We flew to Los Angeles as planned and stayed for a night but then continued to Tucson, where the conference had been moved at the last minute. This allowed Armstrong, who had avoided traveling to Pasadena to appear in court on the grounds of ill-health, to address us.

When we gathered in Tucson in January 1979, I had the intricate timelines of prophetic fulfillment in the back of my mind. It was roughly 1335 days (Dan. 12:12) until the recalculated date for the end of Babylon's sway and the institution of divine rule on earth. Worldwide had initially counted Nebuchadnezzar's seven years of madness (Dan. 4:23) as partial fulfillment of those years, allowing everything to intersect on a date seven years earlier that coincided with internal events in the history of Worldwide. This had to do with Metonic (nineteen-year) cycles. In Worldwide's construction of early church history, the crucifixion occurred 31 C.E., Paul introduced the gospel on European soil nineteen years later, 50 C.E., and the Jerusalem congregation fled to safety 69 C.E. Similarly, Herbert Armstrong began preaching on the radio in January 1934, began broadcasting to Europe in January 1953; therefore, the expectation of a flight in 1972. Now it was seven years after the time we had expected Worldwide's work to end and the faithful remnant to prepare to flee to a place of safety. It was clear that Herbert Armstrong had found his own place of safety by buying a home in Tucson. Here, he was out of reach of the court-appointed receiver. Was there significance in the timing?

So total was my focus on the internal problems of Worldwide that I paid little attention to major developments in the world scene that year, particularly two that, in tandem, set the stage for the continuing confrontation between the Islamic world and the West: the Soviet invasion of Afghanistan and the toppling of the Shah of Iran by radical Islamists. In addition to my preoccupation with Worldwide's problems, another factor was that these were areas of the world that Worldwide hadn't focused on in its end-time speculation. Herbert Armstrong always dismissed the possibility of a Soviet attack on the U.S., since he found no indication of it in the prophets, nor had he ever issued a booklet entitled

Persia in Prophecy. Looking back more than forty years after the fact, one could make the case that these events opened a new era of world unrest. Consequently, 1979 was a significant year, but it did not mark the beginning of a three-and-a-half-year tribulation that culminated in the return of Jesus on Trumpets 1982.

Back to the conference in January: We had been instructed to bring our loose-leaf binders containing the recently issued compendium of Worldwide's teachings, the Systematic Theology Project. Drafts I had written at the behest of Washington pastor Larry Salyer were still recognizable in a couple of the entries. Herbert Armstrong had come to view this project as emblematic of everything wrong with Worldwide that he had been brought back from death to clean up. I was tempted not to comply, or at least to photocopy the contents before leaving home.

An account in the book of Acts made me think again. When the original Jerusalem congregation introduced the community of goods, the account mentions a couple, Ananias and Sapphira. Like the others, they monetized their possessions. Unlike the others, they held back a portion of the proceeds yet claimed they had deposited the entire sum in the congregation treasury (Acts 5:1–11). I wasn't afraid that God would strike me dead if I kept a copy of the contents before turning in my binder. It was enough, though, that God had made his opinion of that kind of duplicity clear in the Bible. I dutifully turned in the complete binder without duplicating any of its contents.

The Tucson conference was notable for a couple of other reasons. Roderick Meredith, reveling in his return to his cherished job as superintendent of ministers, gave lengthy presentations. He commented extensively on the pending divorce case of his former brother-in-law, Raymond McNair. McNair's wife had countersued, naming the church as co-defendant for alienation of affection. Meredith spoke in detail on Leona McNair's alleged shortcomings as a wife, which gave her ample grounds for an additional suit, charging defamation of character.

Another memory of the conference had been totally erased. Even after I came across it in my journal while writing the first draft of this book, I had no recollection of it. Dexter Faulkner, whom I had succeeded as *Plain Truth* correspondent in Washington, was now responsible for the Editorial Department. He told me that most of the staff, including his predecessor, Brian Knowles, had resigned. The editorial team had to be rebuilt from scratch. He asked me to move to Pasadena to join the staff.

Instead of asking for some time to think and pray about it, discuss it with Edel, and then sit down with Dexter in a quiet place to discuss it in detail, I blurted out my spontaneous reaction. I told Dexter that I was relatively inexperienced in the field ministry and therefore ready to conform to Herbert Armstrong's instructions of how to do it. However, with editorial matters, I had more experience, including experience outside of the church's employ, and strong feelings about how things should be done.

Looking back, I think it was best not to accept the offer. Edel and I had a ten-month-old child and had just bought our first home. After being press-ganged into the French Work, I had entered my first pastorate with all the trauma that gave us both.

Dexter and I remained on good terms. I contributed coverage, both articles and photos, of the conference for the church's newspaper, the *Worldwide News*, and in coming years contributed articles to the *Good News* and the church's new magazine aimed at youth.

The conference ended on a Friday morning. As it ended, Herbert Armstrong announced a church-wide fast that would begin at sunset that evening, the Sabbath. Our flight home, via Chicago, had many Worldwide ministers and wives among its passengers. There were two choices for the in-flight meal, chicken or pork. Our seats were aft, and by the time the flight attendants reached us, the chicken was long gone. Worldwide's adherence to the dietary prescriptions of Leviticus meant that there were very few takers for pork. When we landed in O'Hare to change for our flight to Dorval airport, the winter sun had already set; as a result, we didn't even think of getting anything to eat before reboarding. We arrived home jet-lagged, hungry, and thirsty and got as much sleep as we could before getting up the next day so that I could conduct morning and afternoon Sabbath services on an empty stomach.

To starve the receiver of money, the church reincorporated as "Herbert Armstrong—A Corporation Sole." Employees in the U.S., including the field ministers, were terminated by Worldwide and rehired by the new entity. Some of my colleagues south of the border refused because, they said, they worked for God, not man. The change from working for the Worldwide Church of God to the corporation of Herbert Armstrong disturbed them. We in Canada were beyond the reach of the receiver, consequently, there was no change in the name of our employer. I don't know whether I would have taken as principled a stand as my colleagues in the States.

Meanwhile, *60 Minutes* got wind of the story, and Mike Wallace asked Stan Rader for an interview. When the interview aired on Sunday, April 15 (Easter Sunday, and during Worldwide's celebration of the Days of Unleavened Bread), I was appalled. Rader had hoped to use the appearance to portray Worldwide as the victim of unwarranted government encroachment but was mortified when Wallace revealed knowledge of a letter Herbert Armstrong had drafted in January, relieving Rader of his executive duties and retaining him as an advisor. Rader lost his temper, told Wallace, "you're on my list" (whatever that meant), and stormed out of the room. Although I kept my opinion to myself when members asked about the program, it was an embarrassing appearance.

Rader kept his job for the time being.

The receivership also played in fictionalized form in the national media, in an episode of one of my favorite shows, *Lou Grant*. It was handled well; the journalist assigned to cover the fictional story was portrayed as a committed Christian. Only after reading in the Bible repeated statements about false prophets, with God's assurance, "I have not sent them" (see, for example, Jer. 27:15), did he gain the inner freedom to pursue the story fairly wherever it led. Coincidentally, although I didn't know it at the time, since I didn't read the closing credits, my *B. U. News* colleague, April Smith, was a writer-producer for that show.

In the end, the State of California backed down. A series of rulings affirmed that the case had been constitutionally questionable from the outset. Nor had it damaged Worldwide's defense that much of what had been decried as extravagant expenditure—the private jet, the five-star hotels, the gifts of Steuben crystal to world leaders—had been described in letters Armstrong wrote to the church's supporters and depicted on the cover of the *Plain Truth* and other church publications.

Nevertheless, the turmoil augmented my uncertainty and idealism as I sought to be a good pastor despite my inexperience. Things might have been different had I been able to filter out the drama and focus on serving my parishioners' needs, encouraging them in the day-to-day struggle of living a Christian life in this world. I'm sure many of my colleagues were able to do that.

The problem was, neither the members nor I belonged to Worldwide just to live day-to-day lives. We believed we'd been called to support an apostle in his proclamation of an urgent witness. Even our struggles in Christian living took on the dimension of overcoming, of character development, of preparation for rebirth in the divine family and rulership on earth in the millennium. Our conviction of Herbert Armstrong's role and ours fed into the narcissism of the Armstrongs, father and son. We were co-dependent in their on-going psychodrama.

Looking back, I can see how it would have helped if I, in my uncertainty, had been able to view Colin not only as my supervisor but as my mentor as well, as I had Carn. It's no one's fault that didn't happen, certainly not Colin's. It's a matter of chemistry. And he, along with the other area coordinators, experienced more stress than we pastors.

A more mature me would have spotted where I needed a sounding board or some feedback. But I assumed I was expected to know how to deal with my role. It's hard to ask for help if you don't even know what you don't know.

I began frequenting the local university library to supplement gaps in my education I noticed in preparing weekly sermons and Bible studies or answering members' questions. I particularly lamented my lack of biblical Hebrew and Greek. Working with Bible texts in translation, supplemented with the basic reference books I'd acquired while in Ambassador or subsequently often confronted me with an array of positions. I had no basis for deciding among them other than what seemed to fit best the framework of Worldwide's teachings. I bought an introductory textbook on New Testament Greek but lacked the self-discipline and concentration for self-study.

Pastoral counseling left me feeling that I needed to learn much more about alcoholism, spousal abuse, homosexuality, and other issues I was confronted with. The more I read, the more inadequate I felt. Given my nature, I would likely have felt that way even without Worldwide's expectation that the minister was there to answer every question. The struggles of my parishioners were a blow to my naive idealism. An older minister's words, "Henry, you can't live peoples' lives for them," made sense but were hard to apply. I slid into a condition I now know was burnout.

In this continuous turmoil, external and internal, I sought solace not only in nature, but also in music, where I so often found it in the past. Songs like Roxy Music's "The End of the Line," Neil Young's "Hurricane," and an older song by Fairport Convention, "Meet on the Ledge" are indicative of my frame of mind. Curiously, the succor Dylan could offer was ambivalent. In September 1978, while preparing for our move to Sherbrooke, Bob Dylan came to the Montreal Forum, and Edel and I went. It was Edel's first rock concert and my first Dylan concert since Carnegie Hall in the fall of 1965. When Dylan first came to Montreal in 1961, he played in a small coffee house, and there had been room for more. Now he drew 18,000 of us to a hockey rink.

I had bought *Street-Legal*, his first full collection of new songs in two-and-a-half years, when it came out three months earlier. I copied it from the LP onto a cassette and listened to it repeatedly on long drives. I hadn't yet heard the literary-critical term "intertextuality," but I marveled at the way the lyrics wove an intricate fabric of many strands, including mythology, tarot, old Western movies, folk and blues songs, and the Bible—from Eden in flames past Armageddon to the peace that would come when the King (and Queen) of Swords ruled.

The songs included many allusions to Christ, especially his betrayal (sometimes conflated with the holocaust), death, and resurrection. Dylan's own recent legal battles seemed to morph into Jesus overturning the table of the money-changers.

There was always a "she" in the songs as well, Goethe's eternal feminine, appearing here in many guises: temptress, tormentor, succor. The whore of Babylon and a shorn Magdalene with an inscrutable ebony face.

The fact that I was astounded by the wealth of allusion, rather than the songs as a whole, showed the weakness of the collection, aside from one of Dylan's all-time best songs, "Señor (Tales of Yankee Power)." In addition, the album sounded simultaneously thin and muddy, with arrangements that didn't always do the songs justice.

The album opened with "The Changing of the Guards" (one of four songs from the album he played at the Forum), which Dylan begins "Sixteen years, sixteen banners united." It had, in fact, been sixteen years since his first album was released. For fifteen of them, half of my own lifetime, I had been a fan. That's not putting it strongly enough; I hung on his words. They often came to me in situations in my own life (the hallmark of a canonical poet). Beginning with the immediate aftermath of the Kennedy assassination, Dylan had been one of two poles in the oscillation of my soul, a counterweight to the other pole, the teachings of Worldwide. That Dylan drew on the Bible as one source for both imagery and ethics complicated the matter.

It seemed fitting that this was the second time I'd seen him in concert. The first, in Carnegie Hall, October 1965, was at a turning point in his career, reflected in the dual nature of the show (first half solo acoustic, second half backed by the Hawks). Now he was touring with a bigger band, new arrangements of old favorites, and stage mannerisms copied from Elvis Presley (the recent, Las Vegas Elvis) and Neil Diamond. The strain in his voice seemed to reflect the dual ordeal of editing a film (panned on its release) and contentious divorce and custody battles. Once again, the wheel on fire seemed ready to explode, although I couldn't have predicted his next incarnation, despite the many allusions, overt and hidden, to Christ. When it came, would it help unify my soul?

When *Slow Train Coming* appeared at the end of the following summer, it was an avowedly Christian album. The songs were good, and it was well-produced, the message reflected dispensational fundamentalism, similar to Worldwide's. But my reaction was ambivalent. It was a counterpoint to my own inner state. At a time when I was struggling to hold on to my faith, he espoused the absolute certainty and moral rectitude of a true believer. That had been me a few years earlier. At the same time, I couldn't shake the feeling I had, while listening carefully through headphones, that he seemed to be standing beside himself as if he were distanced to what he was singing.

Even more than seven years earlier, when the failure of the church's timeline coincided with learning of Ted Armstrong's failings, my faith that Worldwide was the one true church was seriously shaken. Yet as then, I continued to cling to three pillars that, to me, supported Worldwide's claim. They were the Sabbath (not only its observance, but as shorthand for the notion that the death of Christ on the cross did not abrogate the covenant God made with Abraham), Worldwide's distinctive teachings on the nature of God and the nature and destiny of man, and the notion that prophecy was written for our day.

This last began to trouble me. Worldwide lived in expectation of the return of Christ but was not alone in that. The church had a distinctive teaching, though, that set it apart from the many other purveyors of dispensational, pre-millennial interpretation of prophecy: British-Israelism. This taught that the Jews were not the only remnant of the twelve tribes of Israel. The tribes who had broken away after Solomon's death and formed their own nation, were then taken captive a century before the Kingdom of Judah was, came to be known as the lost ten tribes. But now, Worldwide taught, they had been found. They had migrated to northwestern Europe, and two of them, Ephraim and Manasseh, were the Anglo-Saxon people of Britain and the U.S. Worldwide also knew what had become of their Assyrian captors: their descendants were the modern-day Germans.

The plausibility of this rested on the assumption that we lived in the end-time; therefore, prophecy would be fulfilled now. When one compared the promises given to Abraham with the world of the twentieth century, the identification we made seemed clear. Who are the nations that have been blessed, who are the nations that have begun an inevitable decline at this time in history?

Now that I was on my own in Sherbrooke, I wrestled with

that teaching. In my conviction of the truth of the Anglo-Saxon people's identity, I studied history, archaeology, and language. The evidence must be there somewhere, I felt. Yet despite a general pattern of migration from the shores of the Black and Caspian Seas into Europe, it didn't seem to line up with any scenario that would show a mass migration of the Assyrian people, taking Israelite captives with them, who would filter out and move a little farther, to the shores of the North Sea. Nor did linguistics show any significant Semitic component in the Germanic or Celtic languages (aside from a few tantalizing coincidences, such as the Hebrew word for "mourn," *kinah*, and the Irish word for lamentation, "keen").

I began to think the unthinkable. Perhaps, when Isaiah, Jeremiah, and others spoke of the Assyrians, Babylonians, Egyptians, Edomites, and other nations, they simply meant the nations of their day. Perhaps they were not leaving clues of the identity or fate of significant nations in our day.

Further, I asked whether, in our frequent reference to the so-called Olivet prophecy in Matthew 24, we had been wrong to downplay Jesus' next words after warning of wars and other catastrophes: "the end is not yet" (verse 6). Was the only sign of the end a second destruction of Jerusalem and its temple? And when Jesus said "this generation shall not pass"—was it conceivable that he meant the generation of his listeners then, and not a different generation nineteen hundred years later?

Indeed, within forty years of when he spoke, days before his arrest and crucifixion, terrible calamity did fall when Rome crushed Jewish revolt. Yet the Messianic kingdom had not been established on earth then—at least, not in the way we expected it.

I kept these thoughts to myself. I studied not to disprove Worldwide's teachings; I was convinced of them and was confident the evidence had to be there somewhere. But it proved elusive.

The other two pillars, the Sabbath, as the center of Christian Torah observance, and the nature and destiny of humankind, remained solid. At least one of my parishioners had been treated by Dr. Wilder Penfield, a brain specialist who had concluded that the human mind could only be explained by a non-physical component. I read his book, *The Mystery of the Mind*, and others on the subject. One was disturbing, however: *The Origin of Consciousness in the Breakdown of the Bicameral Mind*, by Julian Jaynes. This suggested that the mind as we knew it had developed not earlier than Adam's time but much more recently. Jaynes adduced evidence from the Psalms that demonstrated that David still had what Jaynes called a bicameral mind, with less connection between the two halves than the modern brain.

Despite my nascent doubts about the accuracy of Herbert Armstrong's predictions, the two remaining pillars were stable enough for me to remain convinced that Armstrong, despite his spotty record in interpreting prophecy, was God's servant.

Nevertheless, I chafed under Armstrong's repeated use of the term "liberal" to decry everything he felt was wrong with the church. To me, liberal was the term for one of two respectable political philosophies, alongside conservative.

Many liberal ideas—the value of education, free trade, self-determination of nations—attracted me. I had difficulty understanding how that term could apply to dissidents in the church. Perhaps the inner-church relevance was that liberals were basically open to change while conservatives clung to traditional ways. Yet those of us who remained associated with Worldwide had accepted several changes in recent years: a loosening of our strict stance against remarriage after divorce and the day we observed Pentecost were two examples. At the time, conservatives opposed him, even to the point of starting competing churches, while it was the so-called liberals who remained loyal.

Perhaps, I thought, the relevance of these two terms borrowed from the realm of political philosophy had a different meaning when applied within a church context. Perhaps they referred to two approaches to the law of God, what I called an old covenant (conservative) and a new covenant (liberal) approach. Unlike many Christians, Worldwide did not believe that the law had been done away on the cross. The new covenant had been announced in the Old Testament. In Jeremiah 31, where the term is used, there is no mention of changing the law but of changing its location—no longer external, but internal, in the heart. The essence of Christianity involved seeking guidance both from Mount Sinai and from the Sermon on the Mount. This involved going beyond the letter of the law to its spirit (which didn't annul the letter). A conservative, to me, took more of an old covenant approach, of insisting on seeing the will of God spelled out and then following it literally.

Yet even that was not what Armstrong meant when he used the term. A liberal, in his eyes, was anyone who balked at any of Armstrong's interpretations of Bible teachings on questions of faith or morals. Such a one, in his eyes, said, "unless I see it spelled out in scripture, I won't accept it."

Defined this way, I wasn't a liberal. In conferring the keys of the kingdom on Peter and the other disciples (Matt. 16:17–19; 18:18), Jesus spoke of the power to bind and to loosen, which, in our understanding, meant that Herbert Armstrong, as the modern-day successor of the original apostles, had the authority to decide points of doctrine and practice. If he were wrong, we believed, it was God's responsibility, not ours, to correct him.

Once the State of California dropped the receivership, the search for disloyal or liberal (the two terms were interchangeable) employees, including ministers, intensified. At first, we felt it less in Canada, where Les McCullough had become the regional director when Wayne Cole returned to Pasadena. McCullough was one of the more easy-going of the leading ministers, the evangelists, and left us to do our jobs.

Nevertheless, I was put on the spot locally when two members of the congregation complained to Colin Wilkins. One of the complaints lodged was that I had been seen wearing blue jeans at the shopping center. One of the complainants had forbidden her son to wear jeans, and he had appealed to my example. A more serious charge was that I was not dealing severely enough with local members wrestling with moral failings.

I was summoned to Montreal and confronted, after which I set out for the two-hour drive home emotionally crushed. Colin later confessed that he had invariably been met with a defensive, counter-accusatory response in similar disciplinary sessions with others. When he saw my face, however, he knew he had overdone it. Nevertheless, his report of the complaints went into my personnel file. Not unusually, that initiated a check of my tithing records in Vancouver, where the Canadian church's office was located. This revealed not only that I had been faithfully tithing and giving generous offerings but that I had been voluntarily paying a third tithe every third year, something from which the ministry was exempt. I got word from Les McCullough that the gesture was appreciated but that our salaries were calculated with the assumption we would not pay the third tithe. We should have enough for a clothing budget that would permit us to properly represent the church (and not wear blue jeans to the shopping center).

I was still reeling from being confronted with my inadequacies when, on July 14, 1980, all the congregations in Quebec were invited for an evening Bible Study in Montreal to be held by Gerald Waterhouse, Worldwide's touring evangelist. The theme of his current tour was the place of safety, a teaching that had been downplayed in the years of Ted Armstrong's ascendancy because of his doubts on the subject, but now reemphasized as part of Herbert Armstrong's reassertion of control. That morning, however, the pastor of the Montreal English congregation telephoned to inform me that Waterhouse had been called back to Pasadena. I had to activate our congregation's round-robin telephone system to let the members know of the cancellation. Before the end of the week, word got back to me that the members, especially in the French congregation, were convinced that the reason was that it was time to flee to the place of safety and that Herbert Armstrong had called Waterhouse back to help plan it. Some members even made flight reservations.

I decided to give my first sermon on the topic that weekend. In it, I traced the vague Bible hints of protection during tribulation. I talked of how the idea that it might be Petra had come into the church. I pointed out that there was no way to be sure that was the place. And for those already purchaing airplane tickets, which airport would you fly to? Tel Aviv or Amman?

As I prepared the sermon, I received more news. Dibar Apartian, who two years earlier had regained direct supervision of the French-speaking congregations in Europe and the Caribbean (Carn's tenure in that job had been brief), had now gotten his long-time wish to have control of the French-speaking congregations in Canada as well.

I have no doubt that Apartian had heard of my exploit during orientation week when I arrived in Pasadena, of achieving the highest score on both the German and French placement exams, which had been offered simultaneously. I had taken both in the hopes of scoring high enough on at least one to test out of the foreign language requirement but overshot the mark. Both the French and German teachers urged me to take one of their courses, I succumbed to the German teacher's blandishments.

When I lived in Brussels, I attended the local congregation, but as an employee of the Editorial Department, not part of the "French Work." Attending the feast in England that first year rather than in the French Alps, the Brussels congregation's assigned site, had seemed to him a small act of betrayal. I tried to rectify that by attending the French site in Canada the following year as part of my honeymoon trip to introduce my new wife to my parents. I was not sensitive enough to church politics to realize that was hardly better since that, too, was outside his area of control. However, it was my first acquaintance with Carn and Colin, and in a way, it led to our assignment in Montreal.

But now, I was part of the French work (despite also pastoring an English-language congregation). Apartian would arrive in Montreal the following Monday and wanted me to meet him at his hotel, the Sheraton Ritz Carlton. He had reviewed my personnel file and found the record of the complaints against me. The next day, Tuesday, he followed up by coming to Sherbrooke. He sat with Edel and me and informed us that I was on probation.

He returned again in the fall. He summoned me to Montreal to meet again with him, just before the Feast of Tabernacles. He stayed for the Feast, the third I had coordinated. He made a significant change in the daily program. Until then, there had been one social gathering for the ministry during the feast, but apart from that, we felt it was vital for us to socialize with the members. But Apartian wanted ministers and wives to meet for lunch each day.

The daily ministerial dining had the air of an orien-

tal court. Crucial was who sat with whom. One who made
sure to take a seat next to Apartian was a fellow pastor with
whom I had a tense relationship. I sat at the other end of the
table. After the Feast, we traveled to Montreal for combined
services on the Sabbath, after which Apartian informed me
that he was removing me from my pastorate.

It's evident in retrospect that the probation was a sham
from the start. Colin, the area coordinator, hinted as much
at the time. There were no clear goals laid out for me, no
benchmarks established to see how I was developing. There
were two charges laid against me. One was that I was indo-
lent, the other, that I wasn't tough enough to run a pastorate. To the degree that the first charge was justified, I can
see now that it resulted from burnout. The simplest tasks—
making a telephone call, writing a letter—seemed burdensome. As for the justice of the second charge: I had long been
dissatisfied at the inability of the church to take seriously
instructions Jesus gave his disciplines when he sent them
out: "Ye know that they who are accounted to rule over the
Gentiles exercise lordship over them, and their great ones
exercise authority upon them. But so shall it not be among
you" (Mark 10:42–43). I noted that Jesus didn't say there was
no authority, but he talked of how to exercise it. It dismayed
me to see how quickly we abandoned that stance whenever
there were problems.

I remained convinced that this was the true church because it was the only one I knew of that took the entire Bible
seriously. I didn't believe that Christ's death on the cross had
somehow made the first three-quarters of the book null and

void. Yet I also took seriously the claims of Worldwide that we were to live according to the new covenant—proclaimed in the "Old" Testament; to internalize the law of God and to live according to its spirit.

I thought of the context in which the commandments are first given: at Mount Sinai, weeks after Israel had left Egypt. The old covenant approach that emphasized obedience to authority seemed to fit the mentality of people just released from slavery. But—and this continued to be an essential teaching, unique to Worldwide as far as I knew—we were called to divine sonship.

I recalled the books I'd read on management and the research of behavioral psychologists, beginning with the class I took in Pasadena. That had been my first exposure to Doug McGregor's hypothesis of motivation, Theory X (authoritarian) and Theory Y (participative). A growing body of experience in business showed that Theory Y was not only "nicer" but seemed to lead to higher productivity, product quality, worker satisfaction and innovation. Moreover, Theory Y seemed more in accord with the new covenant, with its emphasis on obedience from the heart.

I continued to recognize Herbert Armstrong's authority and those between him and me in Worldwide's pyramid. Looking up from wherever one was, the proper response, I felt, was Theory X. Yet I was uncomfortable applying it looking "down." But perhaps the excessive servility that it led to in me was part of the problem.

Apartian offered me the opportunity to fly to Pasadena to look into other employment opportunities. The Sherbrooke congregations, once again, would no longer have a resident pastor. The English congregation would be looked after by ministers of the Montreal English congregation, the French congregation assigned to the Montreal French pastor, the colleague who had placed himself next to Apartian at our common meals throughout the Feast. Within a week, he disfellowshipped the struggling members I had been working with, as well as one or two who had been vocally critical of me behind my back.

I spent a week in Pasadena, staying with the Salyers (Larry now pastored one of the Pasadena congregations). Before my arrival, he had lined up a couple of possible interviews. One was in the television department, looking for a writer, especially for ads promoting the church's literature. The other was in the church's print advertising department. Besides, Larry said that if I got one of those jobs, he would use me as an associate pastor of the congregation he cared for.

I also spoke with many others. I was invited to sit in on lectures organized by Church Administration for pastors from Australia and other places who had been brought in on suspicion of liberalism. Many of them had been my contemporaries in Pasadena or in Bricket Wood. When I took a seat in the lecture hall, many greeted me with the question, "What are you in for?" This lecture series was the beginning of a new ministerial refresher program, which replaced earlier annual ministerial conferences.

In addition to Larry, my other guardian angel was Carn, who was back in Southern California after Apartian's ascension, teaching at the college and pastoring a nearby congregation. He invited me to lunch and offered encouragement.

To audition for the TV job, I had to submit storyboards for spots for booklets. I had no idea how to do that and borrowed books on scripting TV ads from the library. I labored over the drawings for the storyboards and submitted them. Larry Omasta called when he received them, said he was impressed with the quality but that I had taken too long to produce them. The other job also didn't pan out. So, rather than moving back to Pasadena, I had no employment prospect.

Once again, I was in the situation I had been in when Editorial laid me off four years earlier. Bob Fahey, a hardnosed, energetic type, was now in Vancouver. He was one of the first "liberalism" whisperers in Herbert Armstrong's ear and had no interest in taking me on elsewhere in Canada.

The four years living in the province of Quebec were a time of increasing stress, involving work that was both satisfying and agonizing. For all of their struggles and imperfections (and mine), the people I pastored were what Jesus called the salt of the earth. My quest to better understand the Bible and related fields was in the interest of being the best pastor I could be to them. Now that it ended, it was in many ways a relief to be catapulted out of it.

My wife never felt comfortable in French, nor with the feeling that parishioners and supervisors judged both of us and found us wanting. These feelings were most potent during our time in Sherbrooke when she again became pregnant. It seemed to have been the prenatal experience for our child, too, based on our experience of him after his birth.

After losing our firstborn in Virginia through a home birth gone wrong, there was no question in either of our minds that we would use a hospital for birthing in the future. While in Canada, we were blessed with two sons.

There were other good memories. One member was a farmer's wife just south of the border Quebec shared with New England. She invited us for lunch one day, set a big kettle of water on the stove, and, when it came to a boil, ran out to the field to cut ears of ripe corn. She shucked them, threw them into the boiling pot, and we sat down to eat the best corn on the cob I've ever had. There was a family south of Sherbrooke in whose home we were always welcome and who had children slightly older than ours who enjoyed tugging our boys on a sled while we adults went cross-country skiing. Another farmer invited us to purchase a half calf. We drove and picked it up freshly slaughtered. It was winter; when we got home, we left it in the trunk of our car with the garage door partway open, so that it was frozen before we put it into the freezer. Whenever Edel served any of it over the following months, she tried not to think that it was probably the same cute calf she had petted on a previous visit to that farm.

The exposure to the people of Quebec and their history and culture enriched me. After moving to Sherbrooke, I found a used record store in a town in the Eastern Townships and, after getting to know the owner, asked him to put together a package of his French-language recommendations.

Some of the music was political. The Quebeckers sometimes referred to themselves as *negres blancs*. But the defeat of Montcalm by Wolfe had even found its way into my imagination as a child. Once my fever shot up and, in my delirium, I was sure that I was Montcalm and that I had just lost the battle of Quebec City. The grievances felt by the Quebeckers, however, were of more recent date as well. They thought they were newly emerging from many decades of enslavement under the foot of the triad of politician, factory owner, and bishop. They felt an affinity with one of Quebec's native animals, the beaver—hewers of wood and drawers of water.

The exclamations that a stubbed toe or hammered thumb might reflexively evoke reflected this. I was accustomed to an assortment of terms drawn from sex or scatology, areas of life that oppress people all over the world. In Quebec, the preferred source was the celebration of the Catholic mass: "host," "tabernacle," "chalice," or, more generally, "sacrifice."

Much of my time in Sherbrooke was spent on long drives through the countryside to visit scattered members. Once, returning late at night, I thought I saw something unusual in the sky; I stopped the car and got out and experienced the Northern Lights for the only time in my life. I wouldn't mind seeing them again, but some experiences are so profound that they don't need to be repeated. You carry them inside you for the rest of your life.

But it was time to leave Canada. I had mixed feelings. A tremendous weight had been lifted from my shoulders, but at the same time, I felt a failure. I had worked past the point of exhaustion to be a good pastor, trusting that God would equip me to do the right thing. Yet apparently, it wasn't good enough; I felt I'd let the congregants down as well as God. I'd have gladly continued to serve the church in some other capacity, but that led to closed doors. So, for the first time since I'd become a Worldwide member more than a decade before, I felt free to decide where to live and what career to pursue.

We decided to sell our house and return to New Jersey. I returned with a different feeling than I would have had we moved back four years earlier. Then, I would have gone back to work in my father's delicatessen with the feeling that the entire journey since leaving home at eighteen had been one long detour from my fate. Now, I felt confident I could find work in magazine journalism, a world centered in Manhattan, twenty miles from my hometown.

Chapter Two

The phone call from Pasadena to inform me I wouldn't be hired in the Television Department reached me at my parents' home, where we had gone for Thanksgiving. I informed Colin that I would stay in New Jersey for another three weeks to begin my job search. I was shy about my talents as a writer and photographer but confident of my skills as a photo researcher and thought that offered me the best path to a job on an editorial staff.

I reactivated the contacts I'd made working in photo research while a student in Pasadena. My cousin Louise had a friend who worked on the *New York Times* photo desk; she agreed to let me look over her shoulder for a day to become acquainted with her work. I woke early the December morning of our appointment and heard on the news that John Lennon had been shot by a deranged fan during the night. I walked to the station in my hometown, boarded the bus to the Port Authority Terminal in mid-town Manhattan, then took a city bus uptown to the *Times* headquarters. The bus route went past the Dakota, where hundreds of fans staged a vigil. Meanwhile, the soundtrack of my mind played songs that seemed to prefigure this, such as "Happiness Is a Warm Gun," or the line from "The Ballad of John and Yoko," "The way things are going, they're going to crucify me." The Beatles had been second only to Dylan in my cultural pantheon, the soundtrack of my life.

At the *Times*, the atmosphere was concentrated urgency. I loved the palpable adrenaline rush. There were no openings, and any jobs that did open at such a prestigious paper went to candidates who had proven themselves in similar work at smaller daily papers. But I felt that this was work I could do.

We drove back to Sherbrooke December 23, my employment with Worldwide ended on the 31st. We placed our house on the market and packed our things to move back to New Jersey; they would be in storage until we knew where we would settle. In the meantime, we would stay with my parents once again.

I resumed my job search. There was an opening on the photo desk at *Newsweek*, my interview went well, but there was a problem. It was a weekly publication, printed on the weekend, and on Friday, the staff worked until the issue was done. I foresaw repeated conflicts with my observance of the seventh-day Sabbath (Friday sundown to Saturday sundown); so I didn't follow up.

Although I spent most of my time networking with photo agencies and magazines, some who knew me said I was setting my sights too low. They said that working in photo research would use only a part of my skill set, leaving out my experience in public speaking and in one-on-one communication.

I also considered combining my love of books with my ability to interact with people by becoming a librarian. Aptitude tests I'd taken suggested it would be a good fit. But my interviews with librarians and my own research revealed that this would require returning to school for a Master's in Library Science. After that, I discovered, I would enter the field with the lowest starting salaries for any profession that required a master's degree. I was never particularly materialistic, but this didn't sound like a path I should go down with a wife and two infant sons.

My dad urged me to look into computer programming: he was sure that would be a growing field. My cousin Louise had just started an excellent job at AT&T after taking free courses at the Chubb Institute. In the meantime, Chubb had begun to charge for the training, and I had a hard time imagining I would enjoy that kind of work.

As I had four years earlier in Washington, I found that the process of looking for a job was interesting in itself. The need to update my resume and present myself in interviews forced me to focus on what I had to offer. This was therapeutic, after months focused on my deficits. I stressed my communication skills, both orally and in writing. Beyond that, my ability to research, compile, organize, and analyze data. My knowledge of German and French was a plus. And not least, there was my joy in helping people solve problems.

I applied for every job I learned about. One ad in the *New*

York Times was for a magazine located in New Jersey rather than in Manhattan. I researched and identified what the publishing company must be. When I was invited for an interview, I mentioned it to Louise. Small world department: a young woman on the softball team Louise played for worked at that company and had been secretary to the man who would interview me, Jim Reynolds. As a result, I heard a bit about his likes and dislikes before going for the interview, which didn't hurt my chances.

The company, which published *Medical Economics*, had purchased a struggling home building and remodeling magazine, *Hudson Home Journal*, and moved it from the Bay area to the East Coast. Reynolds was an experienced editor who had worked for *National Geographic* for many years before joining *Medical Economics*. He became editor of the new acquisition, now renamed *Home*, with the commission that it had to get better in a hurry, or else the company would fold it (the principal value of the magazine was in the ready-made building plans it featured that builders and private individuals could buy; that division could be monetized in other ways).

Some of the staff received a relocation offer, accepted, and moved east, but replacements for the others needed to be found quickly. It was perfect: a struggling magazine, located outside of Manhattan (where most publishing professionals worked), meant it had two strikes against it in the competition for suitable hires, whereas I had only three years of work experience for a magazine, which had ended four years in the past. And I lived in New Jersey. I was hired as photo editor and threw myself into my job.

It also hadn't hurt my chances that, a few years earlier, Reynolds had hired another pastor looking to change careers, and that had worked out well. Reynolds seemed to enjoy hiring men of the cloth and then exposing them to the saltiest language this side of the Navy.

I had also been interviewed by the executive editor, Olivia. She had worked for the book division of *American Heritage*, and I told her that I had urged my parents to subscribe to it and then become charter subscribers to a sister publication, *Horizon*, as well. Our family also bought most of the books the company published, and I spent hours poring through them, soaking in, without knowing it, how text and graphics could work together on a page.

I began working at *Home* on Friday, April 3, 1981. Edel and the boys soon left for Germany to visit her parents for seven weeks. Meanwhile, I continued living with my folks and began looking for a house. When Edel and the boys returned, I went to Kennedy Airport to pick them up. I saw them through the big plate-glass windows before they saw me. The first to spot me was Mark, our younger son. He had turned one while they were in Germany. The weeks they had been away extended his life by nearly twenty percent. He stared at me in incomprehension, as if he thought I looked familiar but couldn't place me. That was heart-wrenching.

For the first months, Olivia was my immediate supervisor and we worked well together. She coached me on essential work skills, such as the importance of focusing on one task at a time and seeing it through to completion. I realized the inability to do this had been a factor in my feeling overwhelmed in the past: I had tried to do everything, not knowing where to start.

The job was an answer to my prayer for one I could throw myself into and learn better work habits. I fully embraced this return to the world of journalism. An added benefit was the need to reactivate an interest in architecture I'd begun to nurture while at Boston University. I had a lot to learn, though, but enjoyed the challenge. The magazine sought to feature innovative ideas; one story I particularly enjoyed working on was about solar-heated homes. At the time, solar storage batteries were even less developed than now, and an objection to solar heating was that it might be fine in warm, sunny climates, but impractical elsewhere. I took a scouting trip to Vermont, where I visited several homes that were built to take advantage of passive solar gain (hillside sites with southern orientation). The owners reported to me that the challenge was that their homes got too warm on sunny winter days. We chose one of the homes and hired a photographer to take photos for the article while deep snow surrounded the house.

Olivia soon succeeded Jim Reynolds as editor, and I began to report to the magazine's art director, with whom I had a tenser relationship. She demanded much from herself and others and made no secret of her feeling that I was not up to the job. But I continued to improve under her tutelage, and we developed a mutual respect.

My tribulations working for Worldwide and the manner of my departure hadn't shaken my allegiance to the church and its teachings. That's why, when I first learned I wouldn't be going to Pasadena, I called the local Worldwide pastor, to tell him that I'd be settling in the area. My credentials as a minister had not been revoked, consequently, I could serve as a non-salaried elder. He informed me, though, that he had just ended a call informing him that he would be leaving the area, transferred to Washington, D.C.

Early in the new year, I learned who the new pastor would be, Jim Jenkins, moving in from Wyoming. He didn't know me, but one of his daughters had been a student in Pasadena with me, although I hadn't known her well. I considered the situation from his point of view. If I were new to a congregation and there were an elder who had just been removed from a pastorate, I'd want to know with whom I was dealing. I learned when his moving van was due and volunteered to help unload (this was shortly before I began my new job). We found time during the day to talk. We sat in his car, which offered the most privacy while the others were going in and out of every room of the house with furniture and boxes. He listened to my story, and I was impressed that he neither sympathized nor condemned but wrapped up the conversation with "well, let's see what you can do."

So, in my spare time, I served in the local congregation. We bought a home in River Vale to cut down on commuting, less than a ten-minute drive from the office. Although that town was part of the Montvale congregation, I continued serving in the Union area. Herbert Armstrong, after a shaky start returning to television after Ted Armstrong's removal, had begun to build a following. His venerable age seemed to give him additional credence with many viewers. Worldwide's time buyers negotiated an excellent Sunday morning time slot for the telecast on an independent New York station. This generated many new subscribers for the *Plain Truth* and, with time, many visit requests. Jim and an associate pastor did their best keeping up, but Jim began petitioning Pasadena to add a third minister to the team. Finally, the Church Administration Department told him they could send him a trainee from that year's college graduating class. Jim responded that he couldn't use a trainee; he needed someone he could send out with a stack of visit requests. And, he added, he had just the person he needed right in the area: me.

I didn't know any of this and was caught off guard when the office manager of Church Administration phoned to say Worldwide would like to rehire me. I demurred, and he—surprised by my reaction—transferred the call to Joe Tkach, now (after Rod Meredith had once again been removed from the position) director of Church Administration. He asked me what the problem was, and I asked in return if it were wise for me to leave a job where I was performing well to return to a job that I had failed at before. He accepted what I said and told me they'd find another solution for the church area.

One morning a few days later, in my time of prayer and Bible study before going to work, I read of Jesus admonishing those who put their hand on the plow and looked back as not worthy of the Kingdom of God (Luke 9:62). In fear of my salvation, I called the office manager to tell of my change of heart. I was sure they had already made other arrangements for the local area, I explained, but wanted to go on record that I was willing to serve the next time they needed someone anywhere.

It turned out they had not yet found someone else. A few days later, he called to say I could return to work for the church. My last day working for *Home* was Friday, November 19, 1982, and on Monday, November 22, I returned to work full-time for Worldwide, two years after I'd been fired in Canada, but that seemed a lifetime ago. It was also nineteen years to the day after the assassination of John F. Kennedy.

For the next four-and-a-half years, I was part of the pastoral team in central New Jersey. The growth of the congregation soon led to starting a second, in Brick, on the Jersey shore, and then a third, in Hudson County, across the river from Manhattan. Jim Jenkins was an excellent mentor, and I enjoyed the camaraderie with ministers from surrounding congregations. But I also experienced an instance of a flagrant lack of collegiality.

This arose when a young woman from our congregation was vacationing with her husband and children in Florida. The woman, who was emotionally troubled, spoke after services there with the local pastor. She also showed him her locket; instead of a photo of her children, it held a photo of my wife and me. I didn't know about that. Apparently, we represented an ideal family in her mind.

The pastor, rather than checking with me, telephoned Joe Tkach in Pasadena to report his suspicion that I was conducting an affair. Tkach phoned Jim Jenkins, who quickly assured him that there wasn't the least indication of anything

improper going on. More than once in the years of my involvement with Worldwide I was struck by how often, for
all our professed allegiance to the teachings of Jesus, we ignored his instructions to go to your brother (Matt. 18:15).

Paradoxically, my work representing a church that espoused British Israelism was also an education in cultural
diversity. For all the talk in other denominations against rac-
ism, most congregations are segregated in fact, even if not
in ideology.

The congregations I served, part of the New York metropolitan area, by contrast, were integrated and had a large
proportion of black members. A new man who arrived to
pastor a nearby congregation had difficulty acclimating and
wondered aloud whether he should let an Italian member
date a "white" woman; I finally told him, "You left Manasseh
when you crossed the Delaware River" (Worldwide taught
that Anglo-Saxons descended from Ephraim and Manasseh,
two of the lost ten tribes of Israel).

Traditionally, there had been one African-American on
the ministerial team. But after the other associate pastor
was transferred, I did most of the visiting in the urban areas of Newark, the Oranges, and Hudson County. Once, one
of the members asked to speak to me. "Don't take this the
wrong way," he said, "but until now, there's always been one
of us on the team." I understood what he meant, and it didn't
bother me. I smiled and replied: "Well, here I am."

I enjoyed serving the members. In addition to African-
Americans, a large part of my visiting load was to Latinos.
Some three to five million Spanish-speaking people lived in

the New York metropolitan area, as many as in a nation like Costa Rica. None of us on the ministerial team spoke Spanish. I sometimes took a Spanish-speaking member to assist me in visiting those with limited English. After a while, I hit on an idea that improved the quality of visits. When a Bible-related question was posed, I asked the person to turn to the passage I would have turned to for an answer and ask them to read it aloud from their Bible. I had acquired a bit of rudimentary Spanish, enough to recognize which word in the passage provided the answer.

In January 1987, the ministry from all the congregations in the metropolitan area met to discuss a proposal to establish a Spanish-language congregation. One of the arguments offered in favor of it was that Latins had a different way of thinking than Anglos. In the case of the New York area, that meant people from Puerto Rico and Cuba primarily. I asked myself whether this one "Latin" mindset included Mexicans, Peruvians, and Argentinians.

The argument was that they should be served by "one of their own." I wasn't in sympathy with that line of thinking and wasn't surprised when one of the African-American ministers present supported it and said we should do the same for the Black members.

I couldn't stay silent. Cultural diversity was one of the things I liked best about our congregations, and I was not in favor of re-segregating them. At the same time, my experience living in other countries brought home to me how language could indeed be a barrier. One could know enough of a language to function in daily life, yet a message about spiritual issues entered the heart much more deeply if heard in one's mother tongue, as a result, I supported the proposal.

The discussion stayed with me in the coming days. I thought of how the Bible records the crucial role of people working cross-culturally. Among them, Moses and Paul. The cross-cultural experiences I was making seemed in keeping with the plan.

Another education in diversity was in dealing with homosexuals. Worldwide shared the general fundamentalist conviction that the Bible condemned same-sex relationships and that no one who engaged in same-sex behavior would be in the Kingdom of God. I never suspected how many people with homosexual orientation agreed with that and had been baptized into Worldwide. They tried to live God-pleasing lives; for many, that meant a life of celibacy. Others thought marriage would "cure" them. My experiences in counseling them suggested to me that it rarely did.

I had first faced the issue and the various ways of coping in Canada. Now, in the metropolitan area, I was confronted with it to a greater degree. These were the years when AIDS first broke out. The Newark area soon had the third-largest number of cases, after New York and San Francisco. My first direct involvement came within days of the first news reports I'd seen of this mysterious new ailment. A visit request arrived from a young Latino who had contracted it working as a male prostitute. He knew he was likely to die, but the existential question he wanted to discuss with me was whether the disease was God's direct punishment for his behavior. I don't know what I would have thought months earlier, but sitting with him as he asked me directly, I knew the answer was "no." I was sad for him that amid his suffering, he was additionally plagued by that question.

The question soon arose of whether an AIDS sufferer could be invited to attend services. I understood the fear many felt of having any contact with someone infected with this new disease. Still, as I researched the question, I quickly concluded that the main danger ran in the opposite direction. For a person with a compromised immune system, it would be life-threatening to be exposed to the common colds and cases of flu that someone could be counted on to carry to services.

I continued my reading to understand the issue of homosexuality. But the most significant factor in changing my mind was not anything I read but the fact that someone close to me lived in a committed same-sex relationship. Returning to New Jersey meant spending more time with the couple than I had previously done in occasional visits to the area. I simply couldn't view them as condemned in God's eyes. For years, I lived with the dissonance of my personal experience in conflict with my understanding of scriptural teaching.

The congregation continued to grow. Snapshots taken of me from the time invariably show me underweight and haggard, with bags under my eyes. When time came to start a congregation in Hudson County, I was delegated to find an appropriate location. I used family connections to gain us access to the Schuetzenpark, built when many neighborhoods in Jersey City were filled with German immigrants.

Returning to work for Worldwide meant much commuting, this time in the reverse direction from my first months working for *Home*, when I had traveled from Westfield to Oradell on the Parkway. Jim Jenkins urged me to move somewhere in the Union church area. He had rented a home in Kendall Park, along Highway 1. Depending on traffic, it took him forty minutes to an hour to reach Newark, where many members lived. Hardly an improvement over my commute from River Vale. Still, I complied. One change a move would bring was in my phone number. The exchange where I lived was 666. I'll admit I savored the hesitation I sensed on the phone when someone asked for my number and I said "my number is . . ." (see Rev. 13:18).

We looked at houses in Maplewood and other towns closer to the center of the congregation and were surprised to find a house we could afford in my hometown, on a quiet street off of South Avenue. Our oldest boy, Erik, was just about to begin school. When I took him to McKinley school on the first day, I had a flashback. The classroom was furnished precisely like the classroom had been when I started in Wilson school, thirty years earlier. And his teacher was the wife of the high school science teacher who had coached our junior varsity soccer squad. Small world.

Whenever possible, I walked Erik to school in the morning. Our route took us past the A.M.E. church a couple of blocks from our house, and I told him about the most illustrious Westfield resident we were never told of in school, Paul Robeson, an African-American athlete, singer and civil rights advocate. His father had pastored that church. Westfield's historical amnesia has since been remedied—when I returned for my fiftieth high school reunion, I found a commemorative stone.

Westfield was conveniently located at an exit off the Garden State Parkway, which helped when I drove to Brick for services. But my visiting load included the bulk of new visit requests from Essex County, and I found I could reach them as quickly by traveling back roads. This probably saved the church between twenty and forty dollars a month in tolls. To get to Hudson County, my best route included the New Jersey Turnpike however, but it also easily accessible.

Best of all, our new house was just a few blocks from the home my parents had moved to when they sold the house I'd grown up in. That meant my mom often looked after our boys whenever Edel needed to accompany me on visits.

We bought a wood-framed house with yellow aluminum siding and an old detached garage at the back of the yard. The yard was long and narrow, and Edel set to work laying out three long raised beds for gardening. One of the members had a family-owned disposal business and had just disassembled an old water tower. The aged redwood beams he'd salvaged would be perfect for the borders of the beds. Another member had parents who owned a horse farm. He delivered a load of manure. Unfortunately, that was just before we left for the Feast of Tabernacles that year. Our next-door neighbor wondered about her new neighbors who had left this stinking pile close to the fence separating our two yards. Once we got home, though, we spread it on the beds, turned it over, and let that continue to decompose over the winter.

The house had no air-conditioning, and there were the hot, humid New Jersey summers to contend with. My dad installed a large fan in the attic to combat this. This relatively inaccessible space was reached by a ladder in the closet of the smallest of the three rooms on the second floor (actually, there was a fourth room: the top level of a two-story sun porch added to the house). I got out of bed at first light throughout the summer, opened windows throughout the house, and turned on the fan to draw in the cool air. As soon as the outside temperature reached 68 degrees, we closed all the windows and pulled down the shades. As a result, the house remained comfortable throughout the day.

My return to the full-time ministry hadn't meant abandoning writing and photography any more than my work for *Home* had prevented me from serving the local congregation on the side. I contributed a steady stream of articles to Worldwide's publications. In May 1984, a further opportunity arose. The annual meeting of the AAAS, the American Association for the Advancement of Science, would take place in New York. Budget and other constraints meant that no one could travel from Pasadena to cover it, and Gene Hogberg, director of Editorial's news bureau, remembered that we had first met at the AAAS meetings in 1969, while I was still a student at Boston University and that, when the meetings were held again in Boston in 1976, covering it had been one of my last assignments while working in Washington for the *Plain Truth*. Gene called Jim to ask if he could spare me for a week.

Jim agreed, and Gene outlined the sessions they were particularly interested in having me cover. Among them were sessions devoted to recent developments in evolution theory, particularly the idea of punctuated equilibrium propounded by Stephen Jay Gould and Niles Eldridge. Biology had been the weakest of my science subjects in school, and my acquaintance with evolution was limited to the paper "disproving" a book on the subject for the second year Bible course, Systematic Theology, at Ambassador. So, I set out on a crash reading program to remedy my ignorance and understand the sessions I attended. Typically for me, I began with a biography of Charles Darwin. After the biography, I went on to books by Gould and Eldridge and compiled a binder of information on all the topics I'd be asked to cover.

Pasadena's interest in punctuated equilibrium was no doubt the hope that it would mean that Darwin had been "wrong" and that, by default, creationism would triumph. Ted Armstrong had been one of the most prominent debunkers of evolution, making it a frequent topic of his radio and television broadcasts. The church's full-color brochures, such as *A Whale of a Tale* and *Evolution: A Theory for the Birds*, had been among our most popular titles.

My reading revealed to me that Gould and Eldridge had been doing what scientists do: they built on the work of previous scientists yet modified their work wherever anomalies couldn't be explained and where additional evidence painted a new picture. We talk loosely of the "laws" of science as if they were absolute, but the reality of scientific investigation is that there is always more to explain.

These newer evolutionary biologists were well aware of Ted Armstrong's criticisms. Gould introduced one of his books by describing the disjuncture of watching a *World Tomorrow* program back-to-back with a televised presentation by Eldridge. Both cited the same animal. In the first program, it had been an example of the absurdity of evolutionary theory, in the other as evidence for the kind of natural phenomenon for which evolution offers the best explanation.

For all its gaps, I saw that the fossil record did show a sequence, a progression, a development—stretching back billions of years on this planet. Admittedly, a sequence doesn't prove that one came from another. But it does show that one came after the other. I asked myself what in the first few chapters of Genesis, or even in the entire Bible, would have led anyone to suspect the vast panorama that has opened before us?

What does one do, I asked myself, in the face of the evidence of evolution? For every Thomas Huxley, gleeful at the disappearance of any authority who could tell one what to do, there must have been many before me who approached the theory dubiously, noted its flaws and inconsistencies, yet had to admit that it dealt with material the Bible gives us no answer for.

The result of my preparation was that I was converted from a creationist to one convinced that evolution offered the best account so far of the diversity of the natural world. Then, in a break between sessions, I spotted Stephen Jay Gould standing by himself in a hallway. I approached him to thank him for writing in such a clear, reasonable way and enable me to change my mind. He didn't know me, of course, but he could read my name tag with *Plain Truth Magazine* clearly printed on it. He immediately said, "I haven't got time," and turned away. I was momentarily offended—he didn't know what I wanted to tell him. But then I realized that he must have often been accosted by zealous, perhaps even abusive creationists. I regret I never had the chance to tell him what I wanted (I wish I had put it in a letter, but I'm shy about writing people I don't know).

I had an entirely different experience after a session on cosmology. Alan Guth of MIT presented his research into the first seconds after the Big Bang. He demonstrated that, once you posit such an event, everything that happened after that could be explained in terms of known laws of science. Yet, he acknowledged that no one knew where that first hydrogen atom came from. Nor could there be any evidence of what, if anything, existed before that event.

I was fascinated and went to talk with him after the session. I said I might write an article about it for the *Plain Truth* and asked if he'd be willing to review my article for accuracy before it ran, something he readily agreed to. Unfortunately, I never did write that article, but the week covering these meetings made a lasting impact.

I asked myself why evolutionists felt so secure in their belief that creationism isn't scientific. One reason, I saw, was that religion had too often spearheaded rear-guard actions against scientific knowledge and understanding. The fate of Galileo was but one instance. Religion had continually been forced to fall back, like a retreating army, from one position to another. As scientists saw it, progress in knowledge had rolled back the involvement of God in the universe. From specifically sending each rainstorm or placing each star, God had withdrawn to a first cause who released vast amounts of energy at a time roughly fifteen billion years ago.

I was bemused to learn that creationists heap even more scorn, if possible, on "theistic evolutionists" than on scientists who make no profession about God. The idea seems to be that these are compromisers, that they willfully reject the power of God yet want to cling to a cloak of respectability. This may be the motivation of some, but for others, an outright rejection of the historical accuracy of Genesis must have been a painful step, reluctantly taken. It was for me.

A fundamentalist complaint about theistic evolutionists is that their God is too small—that these are people who believe God couldn't have made each species as a full-blown, separate, individual "kind" six thousand years ago. But "could have," I decided, is not the issue. God can do anything He wants. The question is, what did He do? The insistence of many fundamentalists that the universe was no more than six thousand years old was clearly wrong. But a literal reading of Bible-as-science seemed to indicate it. Worldwide's attempt to meet science halfway by assuming room for a gap of fifteen billion years between the first two verses of Genesis was not the most natural reading of the passage. It also seemed increasingly less probable, in light of findings of bones and indications of culture, such as the cave paintings of Lascaux, that Adam lived six thousand years ago.

I learned that the first serious geologists had begun sure

they would find evidence of a worldwide flood from the time of Noah, 4,400 years earlier, but the evidence they turned up told a different story.

By this time, I was aware of the similarities between Genesis, especially chapters 1–11, and the myths of other peoples, dating back to ancient Sumer, long before the time of Moses, the putative author of the Torah. Not surprising, I felt, since Abram, a native of Ur of the Chaldees, could have carried these stories with him and passed them down to his descendants. Still, it undermined a strictly literal, inerrant inspiration of the Bible.

Once I began questioning my previous assumptions, it was hard to stop. Chapter 10 of Genesis says that before the Tower of Babel, all were of one language, then their tongue was confused. Epigraphy shows us older languages than this. Were the tongues confused back into languages that had existed before the flood? Occam sharpened his razor precisely for convoluted explanations such as that.

Even if reluctantly, I decided I must face these things because of my absolute conviction that God, the creator, exists and my passionate devotion to God's way of life as the best way to live.

This didn't lead me to throw out all of Worldwide's teachings. For example, the exciting developments in cosmology known as the New Inflationary Theory showed that the universe could (but didn't necessarily have to) have come from nothing. And, by nothing, they mean not just empty space but no space and time. Also, I had heard Paul Levinson of Fairleigh Dickinson University, in one session, point out that we still have two profound discontinuities: that between living matter and non-living, and that between thinking matter and non-thinking. This last dovetailed with Worldwide's interest in the spirit in man.

On top of that, I continued to believe that the Bible presents a way of life that works, in a way that even the classics don't work, including the dimension of divine intervention.

That possibility of divine intervention was driven home to me when I was called to the hospital because a member had gone into a coma. He was a diabetic but liked to dose his insulin so that he was close to the edge. It made him feel more productive and alert. But it was easy to slip over the edge, and he had. When I arrived, the caretakers said he was totally unresponsive, but I spoke to him, calling his name and identifying myself. He immediately regained consciousness, opened his eyes, and recovered.

Most of my reading wasn't on scientific topics in those years. I continued to read history and biography as well as books on social and psychological issues to better understand matters brought to me in counseling. From time to time, I found myself drawn to the library of the nearby New Brunswick Theological Seminary, a Reformed school affiliated with Rutgers University, as I had been to the university library in Sherbrooke.

Despite my continued commitment to Worldwide, I still wrestled with doubts about the distinctive element in one of its teachings, that of British Israelism. It bothered me that Herbert Armstrong had plagiarized lengthy passages of his book, *The United States and British Commonwealth in Prophecy*, from an earlier work, J. H. Allen's *Judah's Sceptre and Joseph's Birthright*, something for which he'd have received a failing grade on a high school essay. I began to trace the origin of the teaching further back and learned that it had been propagated by Richard Brothers, a strange Englishman who was a friend of William Blake's. More troubling was the adoption of the teaching by the growing "identity" or "covenant" movement on the racist, militaristic fringe of the right-wing.

I also continued to wrestle with the timeline we'd constructed from the book of Daniel and elsewhere. As Trumpets 1982, 2,520 years after the fall of Babylon, approached, many of us wondered whether something significant might happen on this date marking, according to our calculation, the end of the Times of the Gentiles. Few expected the return of Jesus Christ—the signs we expected to precede that hadn't happened. Yet in what way would Babylon fall?

It turned into an instance of theme and variation: German chancellor Helmut Schmidt lost a vote of no-confidence in parliament on that day, and Helmut Kohl became chancellor in his place. Schmidt had been an able leader who had sought to defuse tensions between East and West. He had been bitterly disappointed by the Soviet provocation of moving missiles into Eastern Europe and reluctantly acquiesced to Ronald Reagan's response. But this provoked unrest among the rank-and-file of his Social Democratic party. His coalition partner, the Liberal party, sniffed the wind and jumped ship, ensuring that Germany would allow the deployment of Pershing missiles.

This was a significant event, but not Belshazzar's feast. Instead, this "fall" was the result of a perfectly normal democratic political procedure. So, not insignificant, but again, the return of Christ had been delayed. Was there any new guess? Hardcore speculators (among whom I no longer numbered) suggested January 1991 as a new time for Worldwide's work to end, an additional nineteen-year time cycle after January 1972. I found this less convincing than the original Trumpets 1975 scenario. Still, I remained a little curious about what event might happen in the church in January 1991 or in the world on Trumpets 1994.

I never attached great importance to dreams, but every once in a while, I had one that was so vivid that I remembered it clearly after waking. Then shortly afterward, some development in Worldwide would seem not so much a direct fulfillment of the dream as to be the confirmation of some foreshadowing I had felt. One such had been in the late spring of 1978. I dreamed that Garner Ted Armstrong had been kidnaped and then, after histrionically crying out, "I'm not going to be held captive any longer," committed suicide. Shortly after that came his banishment.

Another occurred a few months later while we visited my parents for Thanksgiving. I was attending a small ministerial meeting with a somber atmosphere at which Les McCullough said, "There are no heroes anymore." Then, five weeks later came the receivership and the allegations about Herbert Armstrong and Stan Rader.

A third happened before waking on a Sabbath morning in July 1981. We hadn't yet moved to River Vale; I was asleep in my parents' home in Westfield. In the dream, I was in Westfield, too. There was a power failure, and then I attended a small ministerial meeting with Herbert Armstrong. He acquainted us with plans for the place of safety (despite my doubts about this, apparently, it still lurked in my subconscious). There was a printed text and pictures along with his presentation. We all took notes on yellow pads. At the close of the meeting, we were asked to put our names on the pads that held our notes and turn them in along with the presentation packet. The meeting took place on a Sabbath in mid-January. The information was to be communicated to the brethren in two weeks, in special services on January 30th.

Armstrong did not give any reasons why he felt our flight was close. He thought that his authority as Christ's messenger should be sufficient. He added that, as always, some ministers accepted it right away, whereas others, also loyal, had many questions that would be resolved. Back home that night, I woke up in the middle of the night (this was still in the dream). The power was still off, and moonlight reflected on the snow. Many homes had gas lanterns in them. Our woodpile glowed as if it were about to burst out in spontaneous combustion. A horde of motorcyclists roared up the street, accompanied by some sports cars and chased by two policemen. They got out of their squad car and chased a few on foot, shooting two. I was filled with a feeling of chaos and fear. Then I woke up. Unlike the other two dreams, I never identified anything this foreshadowed, other than that I had not wholly discarded the belief of a flight to a place of safety, as well as general uneasiness that the (relative) tranquility of life was but a thin veneer.

Armstrong jettisoned Stan Rader soon after we returned from Canada. We learned of this when Armstrong traveled to New York City at the end of April 1981 for combined services in the hall the Manhattan congregation rented around the corner from the United Nations. After the State of California dropped all legal action against Worldwide, the legislature passed an act that would make it harder to act against any church in the future. Now that the threat was gone, Armstrong claimed he had long seen through Rader but that he let things run until we could all see it, too. The immediate occasion was the announcement by Rader of a new initiative, the Herbert Armstrong Peace Prize, to be awarded by the Ambassador International Cultural Foundation (AICF). There had been intense criticism from members, who continued to have difficulty understanding why the church needed to sponsor a foundation. My immediate reaction, given the instinctive mistrust I, along with many members, had felt for Rader, was to give credence to Armstrong's version of events. In retrospect, it seems that, with the threat of receivership was gone, Armstrong no longer needed Rader, who had shielded not only himself but Armstrong. What we weren't told: Rader would continue to serve behind the scenes as Armstrong's consultant.

The foundation, with its concert series in the Ambassador Auditorium, had brought the church prestige. It allowed both Armstrong and Rader to spend time with personalities at the intersection of music and philanthropy such as Arthur Rubenstein. AICF had sponsored many worthwhile projects, beginning with a literacy initiative among refugees on the Thai-Laotian border, then in Bangkok, Sri Lanka, and Amman. Many Ambassador students served on these projects. Student labor helped keep project costs down, while in return, the students gained invaluable exposure to other cultures; it was like a church-sponsored Peace Corps. Once, while I was standing in line at the checkout counter in Vroman's bookstore while in Pasadena on a refresher program, two young women in front of me fell into a conversation: "It's so good to see you! How was your summer in Jordan?" "Amazing. How was your year in Thailand?" When it was my turn to pay for my purchases, the cashier commented, "Ambassador students" (as if I didn't know).

I continued to view Herbert Armstrong as God's apostle in our age, but an increasing number of instances challenged that. One had been the insensitive editorial he wrote in the church's internal newsletter for ministers, the *Pastor General's Report*, after John Lennon's shooting. Another had to do with Worldwide's observance of the Passover one night earlier than the Jewish community, followed on the following evening by a celebration it called the Night to Be Much Observed. This was one way of understanding the indications in Exodus, but some maintained we were wrong to split what Jews understood as one observance into two. Herbert Armstrong decided to settle the question by writing that, based on his authority as an apostle, the Passover of the Exodus was "officially" on the evening beginning the 14th of Nisan and that the Israelites had left Egypt the following night. We had always used the power to bind and loosen (Matt. 16:19; 18:18) to cover many things, such as refusing to baptize anyone who refused to quit smoking, even though tobacco is not mentioned one way or the other in scripture. Still, his reasoning for that decision was based on scriptural principles: The tenth commandment, against coveting, covered, in principle, any form of addiction.

Yet while it was clear to me that our interpretation of scripture was something for Herbert Armstrong to decide, the issue of when Israel had left Egypt was a historical issue and not, I felt, something that he could "officially" declare thirty-five centuries later.

Armstrong was given to increasing speculation about the pre-Adamic world as well. He became convinced that the earth had first been created for Lucifer and the angels to inhabit and govern. Then, after Lucifer's rebellion and transformation to Satan, God decided that the only way to achieve his goal was to reproduce himself, creating man with the destiny to develop character and be born into the God family. This made it seem as if humankind was something like an after-thought, a plan B. And there was more. He was inclined to believe, he said, that there had been no physical reproduction before Adam and Eve. I contemplated this when standing before an exhibit of dinosaur eggs at a natural history museum.

Armstrong began to expound those ideas in *The Incredible Human Potential*, which he wrote to replace the abortive

Systematic Theology Project as a summary of Worldwide's teachings. In it, he outlined his teachings of the spirit in man and human destiny. Now he revised it to incorporate more of his new speculations. The result, *The Mystery of the Ages*, was the last book he wrote, a summation of his lifework. After it appeared, I would often field questions about it when visiting members and prospective members. This put me on the spot. To me, these speculations were unbiblical, but I also felt it would be unbiblical for me to say as much. I replied by reminding the person I was talking to that one of Armstrong's oft-repeated slogans had been, "don't believe me, believe the Bible." My counsel was to read what he wrote respectfully, compare it with the Bible, and believe it if they found it supported there.

For all of our rhetoric against the Roman Catholic Church as the seat of the False Prophet, Worldwide's view of Herbert Armstrong's authority had become very similar to the (relatively recent) Roman dogma of papal infallibility. In fact, as Armstrong grew older and insisted on the prerogatives of his office, he revised Worldwide's view of early church history. Worldwide had long rejected the notion that Peter had been the first bishop of Rome or the supreme leader of the early church. A key text for us was the report of the council in Acts 15, at which James, the brother of the Lord, presided. It was he, not Peter nor Paul, who promulgated the results of the confab.

The role of James as presiding apostle also suited Worldwide well because, in the epistle bearing his name, he teaches against the notion that faith without works suffices for salvation (the same passage that caused Luther to call the writing an epistle of straw). But now, Peter became the new model for the aging Armstrong.

The last time I saw Herbert Armstrong was in April 1985, when Edel and I were in Pasadena for the two-week refresher program. He addressed us on the first day and told us he had finished his final book, *Mystery of the Ages*, that morning. While speaking, Armstrong seemed much as he had in the previous years, yet when he got up to leave the room, his step was halting and labored. One afternoon I happened to look out the window of the church-owned apartment used to house visiting ministers and saw his chauffeured limousine drive along South Orange Grove Boulevard. I spotted him sitting in the back. My eyes may have deceived me, but it looked as if he were waving to crowds lining the sidewalk— crowds that weren't there.

It was a wrenching sight, and my prayer for him became that he could soon rest from his labors. God was only keeping him alive, I felt, because we weren't ready to carry on without him. I prayed we would be ready.

The following January, I was out one evening doing parish visits. My wife knew where I was, and she called to tell me that Herbert Armstrong had died. I wrapped up the visit and returned home. I heard the news confirmed on the car radio, first in a brief notice on the hourly news, then in a feature on National Public Radio's *All Things Considered*. Whereas the CBS radio notice had been brief and neutral ("a voice known by millions"), the NPR report included an interview with Joseph Hopkins, a scholar at Rice University. He told of some of Worldwide's more controversial teachings, receivership battle, and rejection of mainstream Christianity as false worship. His final words hurt: "Frankly, I'm glad he's dead."

My own feelings toward Armstrong were more complicated. The obstinacy with which he insisted on dubious positions, the insensitivity he displayed in his hurtful editorial after John Lennon's death, the increasing fantasy of his speculations about the pre-Adamic world—all of these made him hard to take. Yet he remained to the end for me an inspirational figure. A few years earlier, I had noted a passage from David McCullough's *Path Between the Seas* (Simon and Schuster 1977. 137). It was a reference from the *Illustrated London News* in 1869 written about Ferdinand de Lesseps. I felt it applied to Herbert Armstrong as well: "Perhaps no other man ever possessed to such a marvelous extent the power of communicating to other minds the faith and the fervor which animated his own."

Armstrong's health had been failing for months. A few days before his death, he appointed Joe Tkach as his successor "in the event of his death." He had auditioned new presenters for the *World Tomorrow* telecast and was active in selecting three, David Hulme, Dave Albert, and Richard Ames. The television department worked intensely to complete a memorial program that was already in the works. It aired the following weekend and drew a large response to its offer of Armstrong's new book.

To the end, Armstrong had difficulty separating his personal fate from that of the church. If his life were to end, he believed, then that meant that the work of warning the world before the end-time had ended as well. All that remained would be to prepare the church to be the bride of Christ. How did this reconcile in his mind with ensuring the continuation of the telecast? I didn't know. There was a surprise in store, though: the increased response to the memorial program was not just a one-off. Response to the telecast with the new presenters continued rising.

After Herbert Armstrong's death, I was concerned about how Worldwide would handle the legacy of his teachings. I was familiar with how the Seventh-Day Adventist church revered the writings of Ellen G. White; seventy years after her death, hers was still the final word on any question of faith and practice. I shuddered at the prospect of a gilt-edged, leather-bound edition of the writings of Herbert Armstrong. Nevertheless, I continued to respect him for the role he had played and for all that I had learned from him. I hoped that the best and soundest of what he'd written would continue to be available.

When it was announced that Herman Hoeh had been tasked with editing Herbert Armstrong's writings and revising where necessary, I was reassured. The process of revision, however, raised issues that couldn't be settled by tasteful edits.

A few months later, I was raised in rank to a preaching elder during the spring holy days. In the hierarchically organized ministry of Worldwide, local elder, for those on the payroll, was the entry-level designation. The expectation was that one would prove oneself and, with time, be ordained a preaching elder. I had been ordained a local elder in Montreal in January 1977, then let go at the end of 1980. Now, after a little over nine years as a local elder, both on and off the payroll, Jim had recommended me for this step. I had caught wind of it through an overheard conversation in the locker room after one of our racquetball games and suspected it would be during services on the first day of Unleavened Bread (ordinations were usually performed on annual holy days).

That day turned out to be a test of whether I was raising our children for their sake or for the church's. One of the qualifications of an elder was to have his children in subjection (1 Tim. 3:4), but I resisted the temptation to do this just to look good as a minister. Our younger son, Mark, needed to go to the bathroom, I took him. But he took a while. I could hear that Jim was talking about the qualifications of a minister (expounding the same passages Wayne Cole had expounded nine years earlier) during announcements—often the run-up to the ceremony. He rambled, even more than was usual for him. Finally, Mark was finished, and we returned to our seats. As soon as we did, Jim quickly wrapped up his remarks and called me to the stage.

Only a couple of weeks later, I received a call one evening from a hospital. It was from Kathryn, the oldest of three sisters I'd come into contact with through my work in the congregation. A few months earlier, she had requested a visit, and I had met her at her college dorm. As her story unfolded, it became clear that she and her sisters had been the victims of many years of emotional and physical abuse.

Now Kathryn had taken her sisters to the hospital for an examination after their mother had disciplined them. The hospital called the Division of Youth and Family Services (DYFS) and summoned the mother to the hospital. Kathryn wanted me there as well. The mother was informed that the girls were going to be removed from the home immediately. The mother agreed (not that she could have refused) on the condition that they be placed in a church home. I offered to let them stay with us and look for a suitable family. So, at two in the morning, I drove home with Kathryn and her two sisters, Sarah and Deborah, in the back seat.

Since Kathryn was eighteen, therefore no longer a minor, she didn't need to be placed in foster care. But it proved more challenging than I expected to find a family willing to take in her sisters, two teenage girls they didn't know. Before long, though, the girls found their way into our hearts, and we decided to look into becoming their foster parents. I called Larry Salyer, now director of Church Administration in Pasadena. He approved it on one condition. Now that I was a preaching elder, I was at the top of his list in case he needed to fill a pastorate on short notice. Therefore, we would have to be ready to pack and move quickly. I contacted the girls' mother, and she gave written permission for us to take the girls anywhere within the United States.

It caused more than a few heads in the congregation to turn when we walked in as a family of seven instead of four. The girls asked us not to say anything, which didn't keep some in the congregation from explaining it to themselves and others. One woman confidently informed the others that they were Edel's daughters from a previous marriage. When that made its way around to me, I said they were indeed our daughters from a prior marriage in which neither of us was involved.

Until we took in the girls, I had been blind to the number of people in the congregation raising OPKs (other people's kids). For instance, the woman who had taken in her grandson, born addicted to crack; he had been taken away from his mother at birth. There were mix-and-match families after divorce and remarriage, and there were others who, like us, had taken in foster children. It struck me how, until then, whenever I'd talked of marriage, the family, or child-rearing in sermons, my remarks had been based on the assumption of an intact nuclear family.

A caseworker from DYFS visited us to assess whether we were suitable for taking on the girls. However, state aid would not be forthcoming until we had passed a training course and become certified. Attending the classes opened our eyes further to the misery of children who couldn't remain in the home of a parent for one reason or another.

Even after we completed the course, it was a long time before the first support arrived. In the meantime, we needed to equip the home for the girls. We gave them our boys' bedroom, moved the boys into what had been our bedroom, and we slept on the upper sun porch, which had been my office. I moved the office to the downstairs sunroom, which we had used as a television and guest room, and moved the television to a corner of the living room.

The girls needed beds, and we were on a tight budget. I

had a childhood collection of baseball cards and other memorabilia, so, I boxed it all up and took it to a nearby shop for sports collectibles and accepted the owner's offer. That allowed us to get good but inexpensive box springs and mattresses direct from a nearby factory.

We wanted the oldest girl, Kathryn, to spend as much time with her sisters and us as possible. An idealistic young architect in the congregation, when he heard what we'd done, designed a small hideaway in the attic. To reach it, he created an ingenious staircase with alternating half-cleats that took up no more space than the old ladder had done. One could almost stand erect in the middle of the attic. A mattress on the floor under the eaves gave Kathryn a place to sleep. We lined the walls with bookshelves and filled them with paperbacks. He and another member, a carpenter, did the work, donating their labor; I paid for the material. Kathryn felt snug and comfortable there when she came for weekends or college breaks. When she wasn't there, I sometimes went up to read. I called it Walden.

The experience enriched our lives in many ways. I won't say too much more about it, though; it's their story to tell if they choose to.

The assigned Feast of Tabernacles site for our congregations was Mt. Pocono, a church-owned property in Pennsylvania that had been the first site I'd attended in 1969. Edel and I also attended there in 1975, when I assisted the assistant feast coordinator, my friend Randal Dick. After returning to New Jersey, we would attend there in five of the next six years, beginning in 1981 (one year we visited the German-language site, Bonndorf, in the Black Forest, to be with Edel's parents).

The Poconos was a large site, with many ministers attending, most of them with more stripes on their sleeve than I. Combined with the visiting speakers assigned from headquarters, that meant that there was no room for me on the speaking schedule. I would have liked the opportunity, but I didn't mind. Jim Jenkins, the Union pastor, was responsible for the hospitality room; Edel and I helped him and June, his wife. The room was in one wing of the administration building and was open to all ministers and their families. We opened it before morning services, offering coffee and pastry, juice, and fruit. We opened again between services and served party sandwiches, canapés, and vegetables with dip so that many never bothered going out to lunch. My experience working for my dad in the delicatessen, including preparing trays of food for catering, came in handy. The popularity of the room wasn't diminished by the fact that Jim was an excellent bartender. We transported his homemade bar, with a satiny finish, along with all the supplies we needed for the week.

As busy as we were, there was a little time to mingle and chat with the many people who crowded the room. Some had been college classmates. There was also a chance to spend time with the visiting headquarters speakers. One year, sitting with Les McCullough, who had been the regional director in Canada until shortly before I'd been booted out, told me he admired me for staying after the way I'd been treated. In my typical, rapid-response way, I replied that I hadn't asked how I would be treated when I'd been baptized. I simply wanted to help the church.

Mac's question was a good one, though. Why did I stay so long? In addition to my own checkered employment career, there had been enough sex and financial scandals in Worldwide to indicate a seriously dysfunctional organization and cause others to leave the church. Yet I felt that each person was responsible to God for how he handled the trust placed in him. And being head-oriented (despite Herbert Armstrong's frequent rants against intellectualism and Ted Armstrong's disparagement of eggheads), my allegiance to the three doctrinal pillars—prophecy, including the identity of the Ten Lost Tribes; the Sabbath and the Holy Days; the nature of God and the human destiny—was more important to me than the peccadillos of others. Over time, another factor became important as well. I experienced a feeling of camaraderie in the congregations I was a part of that seemed to be genuine Christian fellowship. None were perfect, but by and large, these were the dear hearts and gentle people of the old Bing Crosby song, striving to live a life pleasing to God.

This is not to say that I wasn't bothered by Ted Armstrong's moral failings, the questions of what Stan Rader was hiding from the receiver, Herbert Armstrong's increasingly esoteric teachings about the pre-Adamic world, or erratic doctrinal reversals on issues such as makeup or seeking medical help. One scripture that went through my mind in such moments was the question of Jesus to the disciples in John 6, when many turned back and he asked the twelve whether they were leaving, too. Their answer: "To whom should we go? You have the words of eternal life" (verse 68). Looking back, I'm struck that I had unthinkingly taken words spoken to Jesus and applied them to Herbert Armstrong. I knew of nowhere else that I could find this combination of the three teachings that seemed to me core doctrines. Of course, the breakaways, including Ted Armstrong's new church, had them as well, but I saw no advantage in leaving the source from whom they'd learned these things.

Another Bible incident that was important to me was the transportation of the ark in 2 Samuel 6. It had been placed on a cart rather than carried by poles strung through metal rod-holders. At one point, the cart jolted, the ark was in danger of falling off, and Uzzah reached out his hand to steady it, for which he was punished. The lesson to me (and this was driven home repeatedly from the pulpit) is a warning not to step in to do God's job for him.

During the Feast of Tabernacles 1986, I became nearly incapacitated by severe pain in my left arm. It turned out to come from a pinched nerve in my neck. I'd had an auto accident a few months earlier. Euphoric about getting out of the car without a scratch, I turned down the offer of a checkup. That was a mistake. Now months later, at the Feast, I attended services, helped in the hospitality room, but otherwise laid in bed. That was how I heard the radio description of the unlikely end of the sixth game of the World Series, as my beloved Mets came from behind because of a ground ball squiggling through the legs of Bill Buckner.

After the Last Great Day, the drive home was agony. That's why I contacted one of the two physicians in our congregation. He told me that knowing me as he did, he would give me his honest opinion. Most who came to him didn't want to hear it, he'd learned, so, he gave them a shot of painkillers or scheduled an operation. But he told me his preference would be not to do anything until I had spent two weeks in bed lying absolutely flat. Edel kept me supplied with alternating hot water bottles and cold compresses.

With my love of reading, I had never minded a day sick in bed. But now, that would put a strain my neck and hinder my recovery; as a result, I couldn't read. This had happened once before, when, at age twelve, I had chickenpox, measles, and German measles in succession. Reading was forbidden then out of fear of eye strain. That led to my discovery of rock and roll from a small clock radio on my nightstand. Now, twenty-seven years later, radio was once again my lifeline. This time, I kept it tuned to WNYC-FM, a local outlet for NPR.

I soon learned the daily program schedule by heart. The day began with *Morning Edition*. The morning passed with classical music moderated by Steve Post and Sara Fishko. In the afternoon, Tim Page offered what his program's title promised: *New, Old, and Unexpected. All Things Considered* began the evening program, leading eventually, on those nights I couldn't sleep, to John Schaeffer's program, *New Sounds*. There was a bit of variety on the weekend, including Garrison Keillor's *Prairie Home Companion* on Saturday night. Nevertheless, I was happy when I had recovered enough after ten days to get up with no need for further treatment.

On Second Thought

Before we took in the girls, we had already booked vacation flights to Germany for July 1986. We hadn't seen Edel's parents since attending the feast in Bonndorf in 1983. We arranged for the girls to stay with another family and flew to Hamburg. While there, my Ambassador classmate Paul Kieffer, who pastored the Hamburg, Hannover, and Berlin congregations, stopped by. He said he'd been asked to work on me but that I'd be crazy if I accepted what he'd been told to propose. He was looking to return to the States next year, and one of the other pastors, Tom Lapacka, who pastored three churches in Switzerland and southern Germany, had also spoken to the German director, Frank Schnee, about returning to the States. The church had a candidate to replace one, but that would leave them one pastor short and they had no idea whom to recruit. I listened and didn't say anything. I wasn't against the idea of returning to Europe but was happy where we were. No one asked me directly, and I didn't offer my opinion.

Chapter Three

Someone would be going to the German-speaking region in the summer of 1987. I heard nothing more for a while, but Larry Salyer called just after the turn of the year to sound me out. I reminded him of our responsibilities as foster parents. I'd gotten their mother's assent to take them anywhere in the U.S. in the case of a transfer, but taking them out of the country was another matter. Nor did I think it would be in the girls' best interests to move to another family. Larry said that he understood and that he'd find someone else; for a while, he thought he had. But then Larry called again to ask if I had gotten permission to take the girls out of the country yet. I knew that refusal wasn't an option at this point, and so I said, I haven't, but I will.

This was at the end of March. The following days were filled with phone calls with Pasadena, Tom Lapacka (the pastor I would succeed in Switzerland), Worldwide's Bonn office, and, finally, on Friday, April 3, we called Edel's parents to share the news with them. The next day, April 4, Jim announced the transfer to the congregations.

Two weeks later, on the weekly Sabbath during the days of Unleavened Bread, I gave a sermon in the morning in Union, then kissed Edel and the kids goodbye. Two friends from the congregation drove me to Jersey City, where I gave the sermon in the afternoon, then they took me to Kennedy airport to catch my flight to Frankfurt. Edel's brother Wolfgang and Linda, his wife, were at the airport when I landed the next morning. It was Easter Sunday; the autobahn was nearly empty at that early hour as we drove to their apartment near Bonn.

The next day, Monday, was the last day of Unleavened Bread, and I gave the morning sermon, in English. The congregations throughout the German-speaking area were equipped with wireless headsets so that an interpreter could give a simultaneous translation to those who spoke no or little English. There were two days of ministers' meetings after that, then, on Thursday (my 39th birthday), I drove with the Lapackas to Switzerland. They had guests and arranged for me to stay with the deacon in the Zurich congregation and his family in Neuhausen. That evening I watched the national evening news with them and got most of what was said, but then the weather report was delivered in Swiss dialect, and I didn't understand a word.

Friday was hectic. Tom picked me up and took me to Zurich to meet the lawyer who would help with my immigration. Then he introduced me to a Volvo dealer to begin preparing to buy the car the church would lease for me.

Worldwide had an office in the Oerlikon section of Zurich to use as a mail address; Tom took me to see it. I gave a sermonette in Stuttgart the next day, again in English, then on Monday flew back to the States.

I had heard that international assignments were typically for five years. From conversations with people in the congregations, I gleaned hints that the members were sensitive to anything that seemed to be a provisional arrangement. The next time I was on the telephone with Larry, I said that I didn't want to hear, going in, anything about a time limit. I didn't want Edel and me to be watching the calendar for five years. "If I go," I said to Larry, "I'm there until you send me somewhere else."

For the next ten weeks, I continued to work a full load in the New Jersey congregations, but my attention was divided. What should we take with us? What should we discard? Were there things that would be hard to get in Europe that we should acquire before we went? There was much back-and-forth with the girls' mother, but eventually, she consented. As a result, the girls could come with us. Sarah would graduate from high school (the same high school from which I'd graduated) just before we left, and Deborah would complete high school via distance learning. The evening before Sarah's graduation, my mother graduated from high school, too. She had dropped out to marry her sweetheart when World War Two broke out and he was drafted (he died seven months after their wedding). I was proud of her when she received her diploma.

I began reading the Bible in German and listing unfamiliar vocabulary. Some words frequently appear in the Bible but aren't part of the basic vocabulary either in German classes or in conversation with Edel's parents whenever we visited Germany. In addition to expanding my vocabulary, reading familiar passages in a different language made them appear in a new light. In some passages, the difference was so significant that it took on a new sense. The inadequacy I felt in Canada in not knowing the Bible languages returned. How was I to know whether the German or English translation had come closer to the mark?

To help me prepare for my new assignment, Worldwide agreed to sponsor German immersion classes. I drove four days a week to Berlitz in Summit for three-hour one-to-one lessons over six weeks. During that time, John Karlson called from Bonn, where he managed the church's office under the direction of Frank Schnee. He also supervised the ministry, now he had a question. Parallel to our move to Switzerland, Winfried Fritz, who pastored the churches in Austria and Bavaria, would be moving to Bonn. Bob Berendt, who had pastored in Ottawa, just to the west of me when we began in Montreal, would become my pastoral neighbor to the east, replacing Winfried there. But John now proposed that Winfried and I swap assignments: that Winfried take the Swiss-Stuttgart circuit and I the Bonn-Darmstadt. He painted the advantages: we'd be several hours closer to Edel's parents, and Edel's brother Wolfgang worked in the office. The little I'd observed of what it was like to live in the orbit of the Bonn office flashed through my mind, and I replied that if it was all the same to him, I'd rather stay with the original plan.

A wrinkle in the arrangement was that legally the Zurich and Basel congregations were part of a Swiss church association founded in the name of the French version of the *World Tomorrow* broadcast, *Le Monde à Venir*. For that reason, I had to be hired by the Geneva office, even though I would report to Bonn. That meant that Dibar Apartian would have to write the application, an interesting turn of events in light of my departure from Canada.

Yet when I attended the annual Swiss association meeting for the first time, I was exposed to a different side of Dibar Apartian. He would typically spend the days of Unleavened Bread in Europe and chair the association meeting in Neuchatel in addition to speaking on the feast day. Apartian took the form of a Swiss association seriously, and he was very open with the members and answered their questions. Perhaps his years living in Switzerland as an Armenian refugee, working in the U.S. embassy, had a hand in this affinity for the country and its ways.

The move meant a change in our summer plans. Our oldest, Kathryn, was transferring from the college she was attending in New Jersey to Ambassador Big Sandy. We'd planned to drive her, with stops along the way to places I'd never been, such as Nashville, but we canceled that.

Before leaving the States, I spent time reviewing the years since my ordination nine years earlier. Working as part of a team had been good for me; I had been productive. I worried that once I took over my own pastorate, I would revert to some of the habits that undermined my effectiveness in Canada. Colin Wilkins had mentioned that I hadn't stayed in close enough contact with him. So, I resolved to communicate fully with the Bonn office, primarily with John Karlson, who would be my supervisor. I also outlined traits I wanted to include in all my sermons: balanced, practical, positive, and Biblical (but not scholarly). Recent sermons exemplified this, I felt, but many of those I'd given in Canada lacked one or more of these elements. Finally, I resolved to remember maxims that Jim had drilled into me: you can't live people's lives for them, you can say anything you need to with a smile (that is, be friendly and firm), and, at all times, be loving and encouraging. He had been a good mentor in my second start in the ministry.

Edel and I had left Europe twelve years earlier, in 1975, less than one year after we married. Now we returned with four children to pastor a three-church circuit, Zurich, Basel, and Stuttgart. All three congregations met on a biweekly basis, the two Swiss congregations one week, morning and afternoon, the Stuttgart congregation the other. In addition, we met in Schluchsee in the Black Forest for holy days, with a combined attendance of over three hundred.

Near Schluchsee was the German feast site in Bonndorf, which we had visited once for the Feast of Tabernacles in 1983. As the pastor closest to Bonndorf, I would serve as the coordinator, a responsibility I was familiar with from the three years in Sherbrooke. It involved dealing with the local tourist office as well as the hotels and providers of vacation properties. I oversaw the various crews that set up operations, and I drafted the speaking schedule, subject to

Bonn's approval. Bonndorf was a popular site for transfers from overseas, including guest speakers; others who came through on their way to or from other feast sites spoke in Zurich immediately before or after the Feast.

My responsibility as feast coordinator brought me into frequent contact with the mayor of Bonndorf, Peter Folkerts, a dynamic personality not much older than I. He thought highly of Ambassador College. Tom and Linda Lapacka before me had formed a personal friendship with him and his wife, Regina; we quickly became friends, as well. It was the first new friendship with someone outside of Worldwide since I had become a member.

We saw each other often in the next five years until in June 1992 Peter Folkerts and three others died in a plane crash in the Allgäu Alps. It hit me hard, but it was a shock for many others as well. He had become mayor twenty years earlier, when only 26, and had been an extraordinarily good one. On the first day of German unity, the previous fall, October 3, 1991, Bonndorf celebrated one thousand years of its city charter. Although not yet 45, he was awarded honorary citizenship. Ralf Dahrendorf, who had been an E.U. commissioner when I was in Brussels, and who had a vacation home in Bonndorf, chaired the occasion and spoke the *laudatio*, and Fritz Stern, the historian, presented a speech he had delivered shortly before to the Bundestag. I was invited to sit on the tribune to watch the parade, and I wore the tie sporting the Bonndorf insignia that Peter had given me.

I was not clairvoyant, but I had been concerned for him. He lived at full speed (he had been a passionate cyclist as a young man). Now he was on the road a lot and at German autobahn speeds. He was a hobby pilot. He was full of energy but drove himself to the limit of his strength. On the fateful day, he wanted to include a young, wheelchair-bound man among the passengers. Unfortunately, the small Beechcraft was so laden that, in the end, it seemed as if they would have to choose between the young man's wheelchair and Peter's own bag. Peter solved it by emptying the contents of the bag into every nook and cranny. The weather was clear, but two weather fronts met over the Alps, producing gusty winds. Nevertheless, they flew only two hundred meters over the mountain, too close to react to sudden turbulence.

The number of mourners far exceeded the capacity of Bonndorf's church. I stood outside as part of the overflow and listened over a loudspeaker. In one of my favorite poems, "Spring and Fall," the poet, Gerard Manley Hopkins, asks Margaret, a young child, why she grieves over the falling leaves, then suggests the answer is because this sign of time passing evokes in her an intuition of her own mortality. I mourned for my friend, who had lived a full life in less than a half-century, having found a spot on earth he could make a better place.

The first summer in Europe was exhausting. From the time the six of us landed in Stuttgart on Thursday, July 2, we wandered from place to place, much of it in a Volkswagen van, reminiscent of the first summer I'd spent in Germany, twenty-three years earlier. John Karlson met us at the airport, delivered the van to us, and flew back to Bonn. We rested on Friday, and I prepared the sermon I would give to the Stuttgart congregation the following day, my first in German. The day after that, we drove to Zurich to meet the congregation there. I held a Bible study followed by a buffet, after which we returned to our hotel in Leonberg, near Stuttgart. The paperwork for our immigration to Switzerland had begun during my trip in April, and we had to be careful not to give the appearance of working or taking up residence in Switzerland until it was finished. There was no guarantee how long that would take.

A highlight of the summer was a visit from Joe Tkach. In the year-and-a-half since he had become pastor general, he had striven to visit as many local congregations around the world as possible. Members from the northern half of the German congregations traveled to Dusseldorf to hear him speak that Sabbath. This included Edel's parents, who came from Hamburg. I introduced them and our four children to Tkach, and someone took a photo of all of us together with Wolfgang's camera. Tkach's theme in the message he gave around the world was "we are family." Gerald Waterhouse adopted that as his motto for his new tour; somehow, that photo ended up in his slide presentation.

That evening, we had dinner with Tkach and his traveling party. The next day we left early and drove south to be at the Stuttgart airport in time to meet the church's Gulfstream executive jet when it touched down. Tkach gave our boys a tour of the plane, after which our oldest boy announced he wanted to become pastor general. Then we went to the hall where Tkach spoke to the southern half of the German-speaking area.

As tiring and chaotic as the nomadic life was, the places we went resonated with me. I have always been sensitive that wherever we stand, other people stood before us, with their hopes, dreams, loves, and hates. That consciousness is one of the things that has always made history come alive for me. And here in Europe, the timeline of recorded memories went back much further than in the "new" world. Of course, the so-called new world is as old, too, but the wave of colonization largely obliterated the memory of what went before. In Europe, however, the present was in continuity with many centuries. After the first service in Stuttgart, we overnighted with members who lived in Weil-der-Stadt. Their home was a few doors down from where Johannes Kepler grew up. The next day, in Zürich, we met at the *Volkshaus*, and I spoke under a wall relief of Lenin. An exile in Zurich, he had spoken in this room on the significance of the 1905 revolution shortly before being smuggled back into Russia in 1917. And our rented bungalow was in Bad Liebenzell, a center of German pietism, near Calw, the birthplace of Hermann Hesse, whose books I still liked having on my shelves as a reminder of the person I was at nineteen when I devoured his writing. The nearby monastery at Maulbronn, where Hesse went to school, had served as the locale for one of my favorites of his novels, *Narziss und Goldmund*. Another family from the congregation lived in Mühlacker, where Henri Arnaud served as a pastor after leading Waldensian refugees to the area.

When the two weeks in Bad Liebenzell ended, we returned to Bonn so that the girls could fly to Britain with other teens, most of whom they didn't yet know, to attend the church's youth camp in Loch Lomond, Scotland. We continued to Hamburg, but then I flew alone to Zurich to meet with the immigration lawyer. I held services on the weekend, then on Monday returned to Hamburg by train. On Thursday, I drove with the family back to Switzerland. The paperwork seemed to be coming along, which meant we could begin looking for a place to live. John's recommendation was that we not even consider an apartment; it would be unreasonable to expect our four children to be quiet enough to please neighbors in an apartment house. He also wanted me to be close to the airport. We looked at three houses the next day, one of which seemed appropriate, then on Saturday moved back to Bad Liebenzell for another two-week stay.

In all, we stayed overnight in more than a dozen hotels, private homes, and vacation rentals in our first five weeks in Europe, leaving some item behind in each place we visited.

In addition to the historical resonance wherever we went, the landscape affected me deeply. For the past four years, I had been making my rounds in surroundings familiar to me, having grown up in the New York metropolitan area. However, much of my visiting load was not in suburban neighborhoods such as I had known but in the inner-city. Many city blocks in Newark still showed the unrestored scars of the riots in the Sixties. As I made my stops in the housing projects and tenements of Essex and Hudson counties, I would look around and think to myself that I had no complaints—the hearts of the people I met and worked with were full of the love of God. I nevertheless couldn't help wondering—especially after Larry warned me that I might be sent to my own pastorate on a moment's notice—what God might have in store for my next stop.

Now I knew. A few weeks earlier, on the weekend I had flown from Hamburg to Switzerland, I stayed again in Neuhausen, and the deacon took me in the evening to the nearby *Rheinfall*, engorged from heavy summer rains. I stood in awe as the water cascaded down and roiled against the rocks. I spent the following evening at the home of the elder in the congregation, near Lucerne. Their teenage daughter had gone to stay with her grandmother so that I could use her room. From the window that evening as I settled in, I could see the two mountains that dominate Lucerne's skyline, gentle Rigi and towering, foreboding Pilatus. The rain and clouds of the day lifted, the evening sun cast a rainbow, and the tip of Pilatus glowed, its snow-covering tinged rose pink. Another visit I made that summer was to a couple who had recently begun attending services. They managed a restaurant in the *Zwissighaus* in Bauen (birthplace of the author of the hymn that became the Swiss national anthem) and served me a fine meal overlooking Lake Lucerne with soaring Alps on all sides on a perfect summer evening. With the Psalmist, I repeatedly said in that first summer, "what is man, that thou art mindful of him?"

When our papers came through at the end of August, we immigrated to Switzerland and moved into our rental home. It was an A-framed semi-detached house with a living room, dining room, and kitchen on the ground floor, three bedrooms upstairs, and an open loft under the pointed roof one level further up. The boys slept there, and the girls each had a room. The owner had lived there himself previously and had outfitted a home office in the basement, which had a separate entrance.

Edel and I decided to enroll the boys in the Swiss public school. They were young enough that they could quickly catch up to instruction in another language, especially since their mother was a native German speaker. For the first year, they had to take supplementary remedial German after school. This enriched their lives in an unexpected way; they formed long-lasting friendships with Turkish boys in their school. And with the help of *Asterix und Obelisk*, *Tim und Struppi*, and Disney's *Lustige Taschenbücher*, they soon had a vocabulary that exceeded mine.

Edel's workload was heavy. In addition to caring for the home and four children and serving as hostess, she did much translating. She worked over each sermon I prepared so that listeners could recognize it as German. On top of that, she translated the feast manual, with its detailed instructions and procedures for each department, and lectures that headquarters provided for our deacons and elders meetings. At the Feast of Tabernacles, she served as one of the interpreters for the simultaneous translations for each service we offered; many commented on her pleasant voice.

I collaborated with Edel on another project. The Bonn office had already compiled a comparative list of Bible passages to help interpreters during simultaneous translations in services. In some cases, especially in the Psalms, the verse numbering differs. In some other books, the chapter breaks differ. We expanded the list to include passages where the sense in the German translation was another than in the English Bible. For example, in Genesis 17:1, the King James Version renders the words of God to Abraham "Be thou perfect." The most recent translation of the Luther Bible (1984), has *sei fromm*, which in everyday language conveys something that English-speakers would call being "pious."

I began to offer the list to visiting speakers. Some of the passages in question were used as proof texts in expounding some of Worldwide's distinctive teachings. Several references to fasting and the holy days were gone from the Book of Acts, the result of using the most recent critical Greek text, rather than the Byzantine, which had been used as the basis for the King James Version. I left it open whether the German or English was more accurate; I simply thought it would be helpful if an interpreter didn't have to explain to the German-speaking listener why a speaker went on at length about words that didn't appear in the German version.

After I'd been in Switzerland for a while, I apologized to a member for speaking such elementary German. "That's all right," was the reply. "We once had a pastor who spoke perfect German. We still didn't understand a thing he said." I was happy, though, that after a few months, congregants only rarely had to suppress a smile over something I'd said that was inadvertently comical (like "checkered teeth" when I meant teeth with cavities).

Once, on a visit, I cautiously asked, "You don't mind having an American for a pastor?" The reply: "As long as it's not a German" (this was forty-five years after the end of the war).

At Spokesman's Club one night, one topic of discussion was about *Ausländer* (foreigners). The general tenor was negative. In my comments at the end, I pointed out that I was a foreigner. "But we don't mean you," protested one. "We were talking about the Tessiner" (Tessin is a canton of Switzerland, and the language is Italian, but the citizenship Swiss).

As exciting as this move was, there was a nagging worry in my mind over bringing my young family to the center of Europe. After all, Worldwide expected Germany was to be the military leader of the European Union, a role it was destined to fill, we believed, because of its identity as the modern-day descendants of Assyria. This oriental empire had first carried the northern ten tribes of Israel into captivity, from which they disappeared into the mist of history.

Despite the difficulty of finding evidence for Worldwide's "key" to prophecy—the identity of the Anglo-Saxon people, and by extension, the modern identity of other prominent nations in the Bible—I hadn't totally abandoned the identification of Germany (at least the warlike Prussians and the *Lederhosen*-clad, knee-slapping Bavarians) as Assyria, nor the expectation that Germany would spearhead a united Europe and take over the U.S. as the opening act of the crisis at the end of the age before the return of Jesus Christ. The dates we thought the tribulation might begin—1972, 1979—had passed, but perhaps the end had been merely postponed, not called off. I had reverted to the fundamental question with which Herbert Armstrong had first introduced the subject: God said that the two sons of Joseph, Ephraim and

Manasseh, would grow into a great nation and a company of nations. Based on the unexamined assumption that the Bible was written for our day, this meant that somewhere on earth, the blessings taken from Israel had been restored 2,520 years later. It seemed self-evident that this had to refer to the United States and the British Commonwealth. If not, then God hadn't kept his word, and we couldn't be sure about anything else in the Bible.

As we grew accustomed to our new surroundings, it seemed increasingly unlikely that this would happen anytime soon, however. It was nevertheless poignant when, between services on the Last Great Day of our second Feast in Bonndorf, 1988, one of the members told me of hearing the news that Franz Josef Strauss had died that morning.

For years, our speculation had focused on Strauss as the type of strongman who could lead the United States of Europe. He had visited the Pasadena campus of Ambassador the year before I enrolled, addressed the student body, been interviewed for the *World Tomorrow* telecast by Ted Armstrong, and had dined in Herbert Armstrong's home. On that occasion, the elder Armstrong had told him, "we" believe that God had big plans for him. When it came time to leave, Ted Armstrong flew him on the Falcon to Washington, D.C. Now it was clear he would not lead the beast of Revelation.

A little more than a year later, on November 9, 1989, I came up from my office and found Edel standing (not sitting) in front of the television. We had followed the unrest throughout the summer in Hungary and Poland and the church-led Monday demonstrations in East Germany (the

DDR). Now the Berlin Wall had been breached, people from the East were streaming over as the guards stood by and held their fire. "I never thought I would ever see this," was all she could say. In the summer of 1988, after being in Europe for one year, we felt it was time to visit Edel's relatives in the DDR. Her maternal grandmother lived there with her mother's brother, a tailor near Weimar, and his wife. Edel's parents traveled there from Hamburg at the same time.

As we approached the border, I reminded all our children that sensitive listening devices would soon pick up any conversation in our van, so, they should be careful what they said. When our turn came to cross, the van was taken apart, as I knew it would be, but the search ended more quickly than expected: as the border guard removed the middle row of seats, our youngest boy, sitting with his brother in the back row, called out, "Look, there's Sarah's bracelet." The guard couldn't help smiling and said we were free to go.

We proceeded along the highway, careful to observe the speed limit to the letter. We hadn't gone far when a Russian military helicopter approached, flying low enough that its searchlights shone into our van, and I could see the faces of the crew. I don't know if that was the standard procedure or particular harassment since our van bore Bonn plates.

As an American citizen, I wanted to be cautious and avoid any incident. I resolved to make no comment of a remotely political nature. I had read books about the DDR as we prepared for the trip, both laudatory and critical, but neither prepared me for the reality of what we experienced. I had taken along something I hoped was innocuous

111

for reading matter, a paperback copy of Goethe's *Sorrows of Young Werther*. The edition also contained some other short texts, including a fable about an elephant and a mouse. That seemed a better parable of life in the DDR than anything else I had read. Like the elephant, it was not malevolent as much as blind to its crushing impact. Meanwhile, it was convinced it had the highest ideals.

Among other things, our visit was an intense sensory experience. I remember the pervasive smell of the soft brown coal used for energy and the strange taste of yogurt and other dairy products. Toward the end of our visit, there was also the rush of trying to use up the currency we'd been required to exchange for the trip but weren't permitted to reconvert before leaving. I went to a record store in Weimar and bought LPs by Ludwig Güttler and other DDR artists. But as I stood in line to pay, I overheard the person in front of me request the new Glenn Gould recording, his second of the Bach *Goldberg Variations*. I asked for it as well; the man behind the counter glared at me (he could tell I wasn't a local) but pulled a copy out from under the counter. On reflection, I realized what had happened. Evidently, the DDR had acquired the rights from CBS to press a limited number of copies. It wasn't openly displayed; only those who heard of it by word of mouth could buy one.

It was clear that life there was carefully monitored and tightly controlled. I was standing in front of Edel's uncle's house, talking with Bernd, the husband of Edel's cousin. We hadn't been there long when a neighbor nonchalantly strolled by, then stopped to say hello. He asked who I was and where I was from in the friendliest of manners, then went on his way. I'm not sure whether Bernd waited until the man was entirely out of earshot before he hissed, *Stasi*.

While there, I held services in Jena in a member's apartment. After services, as we all sat over coffee, I learned of a wardrobe faux pas. Why, one asked me, did all the Worldwide ministers wear red ties? I understood the sub-text immediately. I answered that most of us owned two suits, one blue, one gray, and that red ties went with both. It was not a political statement, I assured him. But I regretted my obtuseness.

Despite my resolution to be apolitical, not only Bernd, but many of those I talked with complained openly about the system. So, finally, I cautiously mentioned *Glasnost*, the policy Gorbachev pursued in the Soviet Union and asked whether something similar was thinkable in the DDR. Never, was the invariable reply. "Never" arrived less than a year-and-a-half later.

After the fall of the Berlin Wall, it seemed at first as if East Germany would continue to exist as a separate nation but open to the West. Events moved quickly, however, and on October 3, 1990, less than a year after the Wall had been breached, the two Germanies reunified. Would this pave the way for a newly self-confident Germany to assert leadership of the European Union? Or would this headlong rush result in chaos, out of which the beast power would emerge? This uncertainty filled my mind as we opened that year's Feast of Tabernacles that evening.

With my apocalyptic mindset, I saw this development darkly. On the morning of the day the currency union took place, the East German Mark was trading at nine to one West German. A five-to-one exchange rate for converting to Western currency would have been generous; the two-to-one the government set seemed irresponsible. I was concerned about its effect on public debt. I was worried that the sixteen million East German citizens had no experience with democratic government since this part of Germany had gone directly from National Socialism to Communism: fifty-six years of unbroken totalitarianism. I felt that East Germans had an idealized version of what life in the West was like and would quickly become disillusioned. At the same time, those in the West would begrudge the massive transfer of capital to rebuild the crumbling infrastructure in the East. I expected the CDU government to fall within a few years, returning the SPD to power, much redder than it had been under Schmidt, and that this, in turn, would lead to a return of inflation and a backlash to the right, paving the way to the German-led revival of the Holy Roman Empire.

Thus, while I was slowly letting go of timelines and date-setting, I was still afflicted by prediction addiction. I voiced none of that in my opening night message in Bonndorf but reflected on the poignancy of meeting on the day that Germany unified and that we looked forward to a time when the "kingdoms of the earth . . . become the kingdom of our Lord, and of his Christ" (Rev. 11:15).

A few months later, I drove past street protests in the run-up to the first Gulf War, as demonstrators hoisted banners that read "No blood for oil." It gave me pause. Germany had reunited but was not remilitarizing. When brutal intertribal war raged in the Balkans—more fallout from the end of the Cold War—I was struck by the reluctance with which Germany played a leading role in NATO intervention. I sensed the inner conflict in Germany's foreign minister, Joschka Fischer, a former firebrand in the days of student protests in the Sixties, as he admitted he never thought he would see the day when he had to choose between peace and justice.

The raising of the Iron Curtain led to some memorable encounters. For example, a group of Sabbatarian "Volga Germans," whose ancestors had migrated to Russia at the time of Catherine the Great, now lived in and around Singen, Germany. This was a new experience for me. Visits to new contacts in North America tended to be to people who shared the same culture but had questions about our doctrinal beliefs. Now, I met people whose difference to Worldwide was more cultural than doctrinal. This was striking. Worldwide felt it was the only true church, charged with a mission to proclaim the gospel to all nations. To call the results of our efforts to do this behind the Iron Curtain "modest" would have been exaggerated. Now I learned there were many Sabbatarians in Russia. Stalin, suspicious of their German ancestry when Hitler invaded the Soviet Union, had resettled those who lived in the Ukraine to scattered areas throughout his empire.

At about the same time these people took advantage of the fall of the Iron Curtain to emigrate to Germany, others had moved to the United States and Argentina and had begun attending Worldwide services, having concluded it was the closest counterpart in the West to what they believed. However, the group located in the Singen area was large enough that their fellowship was sufficient to themselves.

I was invited to speak at one of their services. One difference that to me counted as cultural rather than doctrinal was how worship was conducted. The services were long. The women all wore scarves. Prayer was lengthy and loud, with all speaking at once.

When they had visitors from the Ukraine, they were anxious for me to meet them. One of the men had lost an eye, put out by the butt of a rifle during an interrogation. They were happy to learn that we believed many of the same things but had lingering doubts about whether we could be true Christians since we had not lived in an environment where we were persecuted for our beliefs. The price they paid for their faith was high. The young men refused military service, which meant five years in a prison camp. One came back totally paralyzed and couldn't work.

Our experience in the West, I acknowledged, had been atypical of the history of Christianity. It would have been difficult to explain that every Christian is tried—whether in his personal life or as a part of organized persecution. So instead, I admitted that prosperity can be more dangerous to spiritual life than persecution, but to add that it, too, could be overcome.

The visitors wanted to know about my experience of coming to baptism. They posed several further questions to test my soundness and were pleased with most of my answers, even when they disagreed.

My host in Singen planned to visit the Ukraine soon, his first time back since emigrating twelve years earlier. He planned to tell everyone of his contact with Worldwide. He offered to take me along the next time he traveled there. I was tempted but concerned about my stamina.

In the end, a colleague from the U.S., Vic Kubik, whose parents were Ukrainian, went instead. On his way to the Ukraine, he stopped in Zurich. When he spoke in services, we were both struck by the symbolism of him under the Lenin plaque. Vic had graduated from Ambassador's Bricket Wood campus just before I began in Pasadena, and this was the first time our paths crossed. We immediately became friends; I soon counted him as one of my best friends among my ministerial colleagues.

Although I didn't visit the Ukraine, another responsibility behind the former Iron Curtain fell to me, Estonia. An Estonian refugee, an academic, had come into Worldwide in Australia. As soon as Estonia became independent, he moved back and joined the university's faculty in Tartu. Before long, acquaintances in the city became interested in Worldwide, and we quickly had a fledgling congregation there. I visited three times, including midsummer and at Christmas. Thus, I was able to experience the extremes of daylight so far north. Edel and I were out late with members on our midsummer visit, and walked back to our accommodations at eleven in the evening. The sun had set, but the sky was still as bright as day. Five hours later, a blazing red ball shone on us through our east-facing window. On Christmas day, it barely showed itself over the horizon for two hours before sinking again.

The Estonians were proud of their new independence, but also fearful. Throughout their long history, they had been squeezed on every side by more powerful neighbors. They told me of the suspiciously large number of Russian officers who had "retired" to remain in the country.

I've forgotten the few words of Estonian I learned, but remember the people. There was much to admire in those I met—not only the professor who'd left his position in Australia to help his homeland rebuild, but also those who had, through his example, become part of Worldwide. One had turned her home into a halfway house for underage boys released from prison. I also came to appreciate the rich choral tradition cultivated there. On one outing for the congregation, we visited the large, open-air amphitheater that hosted choral festivals. I couldn't resist trying out the acoustics.

The late eighties were not only a momentous time on the world scene but also in Worldwide. Herbert Armstrong's death in January 1986 hadn't meant the end of the church's mission, as many had expected, but initiated a boom. Responses to the telecast rose, as did the circulation of the *Plain Truth*. The media landscape in Europe was changing as well; one nation after another dropped restrictions on private television stations (most television until then had been state-run). As a result, Worldwide could now run the *World Tomorrow* telecast in Europe, dubbed into local languages.

The boom didn't last long, however. The expansion of the media landscape that allowed us to expand to new markets also meant a dilution of the audience. Our cost per response rose. Joe Tkach began to focus on the congregations' condition and personal evangelism as a source of future growth, something Ted Armstrong had pushed shortly before being expelled. This was unsettling for the members, most of whom had come in (as I had) through media outreach. I was already saturated with Worldwide's teachings before meeting any member. Yet it had been the example of those I met, especially one family, that counteracted the adverse reaction I'd had to the first service I'd attended. Still, we were pioneers in using up-to-date media to spread the gospel (that is, the media as it evolved in the twentieth century: radio, then TV, and the golden age of magazine journalism).

I felt we were correct to recognize we had to update to reach readers of the Nineties. While I thought the telecast excellent, I found the *Plain Truth* not merely bland, but inconsistent. We had some outstanding issues, followed by others with no impact. It seemed as if even in the best issues, there was at least one article that was shallow, ill-conceived, or poorly focused. Edel asked me to let her read each issue when it arrived before I did, because after I read it, it was heavily marked with a red pen. I longed to be more involved, yet I also knew that it was harder to find pastors who spoke German than people with editorial skills.

This continued concern for Worldwide's media efforts showed, though, that I was still torn in how to make a contribution. Before leaving for Europe, I had contacted Dexter Faulkner, the managing editor of the *Plain Truth*. After being rehired by Worldwide, I resumed contributing articles to the *Worldwide News*, the *Good News*, and the church's youth magazine. Now, Dexter was interested in receiving occasional articles from me for the *Plain Truth*, as well. At the time, no one was writing from Europe, and he felt it would be good to have that perspective. I got one proposal approved and had sketched ideas for it before leaving the States. But in the crush of settling in, I never finished it. When Herman Hoeh, executive editor of the church's publications, visited Bonndorf for the Feast in 1987, he also mentioned the need for good material from Europe. When I traveled to Bonn in December of that year for the semi-annual ministerial conference, John Karlson announced that the *Plain Truth* would return to having a window available for contributions of more local interest, similar to what had been done in the mid-seventies, when I worked for the *Plain Truth*. John said that the German office intended to make full use of this, and all eyes in the room turned to me. This was the third tap on the shoulder, and I realized that I would now have to find time to do this even though I didn't feel I was entirely on top of my responsibilities as pastor and feast coordinator.

But when I visited Pasadena for the refreshing program in 1989, however, both Dexter and Larry advised me to put writing on the back burner. Although the editorial staff in Pasadena was small, Dexter found it challenging to find space for what they produced. He also had been burned by editorial contributions from field ministers. Their experience speaking in services didn't carry over to writing for a more general audience. His picture for it: you either ride the bicycle, or you walk alongside it. Larry concurred; he wanted me to concentrate on counseling and other duties of an effective pastor. In addition, they wanted my input in European matters from a European perspective, but as a respondent, not a correspondent. I did, however, continue to contribute short articles to the German edition of the magazine.

I had a vicarious taste of editorial work from time to time, notably whenever Gene and Barbara Hogberg passed through. Once, they had been in New Jersey while I was still there. One of the members worked for the national park service at the Edison Laboratory in West Orange, and she gave us a personal tour outside of normal hours; she looked the other way when Gene slipped under the red cordon so that I could photograph him working at Edison's lab bench. A few years after we moved to Europe, the Hogbergs visited our home. Gene was conducting interviews in Europe and used the stop in our home to summarize what he had learned so far. We worked together in my office as he compiled his report. If we weren't quite Woodward and Bernstein, I felt again the rush I experienced working on a publication.

But for the most part, I remained committed to the needs of the congregations. Much of my week was spent on the road, visiting the wide-ranging area I was responsible for. I prepared sermons and Bible studies, conducted baptisms and funerals, and counseled couples preparing for marriage. One wedding, in particular, stands out because of two strong memories. The groom's brother was one of Switzerland's best-known comedians. He organized entertainment for the reception, involving many of the guests. The other memory is that of the bride's father. He had left Worldwide to follow evangelist Raymond Cole (Wayne's brother) in the early 1970s when Worldwide changed the day it observed Pentecost. From the moment the man walked in, the way he carried himself and the clothes he wore were familiar: it was how we all dressed and acted in the 1960s. I hadn't been aware of how much the congregation's ethos had changed in two decades, but now I was confronted with a time capsule of our past.

Beyond my focus on my duties as pastor, I thought of the present and future needs of the local congregations in German-speaking Europe. There were nine congregations, along with outlying study groups in Berlin, Vienna, and East Germany. The congregations were organized into four pastorates. At the end of my first month in Europe, in summer 1987, I drafted a memo outlining a plan for developing manpower ahead of the needs. It called for adding one trainee or elder per year; I suggested beginning with the Southwest, my circuit. The trainee could live on the German side of the border, thus no residence permit would be needed. After a year, if all went well, he would be ready to become associate pastor, at which time he could move to the Stuttgart area. The congregations could begin weekly services, the associate and I would continue to alternate between being in each congregation on a biweekly basis.

John didn't comment on the memo at the time but carried it out nearly to the letter. In 1988, he sent Wade Fransson to be my trainee. Wade had come to the Bonn office after graduation; his particular interest there was the newsstand program. But he clearly had ministerial potential in addition to his substantial gift for organization and strategic analysis. Wade had had an eventful life; it wouldn't go too far to say tumultuous. He has written about this in three volumes of memoirs, the *Rod of Iron* trilogy.

Wade and his wife, Kay, moved to Waldshut, just across the Rhine River from Switzerland. In my years in New Jersey, I had used the need for a second man on visits as an opportunity to train local men in the area. Now I was responsible for training a young and capable man who could clearly make a good contribution in the ministry.

One of Wade's special interests was youth programs, especially summer camp. For years, teens from the continent had gone to Loch Lomond. Wade had served on the staff there as well as in the church's main U.S. camp in Orr, Minnesota. Now he began a camp in Germany, beginning with summer 1990. Although the primary language was German, it was international in scope; campers, counselors and staff came from other, non-German-speaking countries, including France, the Netherlands, and the U.S., in addition to Germany, Switzerland, and Austria.

Wade tapped me to teach the courses in journalism and video, which meant helping the fifty campers produce a newsletter and film documenting the camp. I also conducted one or two of the morning devotions. We brought our boys; even though they were too young to be campers, they could participate in many activities. They especially enjoyed the pottery class, which Edel also took part in. It was an interesting experience to have our roles reversed; suddenly, I worked for Wade, which I didn't always enjoy. But, on the other hand, I was thrilled to see him step into a leadership role and handle it well.

Our time together was one of iron sharpening iron. Wade's ordination made it possible to begin holding weekly services in all three congregations after the Feast of Tabernacles 1989.

Working in Switzerland meant reassessing some of our teachings, for instance, our strict non-participation in the military. One of the elements of Switzerland's vaunted neutrality was the motto that every citizen was a soldier. There was compulsory military service for each male. Even after basic training, he kept his weapon at home. Yet, at the same time, the likelihood of ever firing a shot in war was minimal. I recalled my abortive contribution to the Systematic Theology Project, when my insight that John the Baptist hadn't required the soldiers who came to him for advice to leave the military had been edited out by Larry Salyer before he forwarded that paper to Pasadena.

Our teaching, formulated in the United States when U.S. troops were on alert in many parts of the world, was meant to pertain universally. It had been challenging to apply for conscientious objector status in Switzerland; one could be jailed for refusing to serve. By the time I arrived, the situation had eased. In addition to the many non-combative branches of the military that had always been available (something our members had been discouraged from availing themselves of; it was seen as partaking "in other men's sins," 1 Tim. 5:22), it was now easier to do alternative, non-military service.

A new wrinkle came when a member of the Geneva congregation decided he wanted to perform his military service. The pastor there called to discuss it with me. He wanted to disfellowship the young man for not following church teaching. I vehemently opposed that, arguing that this would weaken the case for all other members when they claimed conscientious objection. The very name of the status makes clear that it is a matter of personal conscience. We, as a church, were supportive in every way, but we couldn't make a person's membership dependent on it.

Another issue was voting. I had grown up in a country that prided itself on being a democracy, but I was surprised at the extent the Swiss practice it. It seemed as if there were elections for one thing or another every few months. The principle of subsidiarity was vital: Local and cantonal elections carried a great deal of weight; voter turnout was high. Most surprising to me was how direct democracy was practiced by frequent referendums.

I guess I was going native, for after living in Switzerland for a while, I could no longer see why Worldwide should tell its members they shouldn't vote. This seemed especially true because, although political issues were intensely discussed and the citizens informed themselves, there was less of the polarization and hostility increasingly characterizing the American political scene.

Finally, amid a referendum campaign with several important motions, I submitted a memo. Randal Dick called me. When he had shown it to Joe Tkach, Jr., Joe had responded, "What's the problem? We've always felt this." In Big Sandy, where Worldwide members were a significant portion of the electorate, they had consistently voted in the mayoral election. And a member had served on the school board in Pasadena in the Seventies. But they preferred that I say nothing since it was a worldwide issue affecting members living in widely varying systems. Were anyone to ask, I was free to say that I had submitted the question, that it had been well-received, and that the church wanted to take a long and careful look at the issue.

Bit by bit, we were moving away from the stance of total non-involvement in the affairs of this world that had characterized both the early church and the radical wing of the Reformation. In each case, this stance had been combined with an imminent expectation of the end of the world. Thus, whenever Christians began to realize their children and grandchildren might have to live in this world, they began shouldering a share of responsibility.

I supported this, but I also saw a danger. Could we take an active interest in the politics of this world without endangering the unity of the congregation?

A third issue was the way tithing was administered in Europe. I still believed one could find three tithes in the Old Testament; others questioned this, but I couldn't see any other way to account for the inconsistencies in how the tithe is discussed in the relevant passages. I had come to feel, however, that in social democracies like Switzerland and Germany, the government had taken over the role of administering what would be the third tithe. In effect, members paid twice to relieve the needy—once through their taxes and then again in the third tithe. Given the number of deductions before arriving at take-home pay, Europeans had less freedom to determine how to spend their money. I had shared my concerns with John Karlson, and he asked me to write them up. Wade, who felt even more strongly about this, worked with me on a joint proposal.

Aside from these specific topics, the church struggled to define its approach to the broader issue of faith and obedience.

One of Worldwide's distinctive teachings was to practice more of the law than most Christians. As an expression of divine will, obedience to the law was a frequent topic in sermons and literature. Unfortunately, this often obscured the understanding that salvation is according to God's grace. Even when that was acknowledged, it was seldom without the corollary, "but rewarded according to works," and the citation of one of the many Bible passages, such as Revelation 22:12, that state this.

In earlier years, Herbert Armstrong had striven to balance this emphasis on obedience by reminders that salvation is a gift offered as God's grace. The discovery of his letter about this in the 1950s to his personal correspondence staff was crucial to me in my senior year at Ambassador when campus life was torn between hardliner ministers and those who seemed to be watering down the truth.

After Armstrong reasserted his authority in 1978, and for the remaining eight years of his life, his emphasis on "getting back on track" and his railing against what he called liberalism, combined with rewarding of previously sidelined traditionalist hardliners, shifted the balance to an emphasis on obedience.

Soon after succeeding Armstrong, Joe Tkach sought to redress the balance, emphasizing God's desire for his law to be written in our hearts. Worldwide sought to make it more transparent, both to its own membership and outside critics—some of whom taught the law had been done away—how Worldwide saw the balance between law and grace.

Temperament undoubtedly played a role in how we in the ministry heard and applied what we were taught (the same applied to the membership at large). During one refresher program I attended in Pasadena before Herbert Armstrong's death, Joe Tkach presented a session on working with readers who had requested visits. While warning us to be cautious whom we invited to attend services, he asked, "Have they read *Why Were You Born?*" followed by the titles of several other Worldwide booklets. Some ministers asked for the list of the booklets he named; consequently, the list was sent to all of us. Before entering the ministry, Jim Jenkins had been a successful furniture salesman and he used some of those skills in the ministry. He kept a stock of booklets in his office and took two or three of them with him when he visited new prospects. Pasadena indicated which literature the new prospect had already requested when we received new visit requests, and Jim selected titles they didn't yet have. As he wrapped up a visit, he would casually mention that he had a booklet that might interest them, and they could have it if they liked. This not only brought new people along in their acquaintance with our teachings, but it was also a relationship builder. A pastor in a neighboring congregation, with the reputation as a hardliner, used the list differently. When Pasadena sent him a new visit request, he wrote the interested person and included the booklet list and said to contact him when they'd read all of it.

As I settled into work in Europe, it wasn't long before I learned that the elder who managed the correspondence in Worldwide's Bonn office had understood the list in the same way as my neighboring pastor in the States and wasn't forwarding visit requests to me but instead told them what they still had to read before receiving a visit.

By the time the spring holy days came around in 1990, we had been in Europe for nearly three years. I was beginning to feel at home in the area, yet I was still not a local. Between services on the First Day of Unleavened Bread, Edel and I took a walk through Schluchsee after lunch before the afternoon service. As we walked by the village church, I noticed the house next door bore a plaque, *Pfarramt*. That's where the pastor lived and had his office, in the middle of the village. Something about this called out to me as the way it should be. I contrasted it with Worldwide's congregations. In the area I pastored, some traveled an hour or more to attend. One elderly gentleman living high above a village in Prättigau, in eastern Switzerland, had to leave services as soon as they ended to reach Chur in eastern Switzerland before the last bus from Chur to his village left. After reaching that village, he had to climb uphill to reach his home. When I first visited him in the idyllic setting where he lived, I could see that, from the point of his knowledge of our teachings, he was someone I should invite to services, but I wondered if he would come. When I raised the question with him, he showed me he had already informed himself and written out the times and routes.

That's what made our congregations exceptional. In addition to our distinctive teachings, there was the hurdle of traveling to attend. Through a sort of natural selection, the effect was that the chairs were filled with highly motivated people who took this upon themselves because they felt they couldn't find what we taught closer to home. The half-hearted were winnowed out. The downside of it was that the Sabbath was, physically speaking, not a day of rest. Not for me as a pastor, nor for the parishioners.

The village churches, on the other hand, were largely empty Sunday mornings. Moreover, many of those who did attend did so out of routine or social expectation. That's why, rather than wanting to exchange one model for the other, I compared both to circumstances as I imagined they would be in the Millennium when the knowledge of God filled the earth (Hab. 2:14). Yet I wondered: when at last the truth could be married to convenience, how would the zeal stay alive?

From the time I began making the rounds and responding to visit requests from readers in Europe, I learned that our publications had a large following and fit into a strong tradition in German Pietism of reading communities. They had their roots in a phenomenon that grew after the Reformation when the official Lutheran church focused more on correct doctrine than spirituality. At the universities, a new scholasticism arose, rivaling that of the Middle Ages in erudition. Pastors became highly educated—the pastor was often the most educated person in his community. Their parishioners respected them but found themselves unmoved by the messages they heard. This was at a time when the expectation was that someone from every household attended services. Many simply let the service go over their heads, then went on with their lives, but some sat there and hungered for spiritual nourishment. This need was filled by books and pamphlets from authors such as Arnd, Spener, Tersteegen, and Zinzendorf. Their popularity spread by word of mouth.

Now, I found our booklets were filling a similar need. Visits I'd made in North America were guided by the questions of whether God was calling the individual and should be invited to services. In most cases, whenever I concluded that this was the case, the person responded positively to the invitation. Then a second stage began, that of preparing the person for baptism. This involved filling in gaps in their knowledge, especially in our distinctive doctrines, and helping them experience repentance, the necessary prerequisite for believer baptism. But now, throughout southwest Germany (with its long Pietist tradition) and Switzerland, I met many people thankful for the literature but not interested in attending services. Others, however, did begin to attend, so that weekly attendance at worship services in all three congregations increased.

Some of those who wrote in for a visit were themselves

pastors who liked our literature. One Methodist pastor, himself the author of several books (he gave me a couple), thought we should join forces to spread the gospel in the German-speaking area more effectively. We remained on friendly terms. Another visit was more contentious: a retired pastor who had done some teaching at the University of Basel. He despaired of the Protestant church, which he felt had drifted too far to the left. He liked our conservative stance but wanted to set us straight on some of our errors. I did the best I could to defend our teachings, but he waved my answers away with the attitude that I would see my error if I only knew Greek. His grasp of Greek wasn't as firm as he believed it was, however. For instance, the transfiguration (Matt. 17) was evidence to him that Moses and Elijah had literally ascended to heaven, insisting that the Greek word *horama* must refer to something the three disciples were literally seeing (as opposed to *phantasma*, another Greek term that could only mean a figment of the imagination). To him, this was proof that what they saw was a physical reality and that the translations were wrong to call it a vision. He wasn't correct in his insistence, as I determined after returning home by looking at other passages that used that word, but without knowing Greek, I was at a disadvantage.

A month later, the saga continued. One of the finest members of the Stuttgart congregation died unexpectedly of a heart attack while jogging. His brother, who was responsible for the arrangements, wanted the funeral held at the pietistic senior center where our member had worked, with a Lutheran liturgy but with me giving the address. The Lutheran pastor who cared for the center refused; so, we held the funeral in the cemetery's chapel. I chose hymns from the standard hymnal, and there was a eulogy by the director of the center; otherwise, the service was the standard World-wide order of worship. The relatives were pleased; his sister asked for a copy of the sermon.

Then, as we sat together afterward for coffee and cake, the Lutheran pastor sat next to me and began asking about the church. Among other things, he asked if we would be considered Jewish Christianity. I said some scholars would apply that term because of parallels with the *Urgemeinde* (original congregation) in Jerusalem. He nodded pleasantly and then asked if we held to everything in the Old Testament; I answered no, since the Book of Hebrews clarifies what is no longer to be practiced in light of Christ's sacrifice. Next, he began to say conciliatory things about the Sabbath based on his contacts with Jews in Israel. He said he was glad we don't have to live by all 613 precepts but that people missed out by not setting aside a day to focus on God and family. I wanted to hear him go on, but one of the members of our congregation sitting at the same table, a young firebrand, jumped in and said it wasn't just one day in seven, but the specific day commanded in God's law. The pastor became defensive, and I changed the subject, asking about his trips to Israel. He'd been ten times, leading tour groups. He told me he preferred to avoid the ostensibly Christian sites but concentrate on archaeological excavations. Not only did these illustrate the Old Testament, but they gave him more of a feel for how Christ lived.

Before leaving, he touched on the ceremony. He regretted that it had not been more liturgical, especially that there was no recitation of the Lord's Prayer to allow the congregation to participate. As for the message, he said there was nothing in it he couldn't have said.

My curiosity to know more about theology also expressed itself when I was in Basel to perform a funeral at the *Friedhof am Hörnli*, across the Rhine from the old city. After the funeral was over, I chatted with the cemetery gardener and asked whether Karl Barth was buried there. His eyes brightened and he took me to the grave, where Barth was interred between two women. I hadn't known about his unusual living situation, but at first glance understood intuitively. The gardener remembered well the funeral of the second woman, Charlotte von Kirschbaum, who died in 1975, less than fifteen years earlier at the time. Among the mourners was the recently-retired president of Germany, Gustav Heinemann, who arrived in a military helicopter that landed on the cemetery grounds. From there, the gardener took me to the nearby grave of philosopher Karl Jaspers, but his enthusiasm increased as he described what was clearly his favorite funeral, that of an American jazz musician, at which fellow musicians played a somber processional, then took up their instruments for a celebratory recessional.

I was still not, in my eyes, a thoroughly competent pastor. When I read in a biography of Ralph Waldo Emerson about his struggles as a young pastor, I related. This descendent of Waldensians (on his mother's side, attested by his middle name) was the son of a minister who had lost faith in many of the tenets of his church by study in Göttingen. The father had then died when Waldo, the second son, was eight years old, leaving only the memory of a severe and distant man who kept his doubts to himself (on the advice of none other than Goethe, whom the elder Emerson visited before leaving Germany, and who told him he would be carrying out no more than a harmless deception).

Waldo was an introspective and unpromising youth; according to his biographer, Gay Wilson Allen, he was considered less intelligent than his three brothers. Nevertheless, after completing Harvard, he was ordained a Unitarian minister. But he was only partly successful. He preferred "to read, contemplate, and write" instead of performing parish visits and "officiating at funerals and weddings" (*Waldo Emerson: A Biography*, Viking 1981, viii).

Although I was more gregarious than Waldo Emerson seems to have been and enjoyed conducting services, I also sensed a kinship. I noted in my journal: "To his congregation, theological questions had already been answered by the men who wrote the creeds of their church. All they expected from their pastor was a repetition of these accepted 'truths' in soothing and encouraging sermons. But to Emerson nothing was settled; every inherited belief and custom needed to be expressed in the light of modern experience and the individual conscience" (viii–ix).

Knowing that I wasn't the first to experience this feeling of inadequacy didn't help, though. I chastised myself. I felt that if I were a better pastor, the congregations would be in better shape. I worked harder. Meanwhile, new visit requests dropped noticeably. The boom that new avenues for proclaiming Worldwide's message in Europe had brought had been temporary. Part of me still yearned to be more directly involved with our media efforts, because I was convinced they could be better than they were.

And I heard rumors of a third way I might be asked to serve. Larry Salyer was looking into consolidating all the European offices into one European service center based in a cosmopolitan border region like Strasbourg. A European regional director would be based there, supported by an office manager. My name had come up, I heard, for the latter job.

I tried not to be distracted by that, though, and redoubled my efforts as a pastor to increase my visits' quality and quantity as well as the quality of sermons.

Meanwhile, the overwork and stress were taking their toll. I had the worst bout of hay fever I'd had since moving to Europe; no doubt, a sign of adrenal exhaustion. Soon after, we went to Schluchsee to celebrate the Night to Be Much Observed at the *Kurhaus* but I found I couldn't go in and put on a smiling face to meet the members gathered there. I recognized that I had once again sunk into depression. I dropped Edel and the boys off, turned on the car radio just after Beethoven's "Tempest" Sonata began and drove to the lakeside. I pulled over to the side of the road to listen. Its alternating mood of turbulence and lyric calm expressed what I was feeling and soothed me. As I listened, I watched snow flurries dance in front of the sunset over the lake, then went to our hotel room and worked on the next day's sermon.

Apart from that evening in Schluchsee I was able to carry out my duties, despite the numbing darkness I felt inside. From our home in Dällikon to services in Basel every two weeks, our route took us past a psychiatric institute near Brugg. As we passed it, I watched people walk the grounds and wondered how long it would be before I landed there.

Perhaps, however, I was deceiving myself in thinking that I was functioning well enough. I'm haunted by a reference I made in a sermon scorning those who took refuge in depression, as if it were a luxury one allowed oneself. I was preaching to myself (as preachers sometimes do) and was blind to anyone else in the congregation who might be battling something similar. One was, a woman whose homeland was ravaged by civil war at the moment. She was deeply offended and could not be reconciled. When in the Epistle of James readers are admonished that not many should become teachers, "knowing that we shall receive the greater condemnation" (James 3:1), I thought for many years that was a reference to divine judgment. I'm no longer so sure. Whatever we say in a sermon can be severely judged by listeners. But this is nothing compared to the self-recrimination one feels, knowing that such words can't be taken back.

Another painful memory of a remark in a sermon: Once at the Feast of Tabernacles I railed against sexual immorality, including same-sex behavior (this was at a time when my understanding of the scriptural references was out of step with the evidence of the lives of people I knew well). Spontaneously, I said that it wouldn't surprise me if one year the earthquake everyone knew was overdue would strike San

Francisco during the feast, while all of "God's people" were safely observing it elsewhere. The very next year, an earthquake did strike there during the feast. Rather than taking satisfaction at the confirmation of my prediction, I was filled with inner revulsion.

One highlight in this dark time: the television department in Pasadena asked me to arrange an interview with Sir John Eccles, a neurologist and Nobel laureate still active at the university in Basel. His position on the brain-mind problem had influenced Robert Kuhn and, in turn, Worldwide's teaching on the spirit-in-man.

Dave Albert, who had regretted that I couldn't stay and join the theology faculty when I graduated from Ambassador, and now one of the presenters of the telecast, would come over to interview him, but there were scheduling conflicts, and the date went back and forth until Eccles backed out, which I understood—he was, after all, eighty-eight. But I reached out to him one more time, he agreed, and we drove to Basel. Dave brought a skeleton crew from Pasadena and drafted my brother-in-law Wolfgang to handle the lighting. It seemed like old times to work with the crew again.

Dave Albert was the most educated Worldwide minister in counseling and psychology, yet I did not avail myself of his visit to open up to him about what I was going through. Our schedule didn't permit it, but even if there had been time to talk one on one, I wouldn't have. I had to show this top minister from headquarters I was competent. To a surprising degree, I was functioning outside the house, dealing with others. At home, it was different. Edel suspected but didn't have the training or insight to know what was wrong. But simply having the crew in town was a lift to my spirits, and had a sequel: over dinner in our home, the cameraman, Ron Prociw, who had noticed the many history books on my shelves, began talking about the Ken Burns series on the Civil War, then playing in the U.S. I hadn't heard of it, and in a few weeks, a box of video cassettes he'd taped off the air arrived via the Bonn office so that I could see the series. That was very thoughtful of him, and the series was well-made. Of course, the pervasive elegiac sadness of the tale was in keeping with my mood, but not in a way that made it worse.

The day after the TV crew left, John Adams, who assisted Carn Catherwood in a fledgling Italian-language outreach of the church, arrived with his wife, Anne, and stayed over-night. Then, two days later, I made repeated airport runs to pick up Larry and Judy, Carn and Joyce, Randy and Susie, and the McCulloughs. These arrivals were in anticipation of the first all-European ministerial conference, held in Colmar in late April 1991. Seeing so many of my favorite people at one time was an encouragement.

I had lunch with Carn and Joyce when they arrived, and I sounded off on my pet peeves about the *Plain Truth* and my suggested solutions. They, like others with whom I shared my concerns, agreed. Yet nothing seemed to change. Mean-while, I was torn. Part of me would have liked to be asked to help in that area, but common sense reminded me how good we had it in Switzerland. I loved magazine journalism and felt Worldwide had a message to communicate. But, on the other hand, I realized that I would not like working in the environment under which the *Plain Truth* was produced. From the sidelines, it seemed a classic case of too many cooks. It didn't look to me as if anyone had identified the individuals best able to do the job and then let them do it.

I retained my conviction that we had a message even though I detected a soft-pedaling of some distinctive teachings such as the destiny of humankind, as well as the conviction that there was a true church and that we were it. At dinner that night with Larry and Judy, we discussed changes needed in booklets and the correspondence course in light of revised understanding, such as born again; Larry hinted there were many more changes to come.

While in Colmar, we discussed the proposed European service center. Speaking for it: in many regions, administration was too high a percentage of the overall budget. We would we save money by consolidating support functions such as data processing, mail reading, literature distribution, and accounting. Nevertheless, it became clear that it would not come about. No one was strongly for it, and many were against it. I felt that neither technology nor organization mattered as much as having a clear idea of our message and mission and saying it with conviction and compassion.

The conference was a ray of light that helped lift my darkness, but I continued to be one who labored and was heavy-laden. I thought it might do me good to get away for a day and thought the perfect opportunity would be Pentecost weekend, in a week's time. I was to speak in Bonn on that day, Sunday, and in Darmstadt the day before that, on the Sabbath. Perhaps we could travel up on Friday. My first idea was to visit Heidelberg, but I dropped it because I realized we'd have to wait until the boys got home from school to set out and would arrive too late in the evening to do the things I wanted to do. Plus, hotels were costly. I studied the area around Darmstadt on a map, and Michelstadt seemed a good choice. Edel volunteered to book a hotel since I had to spend the day in the Stuttgart area. All except one hotel was full. The town would host a bee festival that weekend. The one hotel that still had a room warned we couldn't eat in the restaurant because of a birthday celebration. Edel booked it anyway. Neither she nor I realized what that might mean later in the night. On Friday afternoon, we left an hour later than we had planned. The weather was miserable as we loaded the car. Holiday weekend traffic slowed our journey, and we arrived at 9:15, six-and-a-half hours after we left home.

The way the birthday child and his guests partied, it seemed as if he didn't think he'd get another chance ten years later when he turned seventy. The music stopped at three, after an hour, I dropped off for four hours of sleep. It was not the relaxing getaway I had hoped for.

Whether you called it depression, a mid-life crisis or accidie (one of the seven mortal sins), I was suffering from it. I still functioned, but I felt overwhelmed. Inside I was wailing. The Germans have a word, *Weltschmerz*. It's based on the Apostle Paul's reference to worldly, as opposed to Godly, sorrow (2 Cor. 7:8–9). Perhaps that was also an accurate expression of the deep sadness I felt over my own inadequacy and that of the world in general.

Chapter Four

The Greek language saved my life.

That's only a slight exaggeration. It happened like this:

The semi-detached house we rented was the last in a row of four pairs of houses. Beyond us, to the west, was a large empty field. We were told when we moved in that the lot belonged to the town and was kept in reserve in case the school needed to expand, but that this would likely never happen. But then building stakes went up.

The village had traded with the local Reformed congregation. Their church stood at the intersection in the center of town, with a parsonage next to it. That house became the town's property in return for the field, and construction began for a new parsonage on half of the lot, the half closest to us. I was uncomfortable. It was one thing that most of the people around us weren't part of the elect, but in Worldwide's theology, they simply hadn't yet had their eyes opened. But pastors weren't just the deceived; they were the deceivers. That was something altogether different.

Uncertain how to handle the situation, I asked myself what we would do in America. There, it would have been natural for us to take our new neighbors a pan of homemade brownies and welcome them to the neighborhood. So, that's what we did, on a Sunday afternoon, June 1991.

The couple was surprised and pleased by our visit. In Europe, the custom is the other way around: when someone new moves in, they go around and introduce themselves. In this case, they had moved less than two hundred meters from the old parsonage. And through their duties, they already knew most of the people on our street. But not us.

By coincidence, I had just begun reading a book I ordered from a remainder catalog in the States, *Heretics*, by Walter Nigg. When the book arrived, I found it was translated from German and that the author had been a Swiss pastor. I asked our neighbor, Hans-Ueli Perels, if he had heard of him. Nigg, it turned out, was his predecessor and had died only a few years earlier; his widow still lived in the neighboring village.

In getting to know our new neighbors, we learned that both he and his wife, Doris, were ordained ministers. They had met at university, where he struggled with Greek, and she had tutored him.

At the mention of Greek, I said that I regretted not learning it since it had not been offered where I studied. Doris said she was starting a small reading group for people who wanted to learn a bit about the language and that I was welcome to join. After the first meeting, though, she said that the easiest way to get what I needed was to take the New Testament Greek course at the university. I thought one had to be a member of the Reformed Church to take classes there; she said that there was no such requirement since it was a public university. Besides, I didn't need to enroll but could audit.

So, in the fall of 1991, I sat as one of more than thirty students for the first Greek class. Most were beginning their theology studies and had come straight from high school and were nineteen or twenty years old. But a few were older, such as an anthropologist looking to change careers.

The University of Zurich theology faculty was housed in a square building attached to the walls of the *Grossmünster*, the church in which Zwingli promulgated the Reformation. It had four stories, half of one below the sloping street level (plus archives one level lower). The walls enclosed a cloister garden, a pleasant oasis in warm weather.

I had no inkling at the time of how closely I would become attached to that building and the society of teachers, librarians, staff, and students who came and went, the *theologorum turicensium ordo evangelicus*, as an old Latin inscription calls it. But it soon had the feeling of a homecoming, given my father's supplement of my Lutheran confirmation classes with dinner-table reminders that Zwingli had made his own contribution.

I was clear about my goals: to improve my personal understanding of the Bible, be more accurate in comments and explanations in sermons and Bible Studies, and to hold a necessary credential when representing Worldwide. But even the third was not unimportant. In Europe, I had learned by this time, it was expected that a minister can work with the Bible in the original languages.

More important than any of these stated goals, however, was that learning Greek was a self-prescribed therapy for battling the depression I'd suffered for more than half a year. I never sought treatment or counseling. Instead, I analyzed myself as if from the outside. Many other men in a mid-life crisis change jobs. That could be one reason why I was obsessed with Worldwide's media outreach. But I didn't want to move to Pasadena, and I remained convinced that the field ministry was important. Other men buy a sports car, but I wasn't interested in autos. The tens of thousands of miles I spent on the road each year didn't make driving for a hobby appealing. Still other men had an affair, but I was happy with my wife. Consequently, learning something new that was also job-related seemed the way to go.

I soon felt renewed energy; I was finally embracing a part of me that had long called to me but that I had shunted aside. I had grown up in a book-filled home. In my previous pastorates, I had been drawn to university libraries. The original appeal of the proclamation of Worldwide had been to know things that weren't widely known.

The Greek course was taught by Jörg Büchli, a voluble philologist with an infectious enthusiasm for the language. He enjoyed springing surprises on the students whenever a close examination of a passage in Greek revealed a teaching at variance with common belief. Some of these were no surprise to me, such as the various words translated hell, each with its own meaning. He also took great delight when we translated a passage from 1 Corinthians 8, pointing out that Peter had a wife; therefore, the first putative "pope" wasn't celibate. But sometimes, the surprise went the other way. Shortly before Christmas, we translated the angel's message to the shepherds in the field (Luke 2:14). Büchli pointed our attention to the footnote, containing a variant of the text. That variant was from the Byzantine text tradition, which meant, from what I'd been taught at Ambassador by Herman Hoeh, it was the original, correct text. But when I compared the two versions, I saw much to be said, based on the sentence structure, for the variant adopted in critical editions of the New Testament in Greek. I immediately grasped the justification for text criticism, so-called lower criticism. It didn't dictate results but showed possibilities and assessed probabilities. It was clear that the Byzantine text, venerable as it may be, couldn't be set up as an absolute authority.

The second aha experience was when we reached the verb *gennao* and its family. Herbert Armstrong had supported his insistence that spiritual rebirth happened at the resurrection with a dictate that *gennao* could only mean begotten and that it was limited to the father's role at the time of conception. Now I learned he had been wrong. It was jarring to realize that he would never have made this error if he had even taken one semester of Greek.

At first, my intention was simply to go to class and return home. But there was a fifteen-minute recess halfway through the two-hour session, and I began to fall into conversation. Some were curious about this American twice their age. One of the friendliest was a young man active in an evangelical, non-state church preparing himself to pastor one of their congregations. It turned out he was aware of the

Plain Truth and some of the teachings of Worldwide. Then, after a few weeks, he asked me outright if no one would be saved who didn't keep the Sabbath. That put me on the spot. I answered that the question of who would be saved was God's business, according to his grace, but that this was simply something we felt we saw in scripture and thus needed to observe.

Toward the end of the semester, just after the new year, Büchli began to look ahead to the final exam in a year, at the end of the third semester. Since I was doing the same work as the others, it would only be fitting for me to have a course completion certificate. But since I was only auditing, he would have to arrange a private exam. He urged me to consider enrolling instead. Then, as a matriculated student, I could sit for the exam with the other students and receive the same university-issued certificate.

I asked John Karlson for his advice. He was concerned about the time it might take away from my work as a pastor and from the regular articles I was by now contributing to the German edition of the *Plain Truth*, *Klar + Wahr*, as well as to the church's newspaper, the *Worldwide News*. But he left the decision to me. I understood his reservations, but was convinced that it would benefit Worldwide if I had the standard certification of proficiency in Greek. So, I began the paperwork to apply. Not having completed secondary school in Switzerland made it seem as if it would be difficult to enroll. In the end, my four years at Boston University, with a bachelor's degree, were accepted as equivalent.

Thus, when it came time for the Greek exam in February 1993, after three semesters, I was able to take it together with the others. It consisted of two parts, written and oral. For the oral exam, administered by Jörg Büchli, two experts were present: New Testament professor Hans Weder to represent the faculty, and Walter Burkert, an eminent scholar of religion in antiquity, as the Greek expert. One of my construals must have missed the mark and perhaps have been unintentionally off-color; the two experts shot a look at each other and had to suppress laughter. Nevertheless, the result was good enough overall to have my proficiency attested with a decent mark. Still, as Weder shook my hand to congratulate me, he said it was permitted to keep learning. I invited the entire class, including Jörg Büchli, to our home the next day for a celebration. I also asked Hans-Ueli Perels, our neighbor, to drop by. This gave him the chance to do some advertising for the course he'd offer the next semester on managing a church congregation. The people came and left at different times; thus, with ferrying them back and forth to the train station, I didn't get as much out of everyone's presence as I'd hoped, but it was still a good gathering.

To finally read the New Testament in Greek had deepened my understanding to such a degree that I was eager to learn Hebrew as well. However, unlike Greek, which was taught over three semesters, this was covered in one, an intensive course that met seven hours a week, on four different days. This was an understandable choice since Hebrew is a more straightforward language than Greek, but it put me at a disadvantage, since I continued to work full-time at my pastorate. It was challenging to fit in the classes, to say nothing of the translations we had to prepare outside of class. In addition, most of my vocabulary repetition was while commuting on the train. Yet any time taken from the congregation was more than compensated, I felt, by the feedback from many members that my sermons had taken on more life and gave the feeling of being solidly grounded. And the Hebrew text has delights that can't be translated, such as the word plays in Isaiah and the excitement of Adam's words when he first sees Eve.

I also received my Latin certificate after taking three semesters of it, also with Jörg Büchli. However, it was recommended for all three classic languages to continue for an additional semester after the proficiency exam with a reading course. So, along with Hebrew, I took the Latin reading offered that semester, on the *Rule of Benedict*, taught by Hans-Dietrich Altendorf, professor of early church history.

Altendorf maintained that one couldn't understand the Benedictine Rule simply by reading it; one had to live it. So, he organized a field trip one Saturday split between the monastery at Einsiedeln and the cloister of Fahr. In addition to talking to our guides, we participated in prayers, early and late. I had arranged to have an elder take Worldwide's services that day.

Halfway through the day, we lunched at outdoor tables in the village of Einsiedeln, and Altendorf invited me to sit with him. He had heard that I was the pastor of a strict sect, and he wanted to learn more about it. When I told him of the Sabbath, he said that the Orthodox churches continue to observe the seventh day as a memorial of creation. When we discussed Worldwide's observance of the annual holy days, Altendorf grew excited as I outlined Herbert Armstrong's teaching that they pictured the plan of salvation. He called it a theologoumenon, that is, a new thought based on theological reflection. It is clear that Christianity's spring festivals, Easter and Pentecost, are continuations of Old Testament models. Altendorf said there were indications in the early church fathers of some sort of observance of the fall holy days as well and suggested that it would be a good topic for a dissertation and that I should consider earning a doctorate. It's the first time anyone suggested that to me.

We discussed one more of Worldwide's distinctive teachings: the purpose of mankind. He recognized and identified it as a variant of the early church teaching, the teaching of theosis, which was still taught in the Eastern Orthodox churches. As one fourth century bishop, Athanasius of Alexandria, said: "He [Jesus] was made man so that we might be made God." It became clear that many of Worldwide's claims to uniqueness were seen against the backdrop of the Western church, but that many of these ideas had been in currency in the East and had never totally died out in Orthodox tradition. This thought wasn't a total surprise when I thought back to the Quartodeciman controversy, when East and West had differed on the proper day to commemorate the Resurrection.

Altendorf wanted to hear more, so, I told him of Worldwide's British Israelism. This didn't fluster him either; he delved into the history of the search for the lost ten tribes. Long before Richard Brothers in late eighteenth-century Britain, there was speculation the tribes were among inhabitants of the British Isles since God had threatened to scatter them to the corners of the earth (Deut. 32:26). Pope Gregory I (late sixth century) had been fascinated by the area since glimpsing pale-faced slaves at the market in Rome. I was already familiar with the anecdote recorded by the Venerable Bede: when, in answer to his query, Gregory learned they were Angles, he replied: *non Angli, sed Angeli, si forent Christiani* ("not Angles, but angels, if they become Christian"). What I didn't know until Altendorf told me: Gregory took the great commission to preach the gospel to the ends of the earth to prepare for Christ's return as seriously as Herbert Armstrong. Once he became pope, he initiated a mission to convert the Angles, the Saxons, and the Jutes, who had replaced the Britons in most of the island's east.

There was no question of considering writing a dissertation, though, if I did not have a complete theology program, ending with a licentiate, the equivalent of a master's degree. Altendorf was sure that some of my work at Ambassador could be accepted as partial fulfillment of the requirements. When I petitioned the faculty to that effect, however, nothing was recognized. The only dispensation I was granted was in the church history proseminar, based on an article I had written for the *Plain Truth* on Martin Luther and his translation of the Bible into German. Altendorf attested that it was superior to any proseminar paper.

The reluctance to grant credits might have put the idea to rest had not the university still operated along traditional European lines. One didn't have to earn credits to graduate. Instead, a student listened to lectures, participated in seminars, and read more or less according to his or her interest. Specific requirements had to be fulfilled, but he or she could do as much or as little beyond that as he or she chose. Then, when a candidate felt ready, he or she signed up for a battery of comprehensive exams. There were two levels. One was propaedeutic, that is, it covered introductory matters. The second level was advanced. It was a system that allowed some to gain a depth of erudition and theological maturity and others to spend as much as a decade as "eternal students." Still others, especially those who needed to support a family, took the most efficient way to qualification.

It was a program I wouldn't have been able to pursue even in Europe a few years later. In an attempt to emulate higher education in the U.S. (where, by common assent, many of the best universities in the world were located), a system of credit points and achievement certificates was assigned to each course or sequence of courses. This reform was called the Bologna process since the formal declaration to begin was signed at the university there, the world's oldest still in operation. It wasn't implemented until my final years at the university; thus, I could finish under the old system. I realized the benefit of European-wide quality standards and the compatibility of degrees. Yet, it seemed to sacrifice the strength of the traditional European system without capturing the best of what made American schools good.

My choice of courses each semester from then on was dictated by two considerations. One was strategic: how to fulfill the requirements for the two sets of comprehensive exams. The other was which courses would help my understanding of questions Worldwide was grappling with. These didn't always coincide, and in some semesters, I took more than the absolute minimum required to remain matriculated. I began with the Old and New Testament proseminars. These were designed to give students a practical introduction to the historical-critical method. As a class, we worked our way together through a passage over the semester to practice the steps of the method in an exemplary way. Then we each had to write an exegetical paper on a passage of our choice demonstrating competence in applying the method.

I took the New Testament course in the summer semester of 1993, then the second, Old Testament, a year and a half later. My ears perked up when the teacher of the Old Testament proseminar, Peter Schwagmeier, illustrated the concept of tradition criticism by a reference to the work of the Lomaxes, the father-son team that preserved much of the American folk tradition through field work. I spoke to Peter about it after class, and we soon discovered our mutual admiration of Bob Dylan.

When I told him I'd seen Dylan, backed by the Hawks (later renamed the Band), in 1965, he was impressed. He rarely missed a concert whenever Dylan toured Europe, often traveling from city to city to catch successive nights. In the summer of 1996, he told me of an upcoming appearance during a music festival on Lake Constance. I'd heard that his live shows had dropped in quality; so, I preferred to keep my memories of the two concerts I'd seen. Peter assured me that he was on an upswing and talked me into coming with him.

On a warm, humid day, we drove to Constance, where the concert was held in a tent near the lakeside. Unlike the first two times I'd seen him, this time there was an opening act, the Dave Matthews Band, new to me at the time. The tent was packed; I estimated there were about twelve hundred people (less than one-tenth the size of the crowd in the Montreal Forum eighteen years earlier). The temperature and humidity inside the tent grew steadily. By the time Dylan and his band took the stage, Peter was nowhere to be seen. He had worked his way through the crowd and was standing in front. I was content to remain in the back to have a little more air. The band began the first number, "Down in the Flood," with a guitar riff reminiscent of Creedence; from that first song to the last, the performance was electrifying. Dylan and his band reworked his songs, mixing and matching intros from one song to another. I was taken in from the start. The violinist from the opening band joined in on "Maggie's Farm" toward the end of the set, then Dave Matthews came on for the closing number, "Everything's Broken." After a short interval, Dylan and his band returned for a three-song encore. The violinist, Boyd Tinsley, returned for the second of them, and the rest of the Dave Matthews Band joined Dylan and his band for a shambling rendition of "Rainy Day Women #12 & 35"). Peter had been right to urge me to give Dylan a chance.

Thus, when Dylan's first LP of new material in seven years, *Time Out of Mind*, came out a year later, in September

1997, I wasn't surprised that it was one of his best. It was a brilliant title—an old phrase in colloquial English, especially in the area on both sides of the Scottish border, to refer to something that couldn't be precisely dated because of happening so long ago. In the context of the ghostly songs, it seemed to suggest timeless, and therefore both immemorial and current.

That same month, I traveled with Peter to Bologna, where Dylan performed at a large open-air concert in the presence of Pope John Paul II. We were packed in a sun-filled field with thousands of youths (I was reminded of Woodstock), and I couldn't help but share a little of the excitement when the popemobile passed close by us as it drove to the stage. Then he took a seat on a throne at the edge of the stage as a stream of artists such as Adriano Celentano and Andrea Bocelli performed (many of the young people around us knew the arias Bocelli sang well enough to join in). The pope addressed us in Italian, albeit I found I could follow his sermon reasonably well. He spoke for about twenty-five minutes, using the text of "Blowin' in the Wind" as his springboard. "You ask me how many roads must a man walk down? I will tell you. There is only one, the one who is the way, the truth and the life." (The words "road" and "way" are the same in Italian). It had grown dark by the time Dylan and his band came on, roughly two hours after the event had begun. He opened with "Knockin' on Heaven's Door", and followed with "Hard Rain's A-Gonna Fall", a song whose stark apocalyptic imagery matched the reality of 1997 even better than that of 1962, when he wrote the song. It set a powerful counterpoint to the announced theme of the evening, *canzone d'esperanza* ("songs of hope") and reminded me of scenes from Old Testament Israel when a prophet would confront a priest with the bad news. Then it was time for the Pope to go. As he departed, Dylan sang "Forever Young," which was a touch ironic as a gesture to the stooped figure who seemed that he has been Forever Old.

By placing Bob Dylan in the spotlight of the Bologna concert, not only by having him sing directly after the homily, but also using his song texts in a liturgical way, the Pope staged the ultimate seeker service, for Bob Dylan is the ultimate seeker of our time.

Worldwide continued to hold annual European conferences after the first one in Colmar in 1991. While it had been good throughout the 1980s to return regularly to Pasadena for refreshers, this new program better fit our needs. In addition, the time spent together with ministers from all over Europe helped foster transnational cooperation.

The second was held in 1992 in Pertisau, in the Tirol area of Austria. It would be the last one led by Larry Salyer. Worldwide was restructuring its international operations. Until then, the director of the international work oversaw all aspects of the work outside the U.S.—advertising, mail, budgeting, ministry, and congregations. Now, the job was reconfigured so that, as a part of Church Administration, it was only responsible for ministry and congregations. Other functions would be integrated into the respective headquarters departments and overseen from there.

I saw the potential upside, harmonization of procedures worldwide. But I also saw a downside. For instance, in small offices, one person might be responsible for various departments in addition to being an ordained minister. Now he would interact with several supervisors, depending on the aspect of his job. In addition, I felt it would make it challenging to develop an overall strategy for the European region.

Larry seemed split: part of him saw the positive reasons for the change but left the question open about whether they outweighed the negative. At the same time, he was hurt, which I understood. He felt that he, along with Randal Dick, who assisted him, and others on the international team, grasped what needed to be done in various regions and was beginning to implement it. Soon after the conference, he stepped down from his responsibility.

The following conference, in 1993, in Chianciano, a Tuscan village south of Florence, had a different feel. It was the first attended by Joe Tkach, Jr., now superintendent of the ministry worldwide. It was clear that his father leaned on him heavily as his right hand. While he and I had been classmates in Pasadena, many of the men serving in Europe didn't know him, so it was good they could now meet. I also enjoyed the Tuscan cuisine. The sessions themselves, however, were disappointing. It detracted that more than half were not live. Instead, we watched video presentations of lectures taped in Pasadena. This reduced the value of the conference considerably.

As unsatisfying as it was to have nearly half of the sessions devoted to video, the live lectures were problematic in their own way. While Joe Tkach, Jr.'s presentation was devoted to clearing up misunderstandings about the pace of change, it fell to another of my classmates, my friend Randy, to cover two topics on which there had been modifications in administration: remarriage after divorce and tithing.

Wade Fransson and I hadn't heard anything about the status of the tithing proposal we'd submitted. Now I was surprised to learn that many international regions had already received permission to recalculate the basis on which the tithe was figured. The yardstick had been whenever the combination of three tithes, based on gross earnings, together with taxes brought a person under subsistence level in third tithe year, then he had the option of tithing on the net (post-tax) earnings. The German region, along with the French, were the two exceptions. Randy explained that this was because they hadn't asked. I was frustrated. Given the hierarchical structure of Worldwide, it seemed that denomination leadership could have been more forthcoming. At the same time, I began to grasp why Randy had steered me away from examining the scriptures about tithing when I discussed a draft of the proposal before Wade and I submitted it and told me to focus on the numbers instead. It turned out that the doubts I had about our understanding of the scriptures had been turned up by others asked to research the topic. I wasn't saying anything new, just repeating what had been presented before and rejected by Herbert Armstrong.

My dismay at the "you haven't asked" excuse also pinpointed what I felt was the biggest drawback in John Karlson as regional director: he was overly cautious. This trait had made him a valuable counterweight when he served as assistant to Frank Schnee. Schnee's enthusiasm could manifest itself in impetuosity, even recklessness. John was just the backup he needed. I had returned to Europe just as the onset of Parkinson's made it necessary for Schnee to step down as regional director; thus, John had been my boss for six years now. We had a good working relationship. I felt I could speak openly with him about any topic. He was considerate and wise. The fact that our two wives had been roommates when they were single helped cement our friendship. But now, I realized that we could have relieved the members of an onerous burden years earlier.

The work that Herman Hoeh and others had undertaken of editing Herbert Armstrong's writings increasingly turned up issues that couldn't be resolved with a cosmetic polish. The church was engaging with some of its critics, not to seek their approval but to correct distortions in our message. Yet, as is the way with any honest dialogue, we learned they hadn't always distorted Worldwide's teaching. On some topics, they understood what we taught, reported it fairly, but showed its flaws.

There had been negative things written about Worldwide in the German-speaking area as well. In Switzerland, Oswald Eggenberger, a pastor of the Reformed Church, put out a helpful handbook about sects and other new religious movements. I learned a new edition was in the works; so, I wrote to Eggenberger outlining points in which I felt he had misrepresented our teachings. He responded in a kind letter

159

and was happy to modify some of the descriptions, but he held to his assessment in other points.

My studies at the university progressed. In the weeks leading up to the Passover, 1994, I decided to use my newly gained Greek skills to read through Paul's letter to the Galatians in Greek, without consulting my Scofield Bible or the copious notes I had written in its margins. I proceeded as if I were reading it for the first time, which, in a way, I was, since it was the first time I read it from start to finish in Greek. Soon after that, Greg Albrecht, now the editor of the *Plain Truth*, visited Bonn, and all of the ministers traveled there to meet with him. He and I were picked up by the same car for the morning meeting. Sitting next to him in the back seat, I confided what I had done and that I had come away from the experience with the feeling that our theology was uncomfortably close to that combated by Paul in the letter. I braced myself for the reaction after this confession and was surprised when he replied in a soft voice, "Henry, many of us at headquarters are coming to the same conclusion."

Edel had been aware of the questions I was starting to have and was concerned that if the church leadership found out what was going through my mind, I would be in trouble. And yet, now this.

Meanwhile, I was wrestling with a development that struck the heart of what, to me, was one of the three core teachings of Worldwide, the nature of God. Worldwide now accepted the Trinity, the teaching that there was one God, revealed to us as Father, Son, and Holy Spirit, after long rejecting it as unbiblical and derived from paganism.

Many strands of the left wing of the Reformation, from which Worldwide inherited many of its teachings, such as baptism by immersion and non-involvement in the civil affairs of this world, had rejected the Trinity as well and had gravitated to Unitarianism, an extreme form of monotheism that denied the divinity of the Son and the Holy Spirit. Worldwide accepted the deity of Christ, but in ways that made it unclear whether we should be considered binitarian (one God, as Father and Son) or ditheistic (two Gods). Many of Herbert Armstrong's explanations sounded more like the latter. When the Gospel of John quotes Jesus saying, "I and my father are one" (John 10:30), for instance, Armstrong took this to mean a unity of purpose or moral agreement with the Father.

By the time I arrived at Ambassador, Armstrong's usual way of explaining the teaching was that God was a family. This intersected with the teaching that salvation consisted of rebirth at the resurrection into that divine family. At present, the God family contained two persons.

Here Armstrong made an error common among believers of understanding the word "person" in the way we commonly use it today, to designate an autonomous individual, rather than how it was used when the classic credos were formulated, when it was borrowed from the theater, where it meant "mask" or a role played when wearing a mask. Of course, this mistake was easy to make since the gospels present Jesus as a "person" in the modern sense of the term, a human individual.

Within a year of resuming my studies, I began to wonder

161

about this. It became clear that the Bible offers no systematic analysis of the relation of the Father and Jesus Christ. Instead, it recounts experiences. Most dramatic among them was Paul's on the road to Damascus, and the appearance of the resurrected Christ to Thomas, one of the Twelve, resulting in the latter's exclamation, "My Lord and my God!" (John 20:28), which reads like the climax of the entire Gospel of John. The belief that Jesus of Nazareth was the divine son wasn't the result of reasoning. I realized that theology is simply the record of the struggle to find an adequate formulation of what experience had already shown.

Now Worldwide's adoption of the Trinity intensified my focus. In the run-up to the fourth European conference, held in Megève, near Mont Blanc in France, in 1994, I immersed myself in the mind- and butt-numbing task of watching a set of fourteen videotapes we'd been sent featuring lectures by Dr. K. J. Stavrinides. Stavrinides had taught in Bricket Wood when Edel attended there, then joined the faculty in Pasadena after Bricket Wood closed. He had once tried to explain to Herbert Armstrong why his understanding of the verb *gennao* was defective (it hadn't gone well). Now it fell to him to explain Worldwide's revised understanding of the nature of God. We were instructed to watch these lectures in preparation for the conference and submit our questions in advance. I dutifully did this, in a closely reasoned, step-by-step fashion, which I prefaced by saying that my questions were likely not the same as many other Worldwide ministers and that I would appreciate a personal meeting with Stavrinides to discuss them.

The conference took place a couple of weeks after my talk with Greg Albrecht. I decided to take my Greek New Testament and use that, rather than an English translation, to read any scripture passages referenced. I was soon glad about the decision, but I might have been the only one in the room who was.

One of the first sessions was handled by Randal Dick. His topic was the commission to the church. Our understanding had been that we were called to deliver a message to all the world as a warning. He began by asking us to turn to the end of the Gospel of Matthew, which we had often quoted ("go ye therefore into all the world") to justify our approach. Next, he asked us which we thought was the most important of the four elements of the commission mentioned there. I turned to Matthew 28, and a quick scan was enough to see that verses 19–20 described the commission with four verbs, but only one was conjugated. The others were participial and thus were dependent on the conjugated verb in some way. My hand shot up, and I gave my answer. I sensed a variety of reactions in the room. Many of my colleagues looked at me as if they had no idea what I was talking about. Randy, meanwhile, seemed deflated. He was expecting a long round of tapping in the dark with some saying "go to all the world," others saying "baptize," before he revealed the correct answer: the command to make disciples. But I also noticed the reaction of Stavrinides, who seemed startled that a Worldwide minister would use that line of argumentation to make the point.

When it was time for his own presentation, it soon became apparent that my fears about my submission had been well-founded. He had not read mine or any others as they were sent in. They had gone to a secretary who'd been instructed to excerpt the questions and group them by topic. That may have made sense for most of the submissions since most of the "questions" argued on the basis of our earlier interpretations of relevant Bible passages. Soon he read out one of my questions, torn out of the context it was written in, and dismissed it. I objected and engaged in discussion. I did this once or twice more. I later learned that Carn Catherwood, sitting on the other side of the room, one or two rows in back of me, was fidgeting. He had kept the French ministry from rebelling by reframing what Stavrinides had written in English so that, in French, the ministers were hardly aware that anything had changed. Now they were aghast to find what the changes meant.

Before the conference, Joe had rejected my wish for a one-on-one meeting. Now, during a break in the tumultuous session, he came to me and said that maybe it would be better if I spoke to Stavrinides privately. Edel wanted to go with me, and when Vic Kubik's wife Bev heard about it, she tagged along.

The conversation was exhilarating for both Stavrinides and me. I felt that those who only sat in his lectures missed the best of him as a teacher. In a manner that reminded me of Socrates in Plato's *Dialogues*, he questioned and probed, and nothing delighted him more than a well-founded challenge, such as once when I called him out for shifting the terms under discussion.

In my own grappling with the issues in the run-up to the conference, I had learned that there are scholars who shared many of our traditional arguments against the trinity teaching as commonly understood. I saw how the orthodox position had been hammered out in a centuries-long process and that its classic formulation owed as much to the concepts of Greek philosophy of the time ("substance," for instance) as it did to the Biblical teaching. I also learned that the twentieth century had seen a revival of trinitarian thought partly because of the arguments leveled against the classic formulations. It dismayed me to see Worldwide capitulate (in my eyes) to a traditional form of the teaching. Many of our arguments against that teaching had been around at least as long as the Reformation. Many of those who rejected the Trinity did so because of reservations about the divinity of Christ; they were unitarians. I saw no reason why Worldwide could not refine its teaching about Christ, retain its reservations about the Holy Spirit, and become firmly binitarian, ridding itself of indefensible teachings that had often made it ditheistic instead. When I talked to Joe again after I met with Stavrinides, I summed up my beef: We didn't have to go down this road. But if we did choose to go down it, we needed to do a much better job of it.

Going toe-to-toe with Stavrinides in this way confirmed to me that I had been right to embark on my studies. Furthermore, it equipped me with the tools to soundly evaluate the revision process in Worldwide's teachings. This would help me personally; I continued to hope that it would be valuable to Worldwide, as well.

Soon after the conference, Vic, in his role as assistant director of Church Administration, brought up the question of a transfer back to the States. When Larry had first raised the issue of moving to Switzerland, I told him that I would be there until he sent me somewhere else. Larry, of course, was somewhere else by now.

Now it had been seven years, and Vic said that if I wanted to move back, I could have my pick of two congregations, both known to me, and places I would have enjoyed living. In addition, both were located close to top-notch theological schools where I could continue my degree program.

There were also personal reasons why it was appealing. Our older boy, Erik, had blossomed after his transfer to the American International School. He intended to study in the U.S. Plus, it would mean being closer to my parents (although a loss for Edel's parents, who had enjoyed seeing us often in these years).

Another factor: if we were to stay in Europe, where would we go when it was time to leave Switzerland? (It was rare for Worldwide to keep a pastor in an assignment much longer than seven years). There were only four pastorates in the German-speaking area, and from what I could see, I had the most appealing.

In the end, the deciding factor, however, was the unsettled state of Worldwide. The change of teaching on the nature of God, coming on the heels of many other doctrinal readjustments, had unsettled many. And I couldn't shake the feeling that more changes were coming. So, I told Vic that I had a better chance of guiding a congregation that knew me through whatever might come than a congregation where I was relatively less-known.

No sooner was that issue settled than Paul Kieffer, back in Germany as John Karlson's successor as regional director, contacted me about moves he was contemplating. He wanted to send one of the other pastors to work with me as an associate in the summer of 1995. Paul felt that the man was harsh and control-oriented but could be retrained. The hope was that, after working with me for a while, he could take over my pastorate, at which time, Paul speculated, he might want to send me to the north (this would have been nice for Edel's parents). He felt the current pastor in that area understood what was wanted in principle but often carried things out in a muddled way; therefore, a change would be good for the congregations.

None of this came about because of the events that hit Worldwide in the subsequent months. Ironically, the pastor whose approach Paul felt too control-oriented was the one who followed him when Worldwide split a year later, although they went separate ways when the group they joined split, in turn, three years after that.

The youngest of our three girls decided to marry and set the wedding for January 1995 in Pasadena. She asked me to perform it. It would be the second wedding I performed for the girls we'd welcomed to our family. The first had been nearly three years earlier, in the summer of 1992. I had sensed something was coming when, a year before that, Edel and I attended the sixth round of the refresher program. As we prepared to travel to Pasadena, Kathryn, our oldest girl, said she was glad we were making the trip, for there was someone she wanted us to meet.

Kathryn had recently returned from a year teaching in an AICF project in Thailand and met our plane. She introduced us to Tim. He had graduated from Ambassador a few years before and worked in Worldwide's data processing center. While a student, he had been on a project on the Thai-Laotian border. He and Kathryn had met when she had been chosen for one of the Thailand projects and Tim had oriented the group she would be a part of.

On the way from the airport to the campus, we passed Dodger Stadium. I mentioned that the Mets were in town and wondered if we could still get tickets. Tim looked into it, and the four of us went that evening. Tim and I hit it right off, analyzing the on-field strategy. I hadn't known it, but Kathryn had told Tim that if I didn't approve of him, she wouldn't marry him. I don't know how serious she was in that. As she watched the two of us, by about the third inning, she knew I would have no objection. The following summer, after Kathryn's graduation, our family flew to Pasadena and I performed their wedding.

Now I would do a second, again performing double duty, as both officiating minister and as father of the bride. Unfortunately, as joyous as that occasion was, it was a week of gloomy, wet weather that mirrored church developments. Two weeks earlier, Joe Tkach, Sr., had given a sermon in Big Sandy in which he unsettled many by saying that observing Sabbath and dietary restrictions didn't determine salvation.

During my short stay in Pasadena, I had met with both architects of the changed understanding, such as my classmate Mike Feazell, as well as staunch opponents. I'd already arranged an appointment before arriving with Greg Albrecht to discuss an article on Albert Schweitzer I'd proposed for the *Plain Truth*. The regional directors were in Pasadena at the time for meetings, so, I interacted with some of them. Vic Kubik asked me to dine in his home, just a couple of doors down from where I was staying in the row of townhouses at 360 Grove. Vic informed me that, in addition to the Swensons (Guy was Vic's assistant, and his wife Jennifer had been one of Edel's good friends in Bricket Wood), the Hoehs would be there. Herman Hoeh seemed startled when he walked in and saw me, but Victor quickly reassured him; "don't worry," he said, "he's one of us." The conversation was incendiary. Hoeh had been one of the few to see an advance copy of Tkach senior's letter for the next *Pastor General's Report*. As the evening drew to a close, Hoeh solicited our confidentiality and our prayers.

The next day, I visited two bookstores with John Kossey, who had graduated a year ahead of me and served as Ambassador College's librarian. Something he told me as we scanned the shelves at Archives bookshop gave me pause for thought. We had always been aware of the account of Paul preaching on Saturday evening before departing from Troas (Acts 20:6–12). It hadn't struck us as unusual; why wouldn't he talk into the early hours of the morning before his departure, given the likelihood he would never see them again. But perhaps there was another reason for the evening meeting, John suggested. Given the high proportion of slaves in the congregation, would they have been free to attend services on the Sabbath? Or even observe the Sabbath at all?

That had been on Friday afternoon. That evening, I was invited to the Schnee home. They had moved to Pasadena when Frank Schnee's declining health required him to step down as regional director for the German-speaking area. He let me read the new *Pastor General's Report*, with its not-too-intelligent opening, "now that we know we are a new covenant church." I had always thought we were, and asked in my mind, when did they find out?

I couldn't help commenting to Schnee that the devilish thing about the new teaching was, it was almost right. His answer: "I don't pretend to be able to set doctrine. I could prove Pentecost was on Monday; I could prove it was on Sunday." This gave me pause for thought: even to a minister with a high level of responsibility, the only option open, if one didn't want to be accused of claiming the prerogative to "set doctrine" was to simply parrot what leadership said, even if it meant "proving" from the Bible the opposite to what one had taught before. The freedom to study and draw one's own conclusions wasn't available to us.

The next day, at a Sabbath morning pancake brunch at Tim and Kathryn's, I sounded out how they felt about these developments. They tended to feel not much was changing and that it was a matter of giving the membership more individual responsibility. That sanguine assessment would be challenged when we went to services in the Auditorium that afternoon. In his sermon to the headquarters congregation,

Tkach made it clear he had no intention of backing away from what he'd said two weeks earlier in Big Sandy. Nor had I expected him to after reading his letter in the latest *Pastor General's Report* the evening before.

The impact of the sermon was dulled, though, by the delivery. Whenever Tkach departed from his prepared remarks, his tone and vocabulary shifted. Moreover, the illustrations he used in these extemporaneous remarks often reflected Worldwide's traditional teachings rather than the new understanding he was imparting. For instance, when Tkach referred to Mark 7 (the discussion of whether what one eats can defile), he read from the King James Version, which renders the last phrase of verse 19 as "purging all meats." In a brief comment, he remarked, as Worldwide traditionally did, "it goes through the digestive tract." Then he returned to his prepared typescript and added: "This is the most revolutionary statement in the New Testament. With one stroke he abrogated a practice for which Jews had died in the Maccabean epoch." That comment was apparently prepared with the New International Version in mind, which clarifies the obscure Greek according to the understanding of the translators: "(In saying this, Jesus declared all foods clean)."

Throughout, there was a striking contrast whenever he switched from speaking extemporaneously, when he taught just as we always had, to reading the manuscript in front of him, which he had difficulty reading. I couldn't shake the impression that he was reading a text prepared by others that he didn't fully understand.

Nor did another kind of off-the-cuff remark help. Every

once in a while, after detailing some (now-judged) errone-
ous earlier understanding, Tkach interrupted himself to ask,
"How stupid could we have been?" One semester of speech
training, supplemented by a bit of psychology, would warn
against insulting the intelligence of people you're trying to
win over, especially since the only mistake of many of the listeners had been to believe what they had been taught in sermons. Now they were being asked to believe something else.

During the sermon, I thought about similar speculations
I had made along these lines, especially the previous spring
when I was going through Galatians. But even though I had
wondered about many of these things and preached some
of them, I was upset about the overall message. How would
members react for whom this was all new?

The morrow brought a different kind of stress, Deborah's
wedding. I thought I was calm until I picked up my book and
started reading the ceremony to the bride and groom. I didn't
write the ceremony, it was the church's standard, but it was
as if Debbie and I were having one of our father-daughter
talks. And she looked thirteen again (shades of the film, *Father of the Bride*). I was hardly conscious of the others present.
We knelt for the prayer. After the "amen," we looked at each
other, and Debbie asked for my handkerchief. We waited on
our knees while she did what she had to do, then rose.

That night, I had dinner with Randy at Mijares, a Mexi-
can restaurant in Pasadena. We had a great talk, which he
opened with: "We must have a death wish, the way we've
presented this."

On Monday, I was on the go all day, meeting with as

many people as possible. One was Tom Lapacka, my prede-cessor in Switzerland. He now worked for David Hulme in handling Worldwide's public relations. Unlike David, Tom had accepted the new teaching. To him, it was all a matter of perspective. As he put it, if you're standing on Mount Sinai looking toward the New Testament, you won't get it. If your feet are on Mount Zion looking back, you will. But even he regretted that we cut loose from the last remnants of our old identity before being able to give members a clear picture of what makes us distinctive. In other words, why be a part of this church?

This was also a topic when I had lunch with Greg Al-brecht. We quickly got through our discussion of my pro-posed Schweitzer article (he made good suggestions, liked my outline overall), then he asked how the new stuff would play in Europe. For many, I answered, it would be the last straw. Those who disagreed would feel that the time had come to find a fellowship still holding to what we used to believe; those who agreed would wonder why they needed to drive two hundred kilometers to attend.

That evening, I had dinner with Wade and Kay. Wade, too, now worked in Pasadena, in the church's youth program. He was very outspoken in his estimation of why Mike and the others behind the changes were doing this and where it might still lead; he felt that they, having grown up in World-wide, had always smarted under its traditional teachings. As we left his office to go to dinner, we ran into Mike, Joe, and Greg by the elevator. It may have been the darkened building or even Mike's purple fedora, but I sensed an overwhelming feeling emanating from him, an aura that struck me as profound sadness, although it could have been something else. I didn't sense this from Joe or Greg.

The next day, Tuesday, I again packed in as much as I could before boarding my overnight flight back to Switzerland. Kathryn picked me up to go for bagels for breakfast. I'm glad we had time for just the two of us, and equally glad we didn't spend much of that time on developments in Worldwide. Meanwhile, it continued to rain heavily. Back on campus, I dried out a little, then went over to Grove Terrace, where the regional directors were meeting, to see Vic once more before leaving. When I returned to the apartment to finish packing, the roof was leaking in some places. Then I went to the Hall of Administration to see David Hulme. In his role as Worldwide's director of public relations, he had won many friends for the church by engaging in dialog about our acceptance of the Trinity. But the latest developments conflicted with his convictions. He still had a seat at the table when Worldwide's leadership discussed doctrine, but he felt that his input was discounted before he opened his mouth. We talked for an hour, and I shared many of his reservations. After lunch with friends, I returned to the apartment one last time and checked flood reports on television. I wondered whether God's promise to Noah never to again destroy the world in a flood was only an old covenant promise, too.

As the water rose, I decided it was worth praying about if I wanted to fly back. Kathryn called. She had taken off from work an hour early so we could leave for the airport. The next television flood report said the tunnel on Sepulveda near the airport was filled with water and closed. Just before Kathryn and Sarah arrived, though, it stopped raining. We set out through nearly empty streets on a beautiful night. The tunnel had drained, and we made it to the airport in record time, two hours before the flight. They hung around with me for a while, said goodbye, and then I was on my way back to Switzerland.

As I flew east during the long night, I turned the experiences of the past week over in my mind. In the coming months, I felt as if I had been at ground zero when the Enola Gay flew over. It wasn't only difficult for me, though, and I had some advantages. I had long felt the new covenant is about internalizing God's law, although I didn't see that as conflicting with Sabbath observance. I had a three-year head start looking at the issues and, more importantly, acquiring the tools to investigate for myself. Another was the geographical distance from my friends, many of whom coalesced in the breakaway group that soon formed.

When I returned to Switzerland, the first resignations from the congregation were waiting for me. One wrote to say he had heard about the changes, studied into them, decided Mr. Tkach was right, and therefore was returning to his local Lutheran congregation. He reasoned, as I expected, there was no need to travel more than an hour to hear the same message he could listen to locally. Another, however, one of the leading men in the congregation, had what he thought was the full story from friends in the States and made up his mind this was all wrong.

I strove to keep the congregation together. I reminded the members that we were admonished to "prove all things; hold fast that which is good" (1 Thess. 5:21). Church leadership had presented us with a significant challenge to our earlier beliefs, I conceded, and we should respectfully look into it and compare it with the Bible. I stressed that every voice was needed as we worked our way through it. In a sense, I was spitting into the wind. I understood. These were teachings we'd held deeply. We had become convinced of them as part of our preparation to be baptized. It was unreasonable to expect we should be able to change as quickly as flipping a light switch. The beliefs that were now derided as stupid were not our own invention but what we'd been taught by the leadership.

I stayed in close touch with Paul Kieffer in Bonn, and we seemed on the same wavelength. But that would change. One thing made sense within weeks: the issue of holy time. From the conversation Jesus had with the woman at the well, John 4, it was clear that his coming had meant that the old debate about holy space had been transcended, and I could see that the what was true of space could apply to time as well. This made no impression on Paul when I shared the thought with him.

The next book I had planned to go through in the Bible studies I held throughout the area was the Gospel of Mark. When I reached the account of the healing of a leper (Mark 1), I was struck by something I never noticed before. Jesus reached out and touched him (verse 40). In many other healing accounts, he merely speaks the word, and the person is healed. Jesus didn't need to touch to heal, so, why did he? Anyone who touched a leper, who was by definition unclean, became unclean as well. For the first time, I asked myself what the psychological effect was on a person shunned in this way (I was aware of the studies of newborns never touched). For whatever reason, Jesus ignored this prohibition. Perhaps the message was that he had something like a contagious ritual purity that was stronger than the contagious ritual impurity of the sufferer. At any rate, what did this touch mean for our assumption that the laws of ritual purity were still in force?

I shared this insight with Paul the next time we spoke, but he rejected it out of hand. From that moment, our respective paths were vectors that diverged. Thus, I began, a bit at a time, to see the reason for the changes.

As I continued the series, we soon came to Mark 7, which contains the controversy about eating with unwashed hands, the explanation of which I felt Tkach had mangled in his sermon in Pasadena. We had always preferred to read this incident in the Gospel of Matthew, which, to us, made it clear "what Jesus meant." But this time, I was reading it in the context of Mark, after previously noticing the touch of the leper. Taking this account on its own, it seemed plausible that for Mark, this incident led to a generalized teaching that nothing we take into our mouths (including pork) could render us unclean. He also adds the graphic detail that it passes through us anyway (if there is an impurity in what we eat, it simply might pass through more quickly and violently).

By this time, it was three-and-a-half years since I'd resumed my studies. I accepted the conclusion of the majority of New Testament scholars that the Gospel of Mark was circulated first and that Matthew and Luke intended their gospels as revisions of Mark's. I had also grown accustomed to reading each gospel on its own and being sensitive to the tendencies in each. Given the overall concern of Matthew for the continued validity of the Torah (see Matt. 5:17), it was clear to me what might have happened. Matthew saw the implication of what he found in Mark and edited the episode to clarify that the ramifications of the controversy were limited to the matter of eating with hands that hadn't been ritually purified.

Even for Mark, the significance of the incident didn't seem to be the overcoming of one of the identity markers that distinguished Jews and set them apart. Instead, the point for him (and this seems to survive in Matthew's version) was that the locus of uncleanness is moved from the stomach (direction: out to in) to the human heart (direction: in to out).

I had no yearning to resume eating pork or seafood (to this day, my stomach prefers to live old covenant), but Mark's Gospel, with its seeming indifference to ingesting unclean meats, was also in the Bible.

Some pastors held firmly to the old teachings. They found followings. Other pastors quickly switched over to the new teaching. They, too, had followings. Many of the early adopters of the changes did so not because of study but because of following the old model of church government: it must be right because Joe Tkach, as Herbert Armstrong's designated successor, said so. In a sense, both sides were act-ing per Worldwide's history and culture. One side held to the traditional teachings; the other side held to the traditional way doctrine was set.

Among those distressed was my pastoral neighbor to the west in Geneva, who telephoned to talk about the changes. He was particularly troubled that Worldwide no longer taught that the Sabbath was the sign of a true Christian. "What will we be persecuted for?" he asked. My reply was quick: "If it comes to that, I would hope it would be for the name of Christ."

I was uncomfortable with both approaches. I needed time. Nor did I expect any of the members who had proven the old teachings to have held them so lightly they could change their beliefs on command. What I wanted was a community of searchers ready to "prove all things." Herbert Armstrong's mantra, "don't believe me, believe your Bible," rang in my ears. In practice, we thought that this was operative in the days before baptism. Unlike Armstrong's own early practice, we only baptized candidates who had studied the church's teachings and agreed with them. In my case, the need to continue to reexamine came to the fore again in Armstrong's later years with his speculation about the time before the creation of Adam and Eve.

But overall, that was not the culture of Worldwide, or at least had not been after the earliest days of Ambassador College when Herbert Armstrong and the pioneer students fit around a table in the college library and studied together. Sadly, that practice soon gave way to one of doctrine being set from the top down.

My optimistic hope that the Swiss congregations could provide that kind of a community—a tolerant community that respected a diversity of honestly-held opinions as we searched the issues together—was naive.

My imperative at the time, though, was to do nothing that would divide the congregation. I felt I owed it to Jesus Christ to look at these things patiently.

Even while the evidence grew that there was something to the changes, I continued to struggle: I caught myself mourning for what had been. There was less security. And when we feel insecure, old problems reassert themselves. That meant we were challenged to identify the real source of our security.

In March 1995, 130 ministers resigned, saying they could not in conscience teach the new material. Joe Tkach, Jr., director of the ministry, contacted each and offered to talk. Thirty took him up on it, but it didn't change any minds.

In May, many of them, including Vic Kubik and half of the regional directors, gathered in Indianapolis and formed a new organization, United Church of God. David Hulme, who had kept himself aloof from discussions in the run-up to the conference but then decided at the last minute to attend, was elected president.

Vic would have loved to have Herman Hoeh's blessing on the endeavor, but when United formed, Hoeh's objection, which he confided to a friend of mine, was that the planning had been done in meetings while on Worldwide's payroll. He had a point. But based on the pre-United meeting I'd attended on church property and my interactions with the regional pastors in the week I was in Pasadena, I could also see where Vic was coming from. He and the others saw that the administration had introduced such radical and sudden changes that many brethren felt they were losing their church home. Many who criticize the way United was formed charge the leading motivation of these ministers was to preserve their salaries, but I feel that concern for the members was the more critical impulse. I had sympathy for what they wanted to do. Victor was correct in telling Hoeh of me, "he's one of us." I, too, saw the need to treat the members with more respect. Yet, I saw something they failed to: Many of our distinctive teachings were on a shaky foundation and needed to be reexamined.

There had been previous breakaways from Worldwide. Two ministers in Ohio had started a movement in the late Sixties based on the teaching that we had to use "sacred names" (i. e., Hebrew) to address deity. There had been the loosely associated splinters that Ken Westby and other regional directors had led when Herbert Armstrong stonewalled examination of questions that impacted peoples' lives, such as tithing, divorce, and the use of medical care. They also saw a double standard in Herbert Armstrong's refusal to deal with his son Garner Ted's behavior. When Armstrong finally did revise some of the contested teachings, as well as correct the day Pentecost was observed, Raymond Cole and other hardliners broke off.

The most serious split before 1995 had been when Herbert Armstrong severed contact with his son, and Ted Armstrong began his own church. Then, after Herbert Armstrong died and left Joe Tkach, Sr., as his successor, others broke off. I suspect that for at least some, in their own eyes, Armstrong should have chosen them instead.

But none of these had flourished, not even the one bearing the Armstrong name. United had a level of credibility that all previous split-offs, even one led by Rod Meredith, had lacked. It seemed to be serious about the need for more accountable leadership and more humane treatment of members while retaining the core of teachings that Worldwide was now changing.

Not all of those involved in the formation of United shared that aim, though. A friend sent me a tape of the first United service in Southern California. David Hulme gave the sermon. His brother-in-law, also a minister, led the songs. He began the service with a Dwight Armstrong setting of Psalm 119, "O How Love I Thy Law." The fervor with which he introduced it and urged the congregation to sing it with gusto made me wonder if it was the law he loved, or legalism. I was still struggling with the way the doctrinal changes had been introduced, but I instinctively knew that while Pasadena might not be right, this was certainly wrong.

When Worldwide compiled statistics later that year, the degree of the immediate hit became apparent. In 1991, 95,000 people had attended services in the U.S. It had slipped a bit in the next three years, but in 1995 dropped to 54,000. Statistics alone, of course, don't tell the whole story of broken relationships. Among my own friends in the ministry were two pairs of brothers, one of whom (in each case, the one I'd been closer to) went with United, while the other remained with Worldwide.

Paul Kieffer resigned when United formed. He had been a compassionate and effective pastor and a no-frills administrator as regional director; combined with his fidelity to Worldwide's traditional teachings, he was able to draw many members with him. Randy asked me to become regional pastor (pointedly not regional director). The work in the German-speaking areas would be run by a troika. I would be regional pastor, responsible for the local congregations and the ministry, Alois Mair, in the Bonn office, for finances, and my brother-in-law, Edel's brother Wolfgang, would edit the German editions of the publications. All three would report directly to John Halford, whose duties would expand from oversight of the British Isles to become European director.

I would be responsible for strategic planning and for the application of policies and teachings. It would be my responsibility to advise and encourage the other pastors and elders, not only through e-mail and telephone but also in church visits. I would typically arrange to visit a congregation from Friday to Sunday, conduct services, make myself available after services to the members, and spend ample time with each pastor. Unfortunately, one pastor consistently threw roadblocks in the way of every date for a visit I proposed. It was probably not coincidental that he was the least competent of our pastors; his indecisive nature had alienated most of the leadership in the congregations he served.

Yet, he was not the only one in over his head. I was perhaps a competent pastor but was now stretched in my new role, especially following Paul, who had been an excellent regional director in his short time on the job. In a phone conversation with Randy, I recalled the first time I went to a major league baseball game, twelve years old. It was Yankee Stadium, and while I saw many of the stars in action, Mickey Mantle was injured and didn't play. In his place, Hector Lopez. Lopez was a good ballplayer, but not Mickey Mantle. I told Randy I felt like Hector Lopez.

Since Alois and Wolfgang didn't report to me, there was no need to move to Bonn. Had I done so, a professor in Zurich would have ensured I could complete my degree at the university there. But I preferred to stay where I was. For Alois, and to a degree also Wolfgang, this was a change from the days when the regional director, Frank Schnee, then John Karlson, and most recently Paul Kieffer, was in the building and could be spoken with face-to-face.

I began working toward a system of non-salaried elders to support the four pastors on the payroll. My goal was to have one dependable elder for each of the twelve congregations. I thought I had identified the suitable candidates and set things in motion. Soon, however, one of the candidates—in fact, the choice I felt most certain of—decided to undergo gender reassignment. Worldwide was not ready to accept a transgender member, however, let alone an elder caring for a congregation. Another of my choices boomeranged in different way. An Ambassador graduate was living in the Darmstadt area; I felt confident he could adequately serve in the capacity of a local, non-salaried elder. Within two years, however, he had pushed me aside to become the new national leader. I underestimated how difficult it would be for the two managers in Bonn, especially Alois, to not have a shoulder to lean on; the elder in Darmstadt became that.

Amid this turmoil, it was time for me to take the first level of comprehensive exams, the propaedeutic, roughly equivalent to a bachelor's degree in the U.S. It consisted of two written four-hour exams, one in church history and the other in the science of religion, followed by a battery of twenty-minute oral exams in those two subjects and three others, philosophy, Old Testament and New. For the written exams, students were presented with three questions and had to write essays on two of them. In addition, one could name a specialty for the oral exam, although one was also tested on general knowledge.

To be admitted to the exams, one had to have certificates of the three classic languages and have completed proseminars, including term papers, in Old and New Testament, church history, and philosophy.

Ambassador had given me a good grounding in the Bible's contents, kept fresh by years as a pastor. With that head-start, I had been able to present myself for the propaedeutic exams based on part-time study in the same amount of time as others studying full-time. I also saved time by choosing American apocalyptic movements, concentrating on the Seventh-Day Adventists and Watchtower Society (Jehovah's Witnesses) in addition to Worldwide, as my specialty for the oral exam in the science of religion.

Most other students were members of the Reformed Church and considered candidates for its ministry; so, their exams were administered by the university on behalf of the church. There was no requirement to be Reformed to study theology there, though, since it was a public university. Non-Reformed students sat for an equivalent faculty exam, reputed to be a little tougher than the exam the university administered on behalf of the church.

I was the only such student taking the exam that semester, so, I was locked in a room by myself for each four-hour written exam, with a secretary letting me out after two hours for a break.

Each candidate had someone to accompany him to the oral exams, usually one of the faculty assistants. I was assigned Ralph Kunz, assistant in practical theology. He had spent a year in Pasadena at Fuller Seminary, and we hit it off immediately so that this was the beginning of a friendship.

Chapter Five

Midway through those exams, after the writtens but before the orals, Joe Tkach, Sr., died. His death came on September 23, 1995, nine months after he instituted changes in Worldwide's core teachings. I didn't learn about it until two days later, though, just before services on the Day of Trumpets, from a visiting American pastor. Tkach had been pastor general for nine years. In the last months of his life, his contribution had been severely reduced by his battle with cancer. He named as his successor his son, Joe Tkach, Jr., who had graduated with me from Ambassador.

The younger Joe brought a number of strengths and talents to the job—in many ways, he was more qualified than his father had been. But after all the years when Ted Armstrong had been heir apparent to Herbert Armstrong and the troubles that caused, some felt that naming one's own son to succeed was the wrong Worldwide tradition to perpetuate.

Many members continued to struggle with the loss of what had been a distinctive feature of Worldwide membership; being part of a small movement allowed us to feel that we were God's in-group. For some of us, the admission there were genuine Christians outside of Worldwide (even among non-Sabbatarians) was refreshing; it brought the experience we'd had in alignment with the church's understanding. My contact with teachers and students at the university had shown me that Christian conviction can be expressed in ways other than what we were used to in Worldwide. But for others, the feeling of no longer being exclusive made the sacrifices required to be part of such a high-demand group seem worthless.

Some of those who had the hardest time were the few members we had (there seemed to be at least one in each congregation) whose sense of spiritual worth depended on feeling superior even to the rest of Worldwide members. In some cases, this expressed itself in acts of service, which at least served a good purpose. But more often, it took the form of claiming superior insight into the teachings, often propounding esoteric beliefs on minor issues. Some of these now left Worldwide, but rather than leave it behind, communicated with members and former members to build up a following. As regional pastor, I was on their mailing list and wasted more time than I should have in responding to their letters and faxes, trying to maintain dialogue.

Four years previously, the Swiss congregations had held a summer family camp in Rabius in eastern Switzerland, near two of the tributaries that contribute to the headwaters of the Rhine. That time of white-water rafting, hiking, common campfire meals, evening sing-alongs, and relaxed conversation had an edifying effect on the congregation. Then to gather on the Sabbath in the middle of camp for an open-air service gave me a small, idyllic taste of what it might be like to pastor a small village congregation (I knew that beloved Swiss author Gotthelf would have helped me understand it wouldn't be just idyllic, but it was nice to dream).

Now, as the turbulent and divisive year 1995 drew to a close, many in the congregation felt a second camp would help restore cohesion among those who had remained with Worldwide. We planned to hold it the next summer in Jaun, situated on an Alpine pass in the Gruyere area of Fribourg in western Switzerland. Shortly before camp started, though, Tom Lapacka, my predecessor in Switzerland, arranged to attend and conduct leadership training sessions parallel to the planned outdoor activities. I had striven to restore the congregation after the turbulence of the previous year-and-a-half and felt like this was a slap in the face. In addition, to take thirty of the leading members of the congregation away from the rest of the group changed the nature of the camp. Nevertheless, I put on a brave front.

Tom had become Worldwide's chief of public affairs when David Hulme resigned and arranged to meet in Basel with the Seventh-Day Adventist press spokesmen for Germany and Switzerland; he asked me to join him, then drive him to Jaun. The Adventists issued a press release after our meeting that was picked up by at least two German-language Christian magazines, both of which reported the changes in Worldwide in a positive manner.

John Halford arrived just before the camp ended so that he could discuss the Swiss congregations with Tom and me. We agreed that the congregation's biggest challenge was my overwork. I had carried eight responsibilities for the past year. We concluded I could probably handle any three to four of them. The four we settled on were to pastor the Zurich congregation, oversee the other German-language congregations as regional pastor, write for our publications, and study. I would hand the Stuttgart and Basel pastorates to non-salaried elders and step down as coordinator of the Bonndorf feast. Worldwide's pastor in Scandinavia would take over as mentor of the fledgling congregation in Estonia.

A week later, John phoned to tell me that he and Tom had spoken again and concluded that even this mix of responsibilities was problematic. My academic program and my duties as regional pastor, for instance, were both demanding, but each needed a different mix of skills.

John outlined a plan that would both harness my strengths and invest in the long-term future of Worldwide. It would involve active pursuit of my master's degree while maintaining (or even increasing) the amount of writing. In addition, I would serve as a roving speaker in all twelve German-speaking congregations (and elsewhere in Europe as needed). Fairness, he felt, dictated that my salary should be adjusted downward for this mix of duties.

I agreed to consider it and look at ways to cut our living expenses or supplement my salary. The plan was attractive. The chance to bundle writing, speaking, and study seemed a natural combination and one that played to my strengths.

I agreed that the long-term needs of Worldwide would be served by having me complete a degree. This had been confirmed when, as part of my continued outreach on behalf of the church, I visited Heinz Rüegger, responsible for ecumenical contacts for the Federation of Swiss Protestant Churches in Bern. When representatives of various denominations sit at the same table, he told me, he noticed that those without an advanced degree weren't taken seriously by the others. It wasn't fair, he admitted, but it's the way it was.

But how to support my family? I didn't see how we could reduce our income. The most considerable expense was housing; John had been in our home, and knew we didn't live extravagantly.

As for other living expenses, we didn't have much room for maneuver in our budget. All four pastors had taken a pay cut that year in the form of forgoing half of the so-called "thirteenth month." On top of this, I had given myself an additional cut in take-home pay. Until then, I had been working under the same arrangement that Tom Lapacka had when he was here. To help with higher living costs in Switzerland, he had arranged with Frank Schnee for Worldwide to pay the employee part of mandated payroll deductions. This put him (and me as his successor) in a comparable situation with other Swiss workers in take-home pay, without raising his salary. But as of January 1, 1996, I had begun paying the employee part, which lowered my take-home pay.

Covering these two cuts had caused us to reduce our budget to the point where there was little left to slash. Added to that was the fact that I was only seventeen years from normal retirement age. We had very little in savings, with two children still to educate. We didn't own a home, and Worldwide had no pension plan in place, even though it had talked of one for several years.

Another way of covering the shortfall would be for Edel to go to work. She had done some work as a freelance translator a few years earlier, but that source had dried up. Since then, she had been looking for other work (we had hoped to cover the costs of Erik's schooling that way) but had accumulated a stack of polite refusals. It wasn't easy for a woman nearly fifty who hadn't worked outside of the home in twenty-two years to reenter the job market.

We'd placed our two boys in public school when we moved to Switzerland. That had worked well for both boys through primary school and into the first level of secondary school, after which, in Switzerland, compulsory school ends. Those who hope to study beyond that had to qualify to continue at a *Kantonschule*. The others enter an apprenticeship to learn a trade. It's a good system, but it doesn't work perfectly. When Erik took the standard exam in math, German, and French at the end of the compulsory schooling, he had a disappointing result in French, and this brought the average on all three exams a quarter point below what was needed to qualify to continue. Since he was gifted in math and science, we looked for a way to continue. To explore all options, we also visited the international school, which was Erik's preference. Mark, meanwhile, with his gift for languages, was able to make the transition to *Kantonschule* when his turn came two years later.

Given our situation, I didn't think it would be fair to my family to choose to accept reduced pay at that time. In my response, I proposed withdrawing from the university and concentrating on the local churches. Nor would I suggest any new articles until the churches stabilized.

My counterproposal was unrealistic. I was nearing the ten-year mark as pastor of these congregations. The longer a pastor is in an area, the less people tend to see the strengths and focus instead on the deficits. On top of that, the previous two years—with the radical changes in teachings and the severing of long-term friendships as congregants scattered in different directions—created a situation in which the idea that I could reestablish myself and serve these congregations (or what was left of them) effectively was illusory.

John urged me to continue my studies and, at a minimum, finish my licentiate (as the Swiss called a master's degree). To keep the momentum going toward that goal, I took a full course load, including two of the graduate seminars I would need, in homiletics and ethics. Altendorf had recommended that the faculty waive the homiletics seminar in light of nearly twenty years of preaching, but the professor for practical theology insisted that I take it. The seminar was valuable, so, I didn't mind; an added attraction was that it was taught by Ralph Kunz, who had accompanied me in my oral exams. The ethics seminar was taught by Hans Ruh, who had been one of the final two assistants of Karl Barth.

That fall, 1996, I served as feast coordinator in Bonndorf for the tenth and last time. After two years of major doctrinal change, Worldwide had now embarked on renewing its worship style. I was invited to attend a regional ministerial conference in Pennsylvania early in the year and had my first exposure to the mildly charismatic contemporary Christian music that the church was moving toward. In accordance with this renewal, we used a revised order of worship similar to that used in Pasadena and changed the format of the opening service to an evening of praise and music. We replaced some of the preaching services in the schedule with workshops and offered children's worship services on first and last days. All of these generated many favorable comments, especially the praise evening.

The United group booked their feast one town over from Bonndorf, in Schluchsee. One day some members came up to me, agitated, and asked if I knew what the teens were up to. I braced myself for the worst and asked what was going on. It turned out they had gotten together with their friends from United after services. I guess these people were a bit put off by my reply: "Well, good for them. If our generation can't manage to patch things up, maybe theirs can."

That feast also marked the first time I was sent to another feast site as a guest speaker, to Idre Fjäll, a resort in central Sweden. I took our oldest boy, Erik, with me. Mark, his brother, had decided not to take off from school to attend the feast that year; thus, Edel stayed at home with him. Erik and I flew to Stockholm, then took the train to the feast site.

When 1997 began a few months later, we still hadn't submitted a budget for the year. Since I was still regional pastor of the German-speaking area, I had to sign off on it after Alois Mair had prepared it so that we could submit it to John Halford. We had run a deficit in 1996 and struggled to find a way to present a balanced budget, but we were leery of cuts that would perpetuate the downward spiral. After looking for the umpteenth time at projected income and outgo, I noticed that the projected shortfall was equivalent to one pastor's salary and benefits. In 1997 we would pay a total of fifteen months' salary to two pastors we knew we would not employ in 1998; one would transfer to the U.S. in the summer, and the other would retire in the fall. So, I decided to lay myself off. If all went well, I reasoned, I could return to the payroll in 1998.

John accepted my proposal but asked me to wait until summer before stepping down. He must have had other financial resources, for he arranged for a replacement to start then. I didn't ask where he'd found money that I hadn't found; I'd made my decision and didn't turn back.

A few weeks later, during a weekend meeting for the Germany ministry in Worms, John floated the idea of moving to Bonn to become more involved in editorial matters. I agreed to think about it.

The next day, when I returned to the university, Fritz Stolz, professor of religious studies, spoke to me. He was fascinated by the flexibility of those afflicted by prediction addiction. Repeated disconfirmation of their expectations rarely dampened their fervor. Beyond that, he was also fascinated by the paradox that, while their beliefs were pre-Enlightenment, even Luddite, in that they often counted technological progress as one of the indications that the end of the world was nigh, they were often among the pioneers in using each new advance to propagate their message. He knew that Herbert Armstrong had been an example of this, as one of the first to use radio, and later television, in this way. Now he wanted to document how apocalyptic groups were harnessing the internet as the year 2000 approached.

Stolz envisioned a research project, for which he could budget a one-third assistant's position. He asked whether I'd be interested.

I suspected Hans Weder, professor for New Testament, had spoken to him about me. The theology faculty had sponsored a lecture series during the previous semester. At the time, there was concern that the imminent end of a millennium might lead to a new wave of end-time hysteria in the populace. Weder had delivered one of the lectures, and I had spoken to him afterward to offer to contribute in any way I could since I was well-acquainted with the apocalyptic mindset. In a way, it was a bookend to my approach to the Worldwide pastor in New Hampshire, more than twenty-five years earlier (recounted in *Fooled into Thinking*), which had led to spending half of each week performing visits with him in the months before entering Ambassador College.

Once again, as it had been when I left Washington at the end of 1975, I unexpectedly had a choice between options. As I considered the parallel offers, I was governed by the conviction that there was meaningful work for me somewhere. In addition, my mission in life continued to be involvement in the proclamation of the gospel.

Speaking for John's proposal of relocation to Bonn: it fit my mission in life. It would also be a way to continue to serve the faith community in which I'd been involved for thirty years. Even if this movement was in its death throes, I was willing to offer palliative care. An additional reason would have been the possible synergy of working closely with my brother-in-law, Wolfgang.

What spoke against it? It would interrupt Mark's schooling; he was now in *Kantonschule* and coming into his own, well-integrated in his class. Second, it would make it more difficult to finish my licentiate, which John and I agreed I should do. Third, there would be the loss of my residence permit in Switzerland, as well as a weakening of the network I'd built up. And the plan was based on a fifteen per cent drop in Worldwide's income. What if the revenue dropped thirty per cent instead? Would it not be better to be laid off from the church now in Switzerland than a year later in Germany? Above all, for the plan to work, it would require the members to catch the vision of what the magazine, and through it, the church, could still accomplish. In my contact with the members, however, it was clear that vision was lacking.

Words of a soliloquy we'd had to memorize in third-year German in high school often returned to my mind. In Schiller's *Don Carlos*, the Marquis of Posa hoped to exercise a liberalizing influence on the friend of his youth, Carlos, heir to the Spanish throne. In Act 4, however, he ruefully comes to the realization, *In diesem starren Boden blüht keine meiner Rosen mehr* ("In such cold soil no rose of mine could bloom," Boylan translation). That seemed to describe my situation in Worldwide. Still, I was reluctant to leave the church altogether, fearing it would sever friendships around the world built up over decades and making it harder for others who had remained through the upheavals of the past two years. And I feared my departure would be felt as a betrayal.

I decided to remain in Switzerland. When I communicated that to John, he nevertheless offered me a thirty per cent salary for a year as his consultant. Ironically, the arrangement he'd proposed the summer before was now coming to pass. He also arranged for me to purchase my fleet car, which by that time had been written off and had only a symbolic book value. Thus, together with the one-third salary working on Fritz Stolz's project, I could devote the rest of my time to prepare for the comprehensive exams in a year.

Meanwhile, Edel had been continuing to look for work. As a way of saying thank you for the scholarship that made it possible for Erik to attend the American International School, she had been volunteering in the school library. She enjoyed her work and decided to pursue that. She enrolled in a librarianship course at the *Zentralbibliothek* in Zurich and began applying to various schools. Unexpectedly, Edel was offered a forty per cent job for the coming year at the international school (the regular librarian was taking a sabbatical). This meant that at least for the coming year, our income would nearly equal what I'd been earning; thus, we were spared moving to a small apartment.

So as soon as I stepped down as Worldwide's pastor in German-speaking Switzerland, I began working on my research project. Fritz Stolz had a third desk and computer moved into an office shared by his two other assistants for me to use.

I learned much from Stolz. He had a dry wit, at times sardonic. He was a genius at languages. In addition to his proficiency in the ancient near eastern languages, he could read over a dozen modern languages. Whenever he had needed to learn another, he read murder mysteries in that language. He even wrote one, set in our seminar building.

Fritz was an early adaptor of computer technology. He taught himself programming to set up a database to keep track of literature long before programs such as EndNote came on the market. He gave me access to it on my work computer, and showed me how he recorded every article he read with a short summary: point-of-departure, the main points (usually three, rarely more than five), the conclusion, and his own take on it.

Looking back, when I relive the stress of the two years between the earthquake sermon in Pasadena and the decision to lay myself off, I realize that I might not have taken that step without the turmoil in Worldwide and my resultant feeling of helplessness.

A few months earlier, Larry and Judy Salyer had called unexpectedly and said they were between flights in Zurich and asked if we would like to get together. The last time I had seen them was in Pasadena after he had been edged out as director of the international work. At the time, he was hurt and looking for a way to continue to make a positive contribution. But after years in an increasingly dysfunctional upper administration, he wasn't interested in remaining at headquarters.

An open pastorate in St. Louis seemed to be the solution. But as the changes continued, he resigned. A small group of disaffected members in the area asked to meet with him. He agreed and was disfellowshipped from Worldwide (as he undoubtedly knew he would be). Rod Meredith had already started his breakaway church, Global Church of God, and courted Larry. The independent St. Louis group affiliated itself with Global. Soon after, Larry was back in administrative duties as Global's director of Church Administration.

It soon became apparent when we met them in the hotel coffee shop near the airport that it was not only out of friendship but in that new capacity that he wanted to see me. Not that the friendship had lessened. Judy pulled out a bag of Hershey Chips for Edel; she had remembered that Edel liked to use these for cookies and that they were hard to get in Europe. The talk soon turned to the state of Worldwide, and then Larry surprised me by saying Rod Meredith had authorized him to offer me the job of directing their efforts in the German-speaking area. In refusing, I explained that one thing that concerned me about Global was the number of sheriffs that had joined him. That was my term for those who emphasized maintaining law and order in their congregations over caring for the brethren, which, I felt, was what a pastor was primarily called to do. Larry responded by saying that many might call him a sheriff, but I demurred. I had worked closely enough with him in many situations to know that he was not; I named a couple of those I had in mind (one of whom soon chafed at Meredith's leadership and started his own church).

Larry persisted. When I said I was still committed to Worldwide, he said, "Henry, can't you see it's falling apart?" I replied, "If they need someone to turn out the lights after everyone's gone, I'm willing to do that, too."

On July 26, three weeks after I had left the full-time employ of Worldwide, and a little over two years after I became regional pastor, Joe Tkach, Jr., came to Germany. At a combined service in Würzburg he installed as new "national leader" one of the elders I'd identified to care for a local congregation. One of Herbert Armstrong's management principles was that if you would allow someone else to take away your job, then you weren't suited for it anyway. That may be so. But it was also true that it was a responsibility that didn't interest me at the time as much as my studies. The decision not to relocate to Bonn when I first became regional pastor was a factor that cost me the responsibility, but it had been the right decision to stay where I was.

It hurt, though, that in time-honored Worldwide style, Joe made the announcement as a big step forward and that we were returning to something we hadn't had since Paul, the last regional director, had resigned. Not a word was said about my two years of stewardship. In the aftermath, Randy said that they had hoped that I would take the ball and run with it and grow into the role of regional director. I felt that was disingenuous since, when he gave me the job, he had told me that was a route they didn't want to go. Randy is not only one of my best friends but also one of the most character-driven people I know, scrupulously honest. I was disappointed that he hadn't filled me in more on what Pasadena expected from me. Yet in retrospect, I'm fine with how things developed.

The summer of 1997 also included an emotion-wrenching two-week vacation in the U.S. Our older boy, Erik, entered Carnegie Mellon. I drove him to Pittsburgh, accompanied him through the orientation events for incoming international students and their parents, then continued to Columbus, Ohio, to visit the Karlsons. John had become pastor there when he left Germany.

On my way back to N.J., I stopped off in Pittsburgh to see how Erik was settling in. A mistake. We had already cut the cord. This revisit made the separation more painful for both of us. Tuning the radio dial as I drove away, I came across Dolly Parton. She sang it well: "If I should stay, I would only be in your way." The time in New Jersey was also emotional. My parents had put their house on the market and were preparing to move to a senior facility closer to the Jersey shore. This, then, would be my last stay with them in my home town.

For the feast in 1997, I was no longer the coordinator, and we decided to stay in our home and make day trips to Bonndorf. Our schedule that week reflected my new situation, split between the university and Worldwide. John Karlson visited as a guest speaker and spoke on the first day. Before services, I had gone to the offices of the *Südkurier*, the local newspaper, to be interviewed about the changes in

Worldwide. The next day, Friday, I gave the sermon. On Saturday, we attended services, then took the Karlsons to lunch.

We stayed home on Sunday, passing up the workshops scheduled that day. On Monday afternoon, Randal and Susie Dick flew in for the second half of the feast, accompanied by two of their children. I picked them up at the airport and took them to Bonndorf and had supper with them there, getting home very late. On Tuesday and Wednesday, I was at the university, and Edel had her librarianship class. On Thursday, we returned to Bonndorf for the Last Great Day. The Dicks followed us home in their rented van, and we had dinner at a nearby restaurant. Among other things, we had the chance to talk about what I was doing and what my prospects might be. After earning my master's, I planned to go back to full-time employment. If that were with Worldwide, then the only possibility would be to move back to the U.S. and take a pastorate. We agreed that would be a side move, away from what I'd been directed into with the studies. For better or for worse, it seems my usefulness would be in theology and writing. John Halford had spoken of giving me a half-salary starting the following April 1, but his ability to fit it into the budget was uncertain. Randy said not to take any offers before talking with him. The next day I took him to the airport for an early flight to Portugal, then went back to our home with his family for brunch before taking them to the airport to return to the States. When I gave Susie a good-bye hug, she said, "Don't let yourself be discouraged—you're doing a good thing."

The months following the feast were a time of stock-taking and wrestling with the idea of what to do with the rest of my life. I would not be returning to the payroll in the German-speaking area. The income had continued to decline, leaving only the new national leader and Alois on the payroll. All the congregations were being cared for by non-salaried elders.

With Randy's encouragement, I had taken a spiritual gifts inventory, even though I was skeptical about the concept. I wondered how one distinguishes between spiritual gifts and natural aptitudes. Or are all natural aptitudes God-given and therefore spiritual gifts? If that's the case, how do tests to reveal spiritual gifts differ from normal aptitude tests, of which I'd taken more than one?

Every book I found on the subject included the admission that there is no consensus on which gifts are listed in the Bible, what each designation means, whether all are present today, or whether additional gifts are not listed. Despite this uncertainty, these books nevertheless stressed the centrality of gifts for the life of the congregation.

The results of my test came back and showed very high scores in the gifts of teaching and creativity. I shared the results with Randy. He thought they were a fair assessment. So, would my contribution be as a teacher? If so, what? I was late coming to the academic world. Perhaps I should be a high school history teacher—my first choice back when I was in the eighth grade. The high creativity score was an indication that writing was a gift I should continue to cultivate.

Ambassador College finally achieved accreditation but closed soon after, in 1997, putting an end to one possibility of how I might contribute when I finished my studies. I'd continued to watch the back-and-forth drama; the campuses consolidated into one, but it moved back and forth between California and Texas. The size of the student body fluctuated. It sought accreditation, called it off, resumed it. Now that saga had ended.

In the year I spent working with John Halford as his consultant, from the summer of 1997 to the summer of 1998, I traveled a great deal. Sometimes on my own, as his representative, other times together with him. We both enjoyed traveling by rail and spent the time brainstorming ideas for our publications. He had convinced Worldwide leadership that the *Plain Truth* was becoming less appealing to a British audience and gained permission to create a separate magazine, yet still call it the *Plain Truth*. I had contributed an article to the first issue and most issues since. John was one of the most creative minds in Worldwide. He picked up insights everywhere he visited and from everyone he met. He had the irreverent humor of his London origins and an aversion to the executive lifestyle others in comparable jobs as his cultivated. Our work together was fruitful.

Our wide-ranging give and take included all areas of Worldwide's teachings, old and new. Once, I no longer recall where—we met up so many places, perhaps it was while we shared a pint at the *Eagle and Child*, one of the Oxford pubs frequented by J.R.R. Tolkien and C.S. Lewis—I shared some thoughts on the Trinity. Given my historical bent, which meant I hadn't had the foggiest idea of what calculus was until I read in a biography of Newton the kind of problem he was stumped by until he and Leibniz independently developed it, I had to think my way back to the problem faced by the early followers of Jesus. Good monotheists all, yet their experience of Jesus, both before and after the crucifixion, convinced them that it wasn't enough to think of him as a very good man and the latest of the prophets. Similarly, their experience of community and inner renewal could only be expressed as God (not merely a quality of God) in and among them. How all of this could be squared with the belief that when they said "God" they referred to something of which there could only be one, was left to future generations and councils, who did the best they could to understand it in terms of the philosophical categories of their day, but that might need to be reformulated as those changed.

John listened, then paid me one of the most welcome compliments of my life. He'd been in many of Worldwide's doctrinal discussions, both in the run-up to its change of teaching and since, but this was the first time anyone had been able to show him whether it mattered if one accepted the Trinity. He also saw the relevance for Worldwide's understanding of human destiny: that nothing less than God (not just his "power") is at work in us.

Meanwhile, in my project for Fritz Stolz, I immersed myself in the hall of mirrors that the various end-time proponents created. Radio and television had given an outsize influence to those who used them; they became much more influential than the tens of thousands of pastors who labored week by week in local congregations. Now the internet was reversing that trend and leveled the field. An individual with an internet connection had as much chance of winning a following as an established group or broadcast ministry. I was also exposed to the way these movements were impervious to disconfirmation. They were quick to come up with an explanation for why their imagined scenario hadn't come about, as well as new speculation about the way it would. Nor were they shy about inventing tales that were apparent confirmation (something I'd experienced while a correspondent in Brussels and *Moody Monthly* claimed the European Community had a beast computer).

While still a student in Boston, before becoming a member of Worldwide, I had read the classic study of how apocalyptic groups cope with disconfirmation, *When Prophecy Fails.* I had fleeting worries at the time that Worldwide might just be another such group but quickly shook them off. The difference between the group depicted in the book and Worldwide, I told myself, was that they were wrong and Worldwide was right.

But 1975, and its alternate scenario, 1982, receded into the past, and the millennium still hadn't begun. My work on this project, together with lectures and reading on the Old Testament prophets (and the book of Revelation), caused me to reconsider and see that it's not just the timelines and scenarios that had been wrong. Instead, any attempt to use Daniel, Revelation, and the Olivet prophecy of Matthew 24 to construct a roadmap to the immediate future was an abuse of these scriptures.

I hadn't been researching long before discovering that

Richard Landes, a professor at my alma mater, Boston University, had created a Center for Millennial Studies, which planned a conference in a year, December 1998. With Fritz's encouragement, I proposed a paper on the experience of Worldwide with disappointed expectations and, more recently, with its refusal to continue end-time speculation. My proposal was accepted, and I flew to Boston on a Friday in December 1998, twenty-eight years after my (canceled due to Kent State) graduation.

To save money, I'd requested to share a hotel room and was paired with a researcher based in Berlin, Johannes Heil. We had Saturday free, so I showed Johannes around the old city in the morning, then spent the afternoon revisiting the Mugar Library, where on long-past Saturdays I'd first sought to confirm or disprove Herman Hoeh's esoteric version of the history of the true church.

The conference opened Saturday night with a viewing of a film, *The Rapture*, followed by a discussion with Michael Tolkin, the director. We had conference sessions all day on Sunday, followed by a buffet that evening at Richard's home in Brookline.

My presentation, "Surviving the End of the End of the World," was on Monday. The task of preparing it had helped me get perspective on what had happened to the church. Worldwide, I said, was now a shadow of its former self. I asked how that happened after it had successfully coped with so many mistaken predictions in the past. But now it had stopped making predictions. Beyond that, it had abandoned two theological teachings, one concerning the nature and destiny of man, the other concerning the nature of God, that together had given Worldwide the conviction that it had a unique understanding of the divine plan of salvation. Finally, it had backed away from its legalism.

There had been various responses among church members, but for all of them, the changes in Worldwide introduced a need to confront and reconfigure one's own individual experience in the church.

For those attracted to end-time groups, I suggested that the group's outsider status is part of its appeal. Acceptance by the mainstream can be unwelcome. Secondly, wrong predictions do not destroy commitment, but the refusal to predict can. This does not, however, destroy the commitment of all. With time, the commitment to the strict form of Christianity that the group practices can come to outweigh date-setting. For these, a loosening of that discipline—even if it had been burdensome—can be threatening. But a certain number of those attracted to strict, end-time oriented groups can use their experience to develop the skills needed to cope with the complexities of modern life. They either leave the group and go on with their lives, or they welcome and support the attempts of the group to mature.

Late that afternoon, Rachel Kohn, a journalist for the Australian Broadcasting Corporation interviewed me for her program, *The Spirit of Things.* She opened by describing how I had been in the crowd in January 1972 when Herbert Armstrong, rather than lead Worldwide to a promised place of safety, broke ground for the centerpiece of the Ambassador campus, an auditorium. It's heady to be interviewed for radio, but I felt as if my IQ sank when she switched on the microphone.

On the final day of the conference, Tuesday, Landes announced plans for an *Encyclopedia of Millennialism and Millennial Movements* and invited us to participate. I was assigned the article on Worldwide, as well as two others.

The experience of attending the conference and interacting with other scholars on millennial movements brought a momentary swerve in my career path. Perhaps my future, after completing my master's, should include using my experience in Worldwide to academically study it and related movements. However, my roommate, Johannes, dissuaded me. "You've spent thirty years on this way of thinking," he said. "Do you want to devote the rest of your life to it?"

That gave me food for thought. I completed my encyclopedia articles and concentrated on finishing my project on the end of the world and the internet. When it was posted on the university's website, it was the most accessed page on the university's server for more than a year. A satisfying conclusion to my involvement with end-time thought.

I also continued taking the courses I would need to complete my degree. I concentrated on the required seminars, but also attended as many lectures as I could fit in. I heard nearly everything offered by Hans Weder in New Testament and Odil Hannes Steck in Old Testament. When Weder had a sabbatical, Ulrich Luz traveled once a week from Bern to lecture on Matthew. That gospel contained many of the words of Jesus that were crucial to Worldwide's understanding of the continued validity of the Torah; I counted myself fortunate to be able to explore Matthew's Gospel with such an eminent authority.

One degree requirement was a term paper in systematic theology. I attended a seminar jointly offered by the systematic and church history departments on the Lord's Supper conflict between Luther and Zwingli (subject of many a dinner table talk by my dad). For my term paper, I read several hundred pages, mainly in the writings of these two figures, but also secondary literature. This controversy had marred the only meeting of these two men in Marburg in 1529, one of the tragedies of the Reformation. Both were concerned to anchor the Lord's Supper firmly in the teaching of justification by faith.

After submitting the paper, I had a conference with Ingolf Dalferth, systematics professor. He began by saying he wasn't sure how he should evaluate the paper. If it were a study in the history of dogma, then he would judge it excellent. But I had taken the seminar to fulfill the requirement in systematics. Looked at it in that way, he missed a discussion of what my results might mean for current debates about the Lord's Supper.

Nevertheless, he let it stand as a fulfillment of the requirement. He was sympathetic to my overall aim, which was to complete the master's program while working, so he offered some tactical advice. There was a further degree requirement, called an *Akzessarbeit*. It could be in any subject area, perhaps I should ask Emidio Campi, the ebullient, cultivated Florentine Waldensian who had replaced Altendorf as professor for church history, if he would accept the topic as a dogma history paper.

This feedback that singled out the historical parts of my paper as the strongest was mirrored in my six-week paper in practical theology (a further degree requirement; it derived its name from the fact that one would agree with a professor of practical theology on a topic, then turn it in six weeks later). The path to getting this paper approved was not as straightforward as in the case of my systematics paper.

During my time in Zurich, the theological faculty was under pressure to cut expenses because of the small number of students (there were also questions about why Basel, Bern, and Zurich each needed a faculty of theology). Traditionally, each of the major areas of study had been represented by two chairs, which made for a rich learning experience. One proposal for reducing the costs was to reduce the number of full professorships from twelve to eleven. As a way of doing this, the proposal was to leave one vacancy whenever a professor retired or left for another post. This calculation was part of the reason why Altendorf was pressured to take early retirement. The faculty wanted to nab Emidio Campi before he accepted another professorship so that he would be in place to continue the center for Swiss Reformation studies when Alfred Schindler retired.

The area of practical theology also seemed set. Werner Kramer was approaching retirement, but the other chair belonged to Susanne Heine. In the year Kramer was scheduled to retire, however, she received a call to her dream job, in Vienna. Kramer agreed to teach for another two years so that the faculty could search for a replacement, and his assistant, my friend Ralph Kunz, stepped up his teaching load in the meantime. He had earned his doctorate by this time and had embarked on his habilitation (the second dissertation usually required to teach at university level in Europe). Among the rights extended to Ralph in this transition period was that of approving topics for six-week papers.

Since Worldwide was engaging the wider Christian world after decades of isolation, I chose to investigate an earlier example of such a process. The lectures I attended on the Reformation had shown me how much of Worldwide's teaching was the heritage of the so-called Radical Reformation, beginning with the followers of Zwingli who insisted on believer baptism. They were often referred to, both at the time and since, as Anabaptists, those who baptize again. There are two problems, though, with this term. First, in the eyes of those who hold this belief, infant baptism is not truly baptism; thus, they are not performing a second baptism. Secondly, the name reduces the movement to just one of its tenets. For them, as for Worldwide, baptism by immersion, following an experience of repentance, is simply the gateway to a life of committed discipleship and membership in a community of believers.

In addition to my article on Worldwide for the *Encyclopedia of Millennialism*, I had also contributed the entry on the Anabaptists (as well as one on the False Prophet), for which I'd read extensively. Now I proposed to investigate recent ecumenical talks between the Mennonites in Hamburg and the Evangelical Church.

Ralph liked my topic, even though it wasn't in one of the four classic areas of practical theology (homiletics, liturgy, catechetic, and psychology of religion); in his understanding, however, practical theology also included the study of cybernetics, that is, how churches are structured and led. Ecumenical talks are never solely about doctrine; they also touch on reconciling different ways of being church. And the completion of the process between these two churches had been celebrated, appropriately, by a liturgical act, a joint Lord's Supper.

So, I had my topic. In the meantime, the faculty had named Kramer's replacement. There had been pressure to appoint a woman since Heine's departure meant the remaining professors were all male. The choice fell on a woman from northern Germany. She was nearly my age but had only recently completed her habilitation in Hamburg. I took a seminar with her during her first semester; many of the other students didn't take to her, but I could relate to her north German ways, so we got along well.

Trouble came, though, when it was time for me to begin my six-week paper: She refused to accept my topic. I had cleared the next six weeks to investigate it and didn't want to start over. Nor was I ready to accept the fact that a topic that had been approved by a person who had been delegated to decide on these matters could be overturned. It seemed to me that her problem had as much to do with her perception of the gap between her popularity among the students and Ralph's as with the topic. He took the matter to the faculty, and it ruled that I could proceed with the topic and that, since he had assigned the topic, he would evaluate and grade it. When he did, in September 1997, he singled out the historical overview as the strongest part, as Dalferth had with my systematics paper. But in the process, I had unwittingly become the first "incident" in the short, turbulent tenure of the new professor in Zurich. It wouldn't be the last.

John Halford was happy with my regular contributions to the U.K. edition of the *Plain Truth* and looked ahead to the time after I finished my master's program. He proposed keeping me on the payroll and raising it to fifty per cent. In those years, I made several trips to England to attend editorial meetings.

One memorable trip to England wasn't John's doing, however. Emidio Campi arranged a study tour to visit sites associated with the English Reformation and invited me to participate. To earn my keep, I translated a sermon he would give and helped with interpreting throughout the trip.

Even though I had been to England many times, much of what we saw, such as St. Martin's in Bladon, where Winston Churchill is buried, and Bedford to visit Bunyan's meeting house and the prison where he wrote *A Pilgrim's Progress*, was new to me.

In Cambridge, we browsed in the Westminster College's collection of works on the history of dissent and Nonconformism—including a Huguenot collection—then shared lunch with students and teachers. At the University Library, we visited the collection of the British and Foreign Bible Society, viewed an exhibit of the *Genizah* manuscripts, and were shown Waldensian manuscripts from the fourteenth and fifteenth centuries. I was fascinated by the small books their itinerant ministers carried, containing scripture, sermon outlines, and remedies for physical ailments. Finally, in the chapel of Jesus College, a small group of us gathered around an old King James Bible on the lectern, opened to 1 Corinthians 13, and I read it aloud. The evening mood—blue light filtering in through the stained-glass window—created a Sabbath atmosphere.

The next day, Saturday, instead of touring Oxford and the Bodleian Library with the group, I went to Watford to deliver the sermon at Worldwide's service. Karl Moore, who had entered Ambassador during my last year there, was at the time a management professor at one of the Oxford colleges. He and his wife drove me. One of the students in our group, Ursina, got wind of my plan. She knew a bit about my exotic background and wanted to experience a Worldwide service, thus, she came along. Ursina and I then continued on to London, where she met her husband, Jonathan, and I had dinner with John Halford.

On Sunday, we worshiped at Wesley Memorial Church in Oxford, after which students of the John Wesley Society hosted us for lamb stew dinner in the church hall. The weather that afternoon was beautiful, but I hadn't yet been to Blackwell's, Oxford's main bookstore. Michael Baumann, Campi's graduate assistant, with whom I roomed on the trip, wanted to go as well. Thankfully, Ursina and Jonathan joined us, and then dragged me out of the store at four to go to an espresso bar with them. Otherwise the damage to my pocket would have been greater. I've learned to only enter bookstores under adult supervision.

That evening we went to chapel services at Westminster College, where Emidio Campi gave the sermon I had translated for him.

On Monday we went to London. First, we visited City Road Chapel, along with Wesley's house and burial grounds. Then we went to Westminster Central Hall, built by the Methodists in the heart of establishment London for the bicentenary of Wesley's birth. It was built to not look like a church, though. The main hall seats 2,300, and until the 1950s was full every Sunday. After decades of dwindling, membership has stabilized, and an average 250 people worshiped there each week. A few years earlier, faced with the need for extensive repairs, estimated at over eight million pounds, the congregation faced a dilemma. Should they sell or renovate (the money for that would have had to come from operational funds)? Neither option seemed desirable. So, they have kept the building alive by going into the convention business. Such a use had been forced on them just after the war. When the United Nations was founded in London, there was no other suitable building left standing. The pastor didn't want to hold services elsewhere during the conference, but the government requisitioned the building. The pastor's refusal was ironic since the impulse to build in the center of Westminster came from the urge to demonstrate that "Methodism matters" in the nation's life and that it was not a fringe group. Now, they are quite proud that they hosted such a historic event (which Herbert Armstrong had attended as a press correspondent) and it didn't hurt their ability to attract congresses.

Most of us accepted an invitation to climb into the dome, though I and a few others regretted the decision along the way; I was unaware until partway across the catwalk suspended over the apse how far the onset of tinnitus had affected my balance. But the view, once we got out onto the parapet, made it all worth it. We had a spectacular view of Westminster Abbey in the afternoon sun, along with Big Ben, Parliament, St. James Park, and Buckingham Palace. Going down the narrow iron spiral staircase inside the dome induced a claustrophobia that made the descent as challenging as the ascent.

Campi offered to lead a tour of Westminster Abbey and then go on to St. Martin's of the Fields, but a few of us went off on our own. One of the students had heard of a good used book store, and I joined her in looking for it. She thought it was on a side street off of Charing Cross Road. When we got there and failed to find it, she checked her pocket agenda, where she had noted it: Scoob's, Sicilian Street, Holborn. By then, we couldn't reach it before closing and we only had time to browse for a few minutes in Foyle's before heading back to Westminster Abbey in time for Evensong, where we rejoined some of the other students. On our way out of the Abbey, with the mood of the service still resonating in us, we were greeted by a nearly full moon over the roof of the Abbey, then we passed Big Ben just as it struck 6 P.M.

The program for Tuesday, our last day, included Eton and Windsor Castle since they were both near Heathrow Airport.

In Eton, we could not tour any of the buildings, not even the chapel, since school was in session. In fact, the students had received report cards or something that day. There were hundreds of boys of all sizes and ages, all wearing identical black cutaways with white ties. We were allowed to walk through the playing fields of Eton, where Waterloo was won, as the old saying goes. Then we walked over to Windsor Castle, stopping for lunch in a pub on the way. Although the entrance price was exorbitant, most of us went on the tour. It had only been reopened in November, five years to the day after a devastating fire on the queen's golden wedding anniversary. For some reason, I still had clear memories of my first visit there thirty-four years earlier, consequently, I was interested to see the changes. I thought George's Hall was significantly improved, although the guard there told me nothing had been changed. A guide in St. George's Chapel, though, later confirmed my memories.

We packed a great deal into our long weekend. The personal takeaway for me was that it helped me situate the Worldwide Church of God in the broader context of Nonconformism in the British Isles.

Still mindful that my time at the university would soon end, I continued to explore all possibilities as to what I should do next, including a return to pastoral ministry. If it were to be in the context of Worldwide, that would mean returning to the States. There was no need for me in Europe. I contacted Church Administration in February 1998, where the reaction was much different from three years earlier when I had my choice of two congregations that appealed to me greatly. The person who dealt with me now was someone I didn't know, and he informed me I would be treated as a new hire, which meant filling out a new ministerial employment questionnaire. That was a bit off-putting after so many years of service.

Nevertheless, I felt I should explore the option. I submitted the paperwork and he quickly got back to me. They had an immediate need for someone in Toledo, Ohio. The only plus I could see was that my neighbors east and west would be former colleagues from the German work, John Karlson in Columbus and Willi Mandel in Akron.

I explained I was to take comprehensives for my master's in the fall. I was told they'd let me fly back to take them. That wasn't a solution: I needed the remaining months to concentrate on preparation; I said I could come after the exams. That was something the person I was dealing with wasn't willing to countenance. I'm grateful for that. It made it easier for me to say "no thank you" in good conscience.

While wrestling with the decision, I once again was presented with an unexpected choice.

The idea of writing a dissertation had been on my mind since Hans-Dietrich Altendorf had suggested it. In the meantime, he had retired and I had less contact with him. Attending conferences Emidio Campi had organized to commemorate Bullinger and Peter Martyr Vermigli, had made me aware of the steep climb I'd have to get my doctorate in church history or history of doctrines, despite the positive feedback I'd received on the historical aspects of my papers.

And I'd dropped the idea of working on apocalyptic movements as well.

I was also aware that writing a dissertation didn't answer the question of what I would do long-term; it simply postponed answering the question.

The thesis known as the *Akzessarbeit* was the main degree requirement. Many students chose their topic strategically: A candidate didn't have to sit for a written exam in the area of one's thesis. For example, if one's thesis topic were systematic theology (a popular choice), that meant not having to worry about the broad range of possible topics from which the set questions in the exam might be drawn.

Since I was older, my primary motivation was to look into things I wanted to understand better. Many of the questions that occupied my mind were provoked by the challenges that Worldwide's changes had made to the earlier claims that had convinced me that it was, despite all its flaws, the one true church.

One of my problems with Worldwide's recent changes was that the whole issue was framed in terms of covenants, old versus new. Yet I had never believed we were under the Old Covenant, established between God and Israel, mediated by Moses, at Mount Sinai. God had declared that covenant broken and announced (in the "Old" Testament) the New, one in which his law (Torah) would be written in the heart (Jer. 31:32). I believed we were in that time.

I was convinced that every one of the several hundred people I'd immersed had been baptized into the New Covenant through the forgiveness of sins. I knew that no one lived sinlessly after baptism, but the remedy was prayer of repentance, not animal sacrifice in a temple. Therefore, although I believed that everything in the Torah was written for our edification, I believed, as Herman Hoeh had once explained to me, that whatever required a priesthood and altar no longer needed to be practiced. The rest of the Torah should be, especially the Sabbath since this was one of the big ten.

I felt the issue was not covenants but whether one could follow Christ without converting to Judaism. Others who had been in Worldwide at the time of the changes, including some I'd baptized, went in the opposite direction and found a new home in congregations of Messianic Jews. I could understand this. It's an attractive way of life. There had been numerous proselytes in the first century (non-Jews who observed the tenets of Judaism). And I found meaning in keeping the Sabbath and the annual holy days. The question was: Is this what the writings collected in the New Testament called for?

The irony was that, as Worldwide was making its paradigm shift and accepting many of the views of mainstream theology (more accurately, the evangelical wing of it), I was discovering that the world of scholarship had been undergoing a shift in the opposite direction. The so-called Third Quest for the Historical Jesus included a renewed appreciation of his essential Jewishness. A strong impulse for this was the question of how theology had contributed to the Aryan mythology of the Nazis. The *Deutsche Christen* ("German Christians") had sought to portray a non-Jewish Jesus. This, in addition to a stress of the anti-Jewish polemic in portions of the New Testament (the Gospels of Matthew and John, remarks of Paul to the Thessalonians). Now scholars rejected the reflexive dismissal of earlier theologians who had characterized Second Temple Judaism as works righteousness. In some of its proponents' hands, Jesus was such a good Jew that it was hard to imagine why he was turned over to the Romans for crucifixion.

The first graduate-level seminar I'd taken had been on the Decalogue, taught by Thomas Krüger, a professor of Old Testament. Two colleagues and I presented a session on the Sabbath, with me covering the scriptures related to it in the New Testament. After that session, Peter Schwagmeier, who assisted in the seminar, came up to me and said, "Henry, you've found your topic." The longer I thought about it, the more I agreed and decided to write my thesis on that.

That would mean writing my *Akzessarbeit* in New Testament, so I considered which of the two professors to approach. I had attended many of Hans Weder's lectures. With his walrus mustache, he resembled Ford Madox Ford. Weder's dissertation on parables had led to a continuing concern with metaphor and language in general. One insight stayed with me. Working with one of Paul's discussions of law, Weder pointed out that the terms in each language, *Torah*, *nomos*, *Gesetz*, each had its own semantic fields, and that it was a mistake to assume that the terms were exact equivalents. One could not apply the entire meaning of a term in one language to the term in another. That much had already become clear to me since I'd resumed my studies. I had even come to see that applied when working with a term in one language: the "laws" of nature were not the same as political legislation, and both were different from what one meant by law in a religious context. But then he continued by asking whether there was nevertheless a common thought behind all the terms, and offered his own suggestion, *der Anspruch des Gegebenen,* "the claim of what is." On another occasion, the text under discussion treated the spirit. He asked how this was meant. The first to answer referred to the third person of the Trinity, but he asked what the term referred to in the Old Testament. A moment or two of uncomfortable silence before I raised my hand halfway and offered "the power of God"? I was always cautious about bringing anything I learned from Worldwide into a discussion. But this was the answer he'd hoped for, and asked us to keep that in mind whenever interpreting New Testament texts about the spirit and to see that one could go a long way with that meaning in mind. This made the passages where one couldn't all the more interesting.

For all my admiration of Hans Weder and all that I had learned from him, I had noticed that one topic that held little interest for him was the question of the Jewish matrix of the early Christian movement. Jean Zumstein, on the other hand, would be more open to the topic.

I had attended Zumstein's lectures on the theology of the New Testament. When he covered Matthew, I had a small epiphany that I shared with him during the half-time break that day. He was already somewhat familiar with my church background, and I said that it occurred to me that Worldwide's theology was the result of a particular reading strategy.

Classic Worldwide theology, I realized, was what happens when you read the Bible like any other book, starting at the beginning. One doesn't get very far before learning that God is very serious about the law. It's about three-quarters of the way through that Jesus makes his appearance. When you reach the New Testament, you don't start with Paul's letters—chronologically the earliest—but with the gospels. Even then, you don't start with what most scholars believe was the first, Mark, but with Matthew, with those statements about by no means thinking Jesus had come to do away with the law. So, you read all four gospels from that premise, keeping it in mind as you read all the controversies he had with the other religionists of his day.

Done with the gospels? Still can't get to Paul until you read Acts, which presents Paul as never departing from the traditions of the fathers. Thus, whatever he meant when he said he was a Jew to the Jews and a Gentile to the Gentiles, it couldn't possibly have meant what it seems to plainly state.

When you do read Paul, his genuine letters are supplemented by others written in his name after his death; many features of these seem to domesticate Paul so he can't be "misunderstood."

Zumstein agreed. He wondered why more Christians didn't come up with a similar reading.

I approached Zumstein sometime in the fall of 1997 to ask about writing my thesis under his guidance. He asked me to submit a proposal, which I did at the end of October. After reading it, he asked for a more detailed outline, with a bibliography, which I turned in mid-December. My next conference with him was in March 1998, at which he surprised me. First, he said the topic was too big for a master's thesis and more suitable for a dissertation. The next surprise: he said he would have an assistant's position available beginning the following fall semester. Coming as it did on the heels of my abortive approach to church administration in Pasadena about a possible return to the field ministry in the States, this seemed fitting. The moment Jean Zumstein made the offer, inner conviction assured me that this was the right next step, even if it wouldn't yet answer the question of what I would do with the rest of my life.

Since my life was approaching its half-century, I asked whether it made any sense to write a dissertation at my age. Zumstein answered that one could never tell in advance what it might lead to, but at the very least, I would have demonstrated my ability to work at the level that a doctorate required.

Then he got practical: To operate as efficiently as possible, I should write this as my thesis, but not take a degree for it. It would simply be the paper I needed to be admitted to the comprehensive exams, an *Akzessarbeit*. The faculty would balk at awarding both a licentiate (master's) and a doctorate on the same topic. A side benefit of Zumstein's suggestion was that an access thesis only needed to be half as long (eighty pages) as a licentiate thesis.

Then he got even more practical: To be eligible for the

comprehensives at the end of the summer semester, my paper had to be turned in on June 15, in three months. Other commitments, including officiating at Worldwide's observance of the Lord's Supper, meant that a few weeks passed before I could devote my attention to it. But then, for five weeks, from late April to early June, I rose at six each day and then worked until midnight, occasionally until one or two in the morning. I surprised myself by being able to sustain that pace; I certainly couldn't now. The result wasn't brilliant, but it was good enough to be accepted.

Going into my dissertation project, I still felt much as I did two years earlier, when I gave a presentation in Thomas Krüger's seminar, prepared just over a year after I'd been in Pasadena for Joseph Tkach's explosive sermon. I was convinced that the gospels presented material with which the early Christian movement could have developed a Christian theology of the Sabbath. Luke's Gospel initiates Jesus's public ministry with a synagogue sermon proclaiming freedom (Luke 4:18–19), reminiscent of the connection drawn in the Deuteronomy version of the Sabbath command to Israel's experience of slavery in Egypt (Deut. 5:15; the Exodus version, by contrast, ties its observance to God's rest at the close of creation, Exod. 20:11).

There are seven healing episodes reported in the gospels tied to the seventh-day. In no other healing account is any day of the week mentioned. A possible Christian accent in Sabbath observance could have been special concern for the infirm.

In Mark 2:27–28, we read that the Sabbath was made for

man, not the other way around, and that the son of man is lord of the Sabbath, this could have laid the groundwork to make the day a memorial of Christ's work of salvation.

In all of this, I was influenced by Samuele Bacchiocchi, an Italian Seventh-Day Adventist who had earned his doctorate at the Gregorian Pontifical University in Rome, the first non-Catholic to do so, and as far as I know, still the only.

Years earlier, when I was in Pasadena in hopes of finding work after I was let go in Canada, I had discovered his book, *From Sabbath to Sunday*, in the campus bookstore. It purported to be the English translation of his dissertation. It had footnotes and a bibliography: the trappings of scholarship.

Bacchiocchi contended that the church at Rome introduced Sunday worship as an anti-Semitic move. This broke with the usual Sabbatarian claim that Sunday worship was imposed by Constantine in the days of the Nicene council. I noticed he offered interpretations of two passages (Rev. 1:10; Col. 2:14–17) that differed from the official teaching of his church. I thought this a sign of intellectual integrity. While working on my end-time project, however, I came across an exchange in an online forum in which someone challenged him on this departure from Ellen G. White's interpretation. His answer astounded me: he believed the official SDA teaching, but wrote what he did in his dissertation because it's what his advisor wanted to hear.

I also discovered that, of the seven chapters of his original dissertation, only one was published to fulfil the publication requirement. Apparently, the faculty at the Gregorianum had reservations about the quality of the rest of the work. So, the book that I was working with was not what it claimed to be.

When I began work on my *Akzessarbeit*, I returned to Bacchiocchi's dissertation and I began to see its flaws. When he dealt with extra-canonical texts and those from the early church fathers, I discovered instances of late dating of some texts concerning first-day worship and idiosyncratic translation of others. He simply omitted one reference that would have called into question his implied conclusion that there was no first-day worship in the first century.

Beyond those details, I had come to feel more strongly than did Bacchiocchi that the fact that Sabbath observance didn't remain Christian practice was also significant. I continued to be struck by the rapid abandonment of the Sabbath within a century of the crucifixion. To the early Jesus movement, it was self-evident to continue to observe it. A century later, it was equally self-evident—at least for the majority of Christians—that one did not. This made it unique in the Christian reception of the Decalogue: it was the only one not literally observed.

Whereas Bacchiocchi attributed the change in practice to a single cause—anti-Semitism beginning in the second century—I could see additional reasons. For one, the surprising success of the mission to the nations brought with it the question of whether one needed to become Jewish in order to become Christian. In addition, there is the unanimous tradition that the first appearances of the risen Christ were on the first day of the week. Finally, there was growing distance between Christian believers and the synagogue in the wake of the disastrous uprisings in 66–70 and 132–135 C.E. Ultimately, I felt it was the very importance of the Sabbath within Judaism—its status not only as one of the ten commandments, but also as a sign, an identity marker—that meant that non-Jewish believers in effect had to emancipate themselves from it to establish their identity.

At the same time, it seemed to me that both the New Testament and the early church fathers left a record of ambivalence, most clearly expressed by Irenaeus, who wrote that the ten commandments retained ever-lasting validity, but that the Sabbath, like circumcision, only had symbolic meaning for Christians.

John Halford had asked me to present a topic at the second German-language ministerial conference in Worms in May 1998, two-thirds of the way through the weeks when I wrote my access paper. I was happy when he agreed that it would be good to present the state of my research into the question of the Sabbath. It helped me to summarize what I had come up with so far and put it in a presentable form. As I went through it step-by-step, John sat in the back row next to Randal Dick, who was attending from Pasadena. Randy wanted to use the time to catch up on his emails on his laptop. John noticed this and whispered to him: "I think that, if you pay attention, you may see a side of Henry you weren't aware of". That was kind of John to say. It was also an expression of his hope that a few of us would get accredited theology degrees to better equip the Worldwide ministry with the best of what we had previously taught and the insights that were new to Worldwide.

The session went well. However, while I upheld the case for a Christian Sabbath-keeping practice, my admission that other worship patterns were also valid was too much for one colleague. I could tell that with every step of my presentation, he became more agitated. It wasn't long before he resigned from his pastorate and joined United.

I was sorry he did. He was Austrian but had married an American woman who had been present as a little girl the day I had been baptized on her family farm, nearly thirty years earlier.

After turning in the thesis, I set my mind on the approaching written and oral comprehensives. I would take written exams in three areas, Old Testament, Systematics, and Ethics. The six-week paper had fulfilled that requirement in practical theology, although there would be an oral exam in that and in the other four subjects. I outlined a study plan, which called for reading in each of the five areas each day, and I did my best to stick to it, despite interruption, such as a one-week trip to the States in late July. Erik returned with us for a short vacation. The day after we landed, Edel and the boys took the train to Hamburg for a week's visit to her parents while I continued to prepare for the written exams, which were only a month away by that time.

Kathryn arrived the day after the last of my written exams. She had business in Europe but arranged to stop to see us for four days. The day she flew out for her first appointment, I also went to the airport to take another trip to England. John had invited Mike Feazell to a short ministerial conference. In line with his hope that I would be able to use my expertise to help Worldwide, he thought it would be good if Mike and I could spend time getting reacquainted twenty-five years after we graduated together from Pasadena. John, knowing both of us as well as he did, sensed that we were closer in our views than either of us might have thought. If there were a future use for me in Worldwide, it would be helpful if Mike and I were comfortable with each other. As if to test John's assumption, I expressed to Mike my concern that Worldwide leadership was encouraging its local congregations to move their worship services from Saturday to Sunday. I accepted this wasn't wrong but my concern was for members who were open to the changes Worldwide was making yet were reluctant to make the switch. Mike countered that, while it was not wrong for Christians to worship on the Sabbath, in his experience it was rare for one who did so to not feel superior to other Christians because of doing so. I could see his point.

One more interruption to my preparation for the orals was the sermon I was invited to give at the Feast of Tabernacles in Bonndorf on Saturday, October 10.

The orals took place two weeks later, five exams spread over three days. The practical theology exam became an incident. I had named three books for my area of concentration. The night before the exam, the professor sent her assistant to my home to get one of them (I had the library copy). In the end, I wasn't asked about that book, which didn't surprise me, I knew she hadn't read it. The professor wasn't pleased with my exam and threatened to fail me, which would have ended my prospect of writing a dissertation. Once again, my accompaniment was Ralph, her bête noir. As he recounted the grading discussion to me later, he had told her that if she failed me, there would be an appeal to the faculty and that he would speak in my favor. She relented, but gave me a grade that pulled my overall average down, although not far enough to raise a question about my suitability to be a doctoral candidate.

Also memorable, the ethics exam. It was my last exam on Friday afternoon and Hans Ruh's final exam before retirement. My area of concentration was Reinhold Niebuhr. We had a relaxed conversation. I had not gotten around to one of the essays on my reading list. Toward the end of the twenty minutes, he asked about that essay. Thirty years earlier, I would have tried to bluff my way through, but I was slowly maturing, and I admitted I hadn't read it. I asked if we could discuss another essay on my list instead that we hadn't touched on yet, a feminist critique of Niebuhr. He agreed and gave me the best of my five oral exam grades.

Now I could begin my doctoral program.

Chapter Six

The precocious little boy had been the hope repository of his father, whose own plans to study had been thwarted. But the boy fled from the nickname pinned on him in the schoolyard, "professor." That little boy still lived inside me, and I found healing from a midlife crisis by finally embracing that repressed self.

For three years, I lived the life of a scholar, part of a community of scholars. I knew it was no more than an interlude. I came to it too late for an academic career, but that was fine. I could see that those I was rubbing shoulders with were brilliant and that I had to struggle to keep up. A new experience.

Words came easily to me from earliest childhood. Whether as journalist or as pastor, I was in the habit of creating texts. But now I embarked on a project unlike anything I'd ever done before. For most of the next three years, and then part of the three years after that until the final product was published as a book, I worked on a dissertation. Everything I'd done until then—the articles, the weekly sermons—was like running sprints or quarter-miles. Now I ran a marathon.

In a way, that marathon had begun long before, when as a high school student I first learned from Worldwide that the Sabbath mentioned in the Ten Commandments was not Sunday, but ran from Friday evening to Saturday evening. When I left home to attend university, I ruled out one to which I was accepted because of a Saturday morning class required of all freshmen. When I began a serious relationship, our religious differences had centered on this question. In fairness to her, I agreed to meet the campus Catholic chaplain to debate the question with him. Unlike Protestants with whom I'd argued, he didn't base his case on the scripture. Instead, he freely admitted that the Bible can't be used to determine the question. The church of Rome transferred the Sabbath to Sunday, and it had the right to. I had decided it didn't. Now, more than thirty years later, the Sabbath was the last to remain of the three doctrinal pillars that had sustained my fealty to Worldwide despite the church's chronic turmoil and the ups and downs of my own career in it. Hans Weder cautioned me that it's generally not a good idea to write a dissertation on a topic that has personal meaning; it might cloud objectivity.

I saw the wisdom of his words. But I had just turned fifty; that made me aware that this might be my only chance to work on a project of this scope, so I wasn't deterred. Still, I took his words to heart and resolved to follow the evidence where it led, which resulted in changing my mind on an issue that was important to me.

I commenced work on my dissertation, plagued by

doubts about whether I was up to it. Jean Zumstein wanted to see a sample chapter and gave me an incisive critique after reading it, offering me helpful advice on what I needed to pay more attention to. He asked for a second chapter, and said after reading it that it was better, and that if I continued to work at this level, there would be no difficulty getting the finished dissertation approved by the faculty.

Jean Zumstein emphasized the necessity of employing sound method. This meant primarily employing the array of tools known collectively as the historical-critical method: textual criticism, source criticism, form criticism, and redaction criticism.

This was welcome. This historical-critical method had been impugned at Ambassador, but in the course of my work in Zurich, beginning with my recognition of the validity of textual criticism (so-called lower criticism), I had repeatedly seen how application of the principles had supplied what I'd lacked since first laboring to produce weekly sermons: a way of understanding the divergence of explanation in commentaries and other secondary sources and offering a basis for evaluating them and arriving at my own conclusions.

My years in Worldwide had shown me the limits of flawed, dogmatically-driven interpretation. Yet its recent changes seemed to me to substitute one set of teachings with another, one held by the American evangelical mainstream, based on the same way of reading scripture.

Zumstein's own work, which focused on the Gospel of John, supplemented the traditional methods of historical-criticism with narratology, especially based on the French hermeneutic tradition of Paul Ricoeur. For my project, I largely left out narratological considerations. Looking back, I can see how this would have enriched my work. Sabbath and first day of the week are time markers, and as such, important elements of plot.

The years of representing a controversialist opinion had made me familiar with the arguments on both sides of the question. So, I began by outlining some points, beginning with the thesis that the Jerusalem congregation (known in scholarship by the German term, *die Urgemeinde*) continued to observe the Torah. It had long been clear to me that Paul, the apostle of the nations, resisted efforts to impose aspects of Torah observance on non-Jews who became followers of Christ. Worldwide insisted that this opposition was limited to circumcision. If so, this would simply affect the question of access to the Jewish ritual cult. Even in the synagogues of that day, a God-fearing non-Jew could observe the Sabbath without becoming circumcised.

While few non-Worldwide scholars accepted this reading, many did hold a variant of it by proposing that one should distinguish between moral and ritual law. But on what understanding of the Torah did Paul decide what Gentiles had to observe and what not? It was, after all, a passage at the heart of the so-called cultic teachings, Leviticus 19, that provided Jesus with the second of the two great commandments, "thou shalt love thy neighbor as thyself," that he had singled out as the foundation of the law and the prophets (Matt. 22:39–40). The supposition that the Sabbath command was merely a ritual issue seemed also contradicted by its position in the middle of the Ten Commandments, commonly exempt from whatever the coming of Christ had done to the Mosaic law. The exception made for the Ten Commandments was driven home graphically when I visited the church in northern Germany in which my father's family had worshiped from the time it had been built eight centuries earlier. When the Reformation came, the image behind the altar had been replaced with a diptych emblazoned with the words of the Decalogue (in *Plattdeutsch*), still on display.

I simply couldn't find any passage in the New Testament where a supposed distinction between moral and ritual law was discussed. Yet if that had been the basis for "doing away" with the Sabbath, I would have expected it.

A question I hadn't considered before, though, was the behavior of Peter in Antioch, as described by Paul in chapter two of Galatians. Peter is said to have lived as a Gentile. This couldn't have been a matter of circumcision, since Peter would have been circumcised as an eight-day old baby. From the context, it must have involved issues of ritual purity and table fellowship.

In chapter four of the same letter, Paul speaks of time markers, including days, although he uses general terms for them. Worldwide's argument was that Paul did not specifically mention the Sabbath or the holy days. This was a minority viewpoint, but the argument on the other side boiled down to claiming Paul "obviously" meant the Sabbath. This didn't satisfy me. One of the strengths of the Zurich faculty was its grounding in hermeneutics: the reflection on how to understand a text, especially a text far removed from our world through being written at another time, in another language, with another cultural framework. I read and reread the text in Greek, asking myself, if Paul meant Sabbath, why didn't he say it? Then it struck me: He used the general terms on purpose in order to show his readers the common phenomenon behind their new enthusiasm for the Jewish calendar and their old allegiance to pagan cult. This also answered Worldwide's second objection to the common reading of Galatians 4, namely, the question of when these Galatians, addressed by Paul as if they had not known God before their conversion, had become so familiar with the Sabbath that they could be said to fall back.

I was excited. I had not read every commentary on Galatians, but many, and I couldn't recall reading this explanation. I was still fresh with excitement when, a few days later, the newest volume of the Anchor Bible arrived, Lou Martyn's commentary on Galatians. It would be a few days before the book would be processed and shelved by the librarians, but one of them let me take a look at it in her office. When I turned to Martyn's treatment of the passage, my heart sank. Here was my new insight. I wouldn't have anything new to say in my dissertation after all.

After a couple of days' disappointment, I took heart. By simply reading the text carefully, I had come to a valid insight. The fact that I wasn't the first was not so important. It confirmed to me that I could work at that level, so I should keep working in the same way and trust my insights.

Another such turned up in working with the controversy surrounding a healing Jesus effected at the pool of Bethzatha near the Sheep Gate in Jerusalem (John 5:1–18). At the climax of the account, opponents—simply called "the Jews" by the narrator—charge him with doing something destructive to the Sabbath. The offense of Jesus is rendered as Sabbath-breaking in almost all translations, English and German, as well as the French Segonde. In Greek class, though, we had been taught to memorize the simple lexical meaning of all the words in the basic vocabulary and to picture first what the concrete meaning might look like before consulting a lexicon such as Bauer-Aland to see the range of translation possibilities. When I applied that method to this passage, I saw that the verb used here, *luō*, is a common word and that its most basic sense is to unbind or loosen. A concrete use would be to untie a sandal.

This electrified me. I noticed further the form of the verb, imperfect. Whatever Jesus had done to the Sabbath (in the eyes of his opponents), it was not a one-time violation, but something recurring or lasting. Jesus was accused of nothing less than unbinding the Sabbath. In the context of the Fourth Gospel as a whole, with its recurrent use of irony to underline the utter failure of what John calls "the world" to recognize or understand the one sent by the Father into it, one always has to reckon with the possibility that to the evangelist the charge contained an element of truth.

When I finished my chapter on the Sabbath in the Fourth Gospel, I asked Konrad Haldimann to critique it. He had taught the New Testament proseminar that trained me in the use of the historical-critical method and I knew the Gospel of John was one of his specialties. What I didn't know was that he was also a member of the commission charged with revising the *Zürcher Bibel*. He sent me a note to say that, after reading what I'd written, he had suggested changing that verb in the translation. However modest my academic contribution would remain, I had the satisfaction of knowing I had left a small legacy.

The tractate known as Hebrews (it's neither an epistle nor were its first addressees "Hebrews," but I won't go into that here) contains a verse that serves as one of the main proof texts for continued Sabbath observance: "So then there remains a Sabbath rest for the people of God" (Heb. 4:9, NRSV). As part of my background reading to prepare for treating this passage, I read much apocalyptic literature from the first century C.E. in Hebrew. I'm self-conscious of how rudimentary my grasp of that language is; thus, I doubted myself when I noticed that the texts often used temporal terms when they seemed to be describing the place to which the blessed were destined, and then spatial terms when speculating on when this might happen. This appeared so consistently, however, that I finally realized it wasn't my defective Hebrew, but a literary feature of these texts. Behind it, I sensed, lay an insight similar to that with which Dalferth had prefaced his lectures on eschatology: it deals with our hopes, not our certainties and for that reason is not something to be dogmatic about.

With this in mind, I understood why Hebrews repeatedly uses the verb "enter," a verb usually understood spatially, together with "Sabbath rest," usually a temporal term. I saw that Hebrews 4:9 doesn't enjoin Sabbath observance as a condition of future blessedness, but that "Sabbath rest" was shorthand for that blessed state in the future. A modification of the invitation to "enter" the rest of God also suggested itself to me as a title that would express the basic conclusion of my project as a whole: *Encountering the Rest of God.* One "enters" a space, but one encounters a person. The Sabbath was not abandoned for another day. Its importance diminished compared to a relationship with Jesus, as I conveyed with my subtitle, *How Jesus Came to Personify the Sabbath.*

Nothing earth-shaking, you might say. Indeed, Augustine got there first, in his *Confessions: Inquietum est cor nostrum, donec requiescat in te* ("Our heart is restless until it reposes in Thee;" Book 1, Pusey translation). There's no shame in taking the long way around to rediscover an old insight. Our two boys scorned memorizing mathematical formulae. If they couldn't derive them for themselves, they didn't want credit for having the right answer (is there a stubbornness gene?). Jesus as rest: I felt the truth of this more deeply than if I'd read Augustine years previously and believed him. To acknowledge his precedence, though, I used these words as the epigraph of my book.

One of the features of my dissertation is that it gave equal weight to the evidence of early non-canonical writings; I wasn't aware of any book dealing with the question of the Sabbath in the first Christian century that had done this. One such writing was the *Gospel of Thomas*, a popular and controversial topic of study at the time. The first complete copy had been among the manuscripts discovered in 1945 at Nag Hammadi on the banks of the Nile in Upper Egypt, fifty miles before you reach Luxor, and published thirty years later, twenty years before I began work on my project. It held an interesting saying about the Sabbath, Logion 27: "If you do not fast as regards to the world, you will not find the kingdom. If you do not observe the Sabbath as a Sabbath, you will not see the father" (Lambdin translation).

The parallelism of the two statements in this logion suggests that they are both expressions of the goal of human existence, metaphors for salvation. But there was no consensus on the concrete meaning of "sabbatizing the Sabbath," as the Greek version had it. Some saw in this a strong admonition to keep the Jewish Sabbath law but this seemed unlikely. Neither this proposal, nor the five or six others I found in the scholarly literature, were argued on text-internal reasoning. This is what I set out to do.

The parallel saying, which enjoins fasting, contrasts with the general stance of the Gospel, which rejects fasting and other conventional practices of Jewish piety. Used metaphorically, though, as it seems to be in logion 27, it makes sense as a taking over of a term and recoining it. To fast with regard to the cosmos, then, seemed to call for the disciple to maintain distance from the world. This was in line with the general stance toward the world in the Gospel as a whole. What, I asked myself, if to "sabbath the sabbath" were meant in a similar way? Rather than an exhortation to celebrate the Sabbath as a Sabbath, it would understand "sabbath" in its limited sense of cease, as a synonym for fast.

Would this make sense in the overall context of Thomas? I concluded that it did. What may have once been as a traditional saying urging sincere, literal Sabbath observance would have been turned on its head. The Thomasine believer is urged to rest, that is, to desist from Sabbath observance, especially in its signification as memorial of the creation of the cosmos the believer is called upon to transcend.

The result accorded with one of the proposals already in the literature, that of Baarda, but he had not demonstrated it from the text itself. I was proud that my Zurich training enabled me to put it on this basis.

My survey of the texts from the first Christian century convinced me there had been a panoply of practice in the early Jesus movement. There were those who seemed to envision a peaceful coexistence of Jewish followers of Jesus who continued to be Torah observant and non-Jews who were not. That view seemed to be reflected by Luke in Acts. The subsequent practice of the eastern church, in which Sunday is observed as the day of the resurrection, but the Sabbath remained a day of joy as a memorial of creation shows one way this developed. The attitude of Paul seems to have been different: an indifference toward specific days for worship because time was no longer divided into holy and profane, Christ having sanctified all of time. There were certainly those who believed that all should observe the Sabbath. This is known to us only by mirror-reading the letters of Paul for indications of what his competitors propagated. No New Testament writings argued for this, and none, not even Matthew's Gospel, seem to have arisen in communities with that practice. It would be interesting if one day a cache of ancient documents, similar to those uncovered at Qumran and Nag Hammadi, but deposited by Jewish followers of Jesus—perhaps taken by followers of James when the Jerusalem congregation fled to Pella. Were such a discovery to be made, then the question would have to be reopened.

It was clear that no one could claim to adhere to the whole of the scriptural canon and maintain that only Sabbath observance was valid. That would involve a misreading of Paul, as Worldwide had done. I felt one must distinguish between Sabbath observance, which can be a valid spiritual practice, and Sabbatarianism, the belief that the entire early church retained Sabbath observance for more than a century after the death and resurrection of Jesus. This, I concluded, was a historical and theological error.

My self-doubt aside, I loved working at the cloister-shaped structure that housed the faculty of theology. It was attached to the northwest wall of the *Grossmünster*, where Zwingli had introduced the Reformation. The office I shared faced southwest, overlooking the *Grossmünsterplatz*. There was typically a fresh breeze that came from the nearby Limmat River in the morning. I let as much of the cool air in as I could, for the wind often ceased around noon, by which time the sun flooded in the windows and made the office uncomfortably warm. When it was too hot to concentrate, I took my work down to the quiet cloister garden.

The office I shared was just off the small coffee room used by faculty, staff, and assistants. Coffee breaks gave us the chance to interact and share what we were working on, as did lunches in one of the cafeterias up the hill, either in the main university building or in the Federal Institute of Technology next to it. One of my office mates, Daria Pezzoli-Olgiati, made an offer soon after I settled in. She wanted me to read her texts before she submitted them and to be as severe with them as I could. She promised to not take anything I said personally, as long as it was her work I was criticizing. In return, she offered to do the same for me. I hope she benefitted from this even half as much as I did.

The faculty library was housed throughout the building, in open stacks. Some of the shelves were in classrooms, thus inaccessible whenever a class was in session, but overall the arrangement worked well. The librarians were unfailingly helpful. Family vacations in the U.S. included time at libraries in Princeton, Harvard, and Claremont to check literature not available in Zurich. In those libraries, as well as in Zurich, I spent many hours over the photocopy machine so that I could continue reading at home. I soon filled several binders with copied articles. I had to remind myself, though, that possessing a copy of something was not the same as having read and digested it.

I felt blessed to continue and deepen my association with the theological faculty. With a few hundred students and a dozen professors, it was possible to interact with nearly everyone. I don't think I would have learned as much in a larger setting.

As mentioned, a strong tradition at Zurich was hermeneutics, reflecting the lasting influence of Gerhard Ebeling, who long taught there and stopped by from time to time. A basic tenet of this application of the thought of Heidegger and Bultmann to theological texts is to look for clues within the studied text itself as a key to interpretation. It seemed we didn't so much acquire knowledge in Zurich as that we simply learned how to read. Once I visited Zumstein's friend and colleague Francois Bovon at Harvard. He invited me to sit in on a seminar. As it began, he passed me the reading list for that session and asked what I thought. I took a glance and said that in Zurich, that would be about two-thirds of the list for an entire semester. He nodded, but gave no indication of which pace of reading he considered better.

In the fifties and sixties, many promising young theologians from the English-speaking world trekked to Marburg and Basel to study at the feet of Bultmann and Barth. Now the center of theology was shifting to the English-speaking world. One of the contributions I could make was in building bridges. I joined the Society of Biblical Literature (SBL) and encouraged others to, as well. I often translated texts written by faculty members. Even some of those whose English was excellent asked me to read over their texts before submitting them for publication.

Another way that I could use my English mother-tongue to make a contribution was the English-reading course I offered each semester. This began when Ralph Kunz asked me to read and discuss a recent book on liturgy with him. He posted an invitation on the bulletin board and another student joined us. When we finished, the three of us co-authored a review for the prestigious *Theologische Literaturzeitung*. This was the seed out of which my course, English Readings for Theologians, grew; I offered it each semester for the next seven years. I consulted the professors to select the topics and readings, often to coincide with a course they were offering. Some semesters, we went through selected essays, for others, complete books, some of them recent, some classics (in this way, I finally read Milton's *Paradise Lost* and Bunyan's *Pilgrim's Progress* for a course on readings in the English Reformation). I usually co-taught with a specialist in the discipline, sometimes a faculty member, more often a grad student. Participants took turns preparing written summaries of each week's reading assignment, which they then presented orally, after which we discussed the text. All of this was in English. In this way, students and grad students gained confidence in presenting their work in English, helping them at international conferences.

I also gained experience at college-level teaching through the courses at the academy for church musicians jointly offered by the church and the conservatory. Again, Ralph had been instrumental.

In the spring of 1997, Beat Schaefer had contacted me after being commissioned to revamp the training program for prospective church musicians at the music conservatory. His ideal was a cantor in the mold of Johann Sebastian Bach, whose settings of the passion accounts in two of the gospels, Matthew and John, reflected a profound theological understanding as well as consummate musicianship. Schaefer felt that Swiss ministers, by and large, knew too little about liturgy (including hymnology), whereas it wouldn't hurt church musicians to know enough about theology to be able to communicate at eye-level with a pastor as they jointly prepared worship services.

Schaefer had approached Ralph Kunz, knowing that Ralph sympathized with that ideal and would do his best at the university to remedy the deficit on the side of ministers. Ralph turned down the offer to teach in the *Kantorenschule* and suggested me.

Beat and I met to discuss the possibility and hit it off immediately. So, beginning in the fall of 1997, I developed and taught three courses, Old and New Testament and Basic Questions of Theology, all of them tailored to the needs of musicians. After the first cycle of three courses, I passed the theology course to one of the other doctoral candidates better qualified than I. I continued teaching the other two courses for six years, and then, after returning to a full-time pastorate, continued to teach New Testament on the side, working twenty years all told. After a few years, I began writing my own text to accompany the course. I had tried different introductions to the New Testament, but none fit the needs of my students.

Those two-hour classes were often the high point of my week. To teach my specialty (New Testament) to students of music was an ideal combination.

The first group I taught remained among the most memorable. They were in my first class, New Testament, and each week's discussion had been stimulating. There was an eclectic mix of viewpoints, from traditionally pious to radical feminist, and none of them were inclined to simply take my word for anything. We gathered again the following semester for Old Testament, and when we met for the second lesson, I got the feeling no one had prepared. I probed, and it turned out that it wasn't because of lack of time, but because of their preconceived opinions about the Old Testament. So, instead of persisting with my planned lesson, I asked whether they had ever heard of Tamar. No one had, so I simply told her story off the top of my head. They were fascinated, and when I was finished asked if that was really in the Bible. From the next week on, they were as motivated and prepared as they had been the previous semester.

All the greater my shock when, shortly after the semester ended, the radical feminist—one of my favorites in the class—was pinned to the wall of the church where she served as organist by a reckless driver. Not every death affects me equally, this one hit me hard. So much potential and vitality snuffed out at such a young age.

Perhaps it traced back to my fiancée in Boston, a voice major, but I understood the pressures on music students and practicing musicians. The lesson, practice, and rehearsal plan while they study is full, their livelihood afterward is pieced together in various part-time and free-lance work. I made a deal with my students at the beginning of each semester: to get through the New Testament in one semester, and even more so through parts of the Old Testament in another, they had to prepare each week. But I understood that at times it simply wouldn't be possible. Extra rehearsals and performances in Advent, for example, could be stressful. My request to them: not to try to bluff their way through, but to admit that they hadn't prepared, and then I would tailor the lesson so that it would be valuable for them.

Still wondering about my future, I asked Zumstein what my chances were of finding a teaching job. He advised me to write a profile, setting down what I had to offer. He said he could see me in a seminary setting, training future pastors, more than at a public university. But the first three or four years would be hard, he warned me, with much time devoted to develop a repertoire of courses and writing them. Did I want to do that at my age?

This coincided with the feedback I got at SBL conferences. There were jobs to be had, and I stood a good chance of getting one, as long as I didn't mind where I lived, or the reputation of the school where I worked. Getting a tenure-track position at my age would be difficult though; consequently, I would lead a nomadic existence, with time-limited contracts. This put a damper on one post-doctorate career I had envisaged. I had thought that if I got a teaching job in the U.S., then I could do block seminars for Worldwide pastors between semesters. John Halford shared that hope.

Nevertheless, I honed my classroom skills. I read and reflected on the hallmarks of a good teacher, especially in light of the growing body of insight about adult learning. Our youngest, Mark, was still at home attending the *Kantonschule*, and had strong ideas of what worked in a classroom and what didn't. We had fruitful discussions, with Edel joining in based on her experience as a high school librarian.

Working alongside the other graduate students, I came to appreciate the great strengths many of them had, and gain a sense of my own limitations. Part of the reason I lagged was language, since German was not my native tongue. In seminar discussions, others contributed while I tried to sort out grammatically what I wanted to say. At times we had an English-speaking guest, and I found that I could without effort spark the discussion with incisive questions. I had the same experience at SBL meetings. Still, many of the other doctoral students were able to generate brilliant insights into the texts they were studying and have since gone on to sterling academic careers. For my part, I came to feel that my strength lay in understanding and synthesizing the work of others and then communicating that to learners. Most universities, even Zurich, in evaluating potential candidates for openings, leaned heavily on publications, both quality and quantity, as a factor determining hiring. Certainly, a faculty that boasts recognized stars is attractive in the competition for students. But not all who published a great deal were good in the classroom. I would have liked to find work at a school that prized teaching excellence. I analyzed my own classroom performance, and paid attention to the written course evaluations my students provided.

Someone like Hans-Dietrich Altendorf would not have been hired in the current climate. I had the opportunity to chat with Henry Chadwick, one of my favorite early church historians, while sitting on a park bench at Trinity College in Oxford when I attended the quadrennial Patristics conference. He asked what I was working on, and I told him of my project. He asked why I was attending a patristics conference, and I told him of how Altendorf had sparked my interest. He leaned back, thought a moment, then softly said, "Hans-Dietrich Altendorf . . . published little, but every bit of it solid."

Other than that, the conference was indelible for two things. I had just been in California with the family for vacation (a good part of it devoted to translating a paper for Alfred Schindler, the Zurich church historian who'd been invited to deliver one of the main addresses). We returned with just enough time for me to do laundry and repack. Still having California vacation as my mental picture, I packed many of the same clothes—it was after all summer. However, patristic scholars at a conference in Oxford do not dress like that. Not even in the summer.

The second memory is more pleasant. I met Willy Rordorf, the expert on the question of Sabbath and Sunday in the early patristic era. Especially useful was his differentiation of Sunday as a day of rest and as an occasion of worship. The latter set in earlier than the former, he demonstrated. When I introduced myself, we were headed the same way. A heavy summer shower burst suddenly and I opened my umbrella. He had none, so we huddled closely under mine, and I had the chance to tell him of my project. I said that as far as I could see, he had said all that need to be said about the patristic material, but that, given the third quest for the historical Jesus and the new perspective on Paul, there was a need to reexamine the New Testament evidence. He agreed.

The first yearly gathering of the Society of Biblical Literature I attended was in 1999. It would have been momentous for that alone, in addition to being held in Boston, where I'd studied. Not only that, Fritz Stolz decided to go to attend the concurrent meeting of the American Academy of Religion, and we flew together. I found it interesting that this scholar who had traversed the world, even doing field work in places as exotic as Bali, and could converse in many languages, ancient and modern, had never before been to the U.S. and was happy to have a native at his side when he landed.

But this trip became memorable for another reason.

When my parents heard I'd be traveling to Boston, they urged me to come visit them. I thought of my workload in Zurich and the time pressure I was under to finish my dissertation. And I had just visited them in the summer. The university provided some support for my flight out of its research fund, which involved booking the flight through the university. I didn't know what it might cost to fit in a side trip to New Jersey, nor did I look into it.

It was the worst decision I ever made. The next February, my dad was diagnosed with pancreatic cancer, a type of cancer that is almost always discovered late, too late for an effective treatment. I mentioned the diagnosis to our house doctor, who was also a neighbor. He urged me to go immediately. I had some commitments, so I booked a trip in three weeks' time. Which got me there in time for his funeral.

To pack more simply, I wore my suit for the flight. While I waited in line to check in, an agent came over and asked me quietly if I were traveling alone. She took me to one side, asked me to act discretely, then explained that the flight was overbooked and they needed to bump a couple of passengers to first class. It was the second time in my life that it happened, the other when I flew to Brussels after graduation to begin work as a correspondent. I told the agent why I was traveling and how much this meant to me.

Based on my two experiences, I'd say that the difference between first class and coach is not as great as the difference in price, but there definitely is a difference, especially on a long flight. It was a big help to arrive less travel-worn than I otherwise would have.

There was a viewing that evening. Some came who had worked for dad and whom I hadn't seen in years. At the funeral the next day, performed by Bob Harvey, pastor of First Baptist in Westfield, I spoke the words from the family. I mentioned that my dad was from a large family, the youngest of five sons, the second youngest of seven children. I spoke of a large family in the Bible, the twelve sons of Jacob. I said that the description of Issachar always reminded me of my dad, one who crouched between burdens. He was always ready to shoulder a load. When Harvey met with us to plan the funeral, I had mentioned that he had been in pain for most of his life. I told of his fall at his brother's mill when he was twelve years old, fracturing his back, and being told he would never walk again. In the sermon the next day, Harvey told of that, but changed mill to factory, which the word mill can also mean in English. I could sympathize. One wants to personalize each funeral, but it is all too easy to get some details wrong.

There was one good side to traveling when I did. I had booked my ticket to stay a week; thus, most of my stay was after the funeral. I was able to help my mom with the first steps of paperwork. We also cleared out his closet and clothes drawers. We took the wearable items to a nearby men's shelter. I set aside a couple of watches for myself, as well as a classic Stetson fedora.

I also took his copy of *The Old Man and the Sea*, which I read on the flight back, and Goethe's *Faust*, my dad's favorite book ever since he'd read it in his school days and the source of the maxim he repeated every time I brought home a disappointing report card (which it seems they always were): *Wer immer strebend sich bemüht, den können wir erlösen* ("who e'er aspiring struggles on, for him there is salvation," Priest translation).

The regret over not having been there for my dad at the end of his life was assuaged by telling myself that, had I been there, there was nothing I could have said to him about how much he meant to me that I hadn't already said many times. But that didn't compensate for the loss of one of the most important people in my life.

Not being with my dad at the end formed an involuntary symmetry for all the times he hadn't been there when I was a child. He was at work then, now, I had been at mine. There is no satisfaction in that realization. And there is self-reproach at the disappointment the last time I'd been with him the previous summer. He had difficulty getting around, but had always been in pain. I noticed his mind wasn't sharp, and I resented it. I had always admired him for his wide-ranging, well-stocked mind. It felt like a personal affront to see him lose that. I probably won't be any kinder on myself when it's my turn.

Boston was the first of five SBL meetings I attended, two of them regional meetings in Europe. My first time was as a listener, but for subsequent meetings, I proposed papers and presented them. It was valuable to have that experience of speaking to a room of scholars and to respond to their questions. I also profited from the feedback some gave me after my presentations. I gained as well from listening both to leading scholars and to those who, like me, were doctoral candidates. Some of those I got to know in that way have gone on to flourishing careers. It was especially enjoyable to meet scholars whose books I'd found helpful to my own work, such as Lutz Doering, who studied the Sabbath in Second Temple Judaism.

It was also at an SBL meeting that I reconnected with one of those from Ambassador who had gone on to a distinguished academic career, Lester Grabbe. When I spotted him, he was talking with his own *Doktorvater* and introduced me. We then spoke privately for a few minutes, during which he confided to me his opinion that not everything Herbert Armstrong taught had been mistaken, which matched my own feeling. Since I enjoy connecting people, I asked him to meet me for lunch and also asked Thomas Krüger, Old Testament professor from Zurich.

At another SBL meeting I spotted Dixon Cartwright, who published a newspaper that reported on the various groups and movements that had arisen from Worldwide. It was good to see him again, and he invited me to have breakfast with him and Ken Westby, who was attending. Ken had been one of the regional directors who had left the church in 1974. Since I'd last seen him, he had become an ardent proponent of Unitarianism, which was in some ways a logical development of the way that Worldwide had presented its objections to Trinitarianism. I found him as amiable as ever, one with whom one could disagree pleasantly. He began to share his views with me. I responded that I understood the appeal of that teaching, but that I felt that it was not the view of the author of the Fourth Gospel. I cited the words of Thomas when confronted by the resurrected Jesus, "My lord and my God" (John 20:28). Ken said that this was the kind of thing that could slip out of one's mouth when surprised. I didn't think that did justice to the way the entire gospel seemed structured to lead up to this acclamation. Neither of us changed the other's mind, but I was glad to have seen him again.

My final visit to an SBL meeting was the year that my dissertation was published, 2005. It had been accepted by the Theologischer Verlag Zürich, which published the works of Zwingli, Bullinger, and Barth. TVZ had just agreed to a distribution agreement with an American publisher, Eisenbrauns, and was happy to have an English-language title in their catalogue. I soon learned the disadvantage of that. To cut down on costs, Eisenbrauns didn't keep any stock of TVZ titles, but ordered a copy of each when they made a sale. I received more than one e-mail from a potential reader disappointed that they would have to wait eight weeks for delivery. What was worse: I presented two papers highlighting some of my findings at that year's congress. People came up to me later and said they had gone to the Eisenbrauns table at the book exhibit, but there were no copies of my book there. Had I known of the policy, I could have arranged to take copies from the TVZ and give them to Eisenbrauns there. As it was, I gave the copy that I'd brought with me to a Finnish scholar interested in my work on the last day of the conference.

As an assistant, I was part of the *Mittelbau*, the non-tenured teaching staff. The group delegated me as its representative on a faculty committee that would revise the doctoral regulations. It was interesting, although I made little headway in the questions that filled my mind: what habits of mind should a candidate cultivate writing a dissertation? What new skills should she acquire?

Instead, the faculty opted for more of what had brought the candidate to a stellar performance at the master's level. A regime of postgraduate seminars was introduced. The main difference between them and the other seminars on offer would be all the participants were doctoral students. Another innovation was that candidates named two side disciplines and would be examined orally in them after attending postgraduate seminars in them. The final innovation was that the defense was open to the public. Mine was the first under the new regulations.

I chose Old Testament as one of my two side disciplines. This not only made sense as most relevant to my topic, but it was a discipline that interested me. That meant that one of my oral exams would be my third with Odil Hannes Steck, one of Zurich's most memorable professors and one from whom I learned a lot.

Steck was a bit shorter than average, with wiry hair and thick glasses. He was prolific (anyone who published more than he did wrote too much, in his opinion). In seminars one had to be careful. He could be biting if work was not up to snuff. In lectures, he was outstanding, although with a tick. He had his lecture manuscript before him, but he rarely looked at it. Nor did he look at us. Instead, he turned to his left (our right) and addressed the wall. A chain-smoker, he was scrupulous about calling breaks halfway through his lectures, during which he was approachable. I took overview of the Old Testament from him as well as lectures on Genesis and Isaiah and gained a wealth of exegetical insight along with the long view of what the Hebrew scriptures offered as part of the Christian Bible and how much we would have missed out on if Marcion had prevailed with his partial, New Testament-only canon.

Our post-graduate seminars ran from six to eight in the evening, after which we often went out to eat. One evening he reminisced about his first year of teaching, writing his lectures into the early hours of the morning just before giving them. He had been a star student at Heidelberg and was called to a professorship in Hamburg at a young age. He was proud of his career—the rapid rise and the amount and quality of his work. After years of thinking that Christian humility required one to always play down one's accomplishments,

it was refreshing for me to hear him comment, when expli-
cating God's "very good" at the end of the sixth day of Creation, that it was not wrong to experience satisfaction when
one had done good work.

Given his high standards, he could be intimidating in
oral examinations. He confided to me that when he named
the passage for the unprepared translation at the beginning
of the exam, he always paid attention to how the candidate
opened the Hebrew Bible. If the candidate opened from what
would be the front of a German book (which was the back of
a Hebrew book, since Hebrew is printed right to left) or if he
opened it to look for a Psalm in the middle, where it would
be printed in the German Bible (the order in Hebrew differs),
then he knew the entire exam would be bad.

He had been one of two experts for my oral Hebrew
exam, which hadn't gone particularly well (the other expert
was Ernst Jenni from Basel, author of the venerable textbook
we used). Then he had been my examiner for the oral exam
in Old Testament as part of the propedeuticum (first level
exam), and again for my comprehensives. By this time, he
had experienced me in seminars and in private conversation
and he knew that my floundering when translating *prima
vista* was not a measure of my overall ability or preparation.

Nevertheless, I was surprised when it came time for him
to examine me a third time, for my doctoral program. We
sat on opposite sides of the table in a small room under the
eaves of the seminar, each with a Hebrew Bible before us. He
began by suggesting we dispense with the translation and
just have a conversation. I don't know if it was more to spare

me agony or himself, but it was appreciated. I don't know that he ever did that for anyone else.

For Willy Rordorf before me, as well as for me, an important question was how and when the Christian movement abandoned (by and large) the seventh-day Sabbath. Given the Jewish matrix of the movement at its outset, my working assumption was that there would have been more of a struggle leaving some literary remains, even if outside the canon. After coming up empty, I asked myself if the function of the Sabbath as an identity marker for Jews might be part of the explanation. Midway through my work on my dissertation, Gerd Theissen published his *Religion der ersten Christen*, in which he explained the development in a way that struck me as a mechanistic: the Christians abandoned the Sabbath and adopted the first day in order to create a new identity. I wasn't comfortable with that way of formulating it. It seemed to suggest a conscious decision. I had come to feel that the new identity existed already in the relation to Christ. This made the day of worship a matter of indifference and could begin with a practical solution of finding a time when all who followed Jesus, whether Jews or Gentile slaves, could come together. To frame the question in terms of "Sabbath or Sunday," as earlier studies tended to do, misrepresented the development. Time markers no longer had the importance they'd previously held. The Sabbath was not abandoned in order to create a new identity. The new identity (in Christ) led to the abandonment (by many) of the Sabbath. There is no New Testament passage that says this, although Matthew 11:28–30 ("Come to me . . . I will give you rest") implicitly reflects it.

In an ideal world, I would have taken the entire manuscript and reworked it in light of this insight (which came fairly late in my work) so that the whole book pointed more clearly to this result. But there was a limit to how long I could devote to it; it was time for me to get back to work. As it was, I moved on before I completed my dissertation.

Chapter Seven

During the three years I worked on my dissertation, it gradually became clear what I should do after finishing it. The first step was to see that my plan to use my education to enhance the skills of Worldwide's ministry was illusory.

In the summer of 1999, nine months into my project, we flew to the U.S. to visit family in New Jersey and California.

All three of our girls still lived in Pasadena, so being there also allowed me to talk with Worldwide leaders. One was new to me, John McKenna, a theologian who'd recently joined the staff. He'd had no previous association with Worldwide. His first acquaintance had come two years earlier when Ambassador University ceased independent operations and established an Ambassador Center at Azusa Pacific University. McKenna was an adjunct professor at Azusa and when he heard of Worldwide's doctrinal turnabout, he felt called to help.

My first reaction when I met him was to realize that with him on the staff there would likely be no need for me in a similar capacity. But I warmed to him. John had a welcoming personality, and I immediately recognized his energy and drive. And perhaps his lack of involvement with Worldwide in its previous form was an advantage.

I then had lunch with Ron Kelly, a long-time Worldwide minister. For most of his career, he had been a teacher and administrator at Ambassador's Big Sandy campus; I'd had little contact with him in those years. He then joined the editorial staff in Pasadena and served as one of the four presenters of the *World Tomorrow* telecast after Herbert Armstrong's death in 1986 until it was discontinued in 1994. Now he was Worldwide's financial manager; in addition to catching up and spending time together, I wanted some insight into the church's economic outlook.

Both encounters were good preparation for talking with Joe Tkach, now in his fourth year as Worldwide's pastor-general after his father's death. Edel and I went one evening to Hamburger Hamlet with him, his wife Tammy, and their two children. We ordered and shared family news while sipping a draft lager and waiting for our meals. Then Joe asked how my dissertation was going. I said it would likely contain things to upset people on both sides of the question, to which Joe replied that I was probably on the right track.

Then I forced the question of my future after completing my doctorate. Joe said, "we want to use you." Part of me wished that I still could make a contribution to educating Worldwide's ministry. But, as I pointed out, the church's income continued to decline, and it was laying off ministers and other workers who had faithfully stuck with Worldwide during the change. It made no sense, I continued, to bring someone back on the payroll who was already off it. "But we want to use you," Joe interjected. "I appreciate that," I answered, "but you can't afford me."

The outcome of these conversations was that it became clear that the best way I could make a contribution would be to enter the ministry of the Reformed Church in Switzerland. In a way, it felt like a homecoming since my ancestors on my father's side had been Reformed for five hundred years. Often, as I approached the seminar building attached to the *Grossmünster*, where Zwingli had preached, I recalled my father talking of him at the dinner table.

Aiding me in my decision was the recognition that Worldwide had found its new home as part of the wider evangelical movement. I felt I'd been able to help those who remained in the congregations I pastored to move away from being a sect—a group that was cut off from other Christians—to one that understood it was part of a wider family. The congregations in Switzerland now had contact with the Evangelical Alliance. To me, the congregations were in a healthier place than they had been, one in which they felt at home. But it wasn't my home. My experience had shown me that Worldwide's problem had not necessarily been its specific teachings, but its basic assumptions about the Bible and how to use it to establish doctrine. The Bible, it was assumed, was in a literal sense the word of God. Doctrines could be formulated by putting together statements from the entire canon; any contradictions must be denied or explained away.

To me, the evangelical movement, especially its more

fundamentalist wing, shared these assumptions and methods. The difference lay solely in the conclusions they reached. As far as that went, I still thought the classic Worldwide conclusions were in many cases more consistent, if one were to interpret the Bible that way.

Some of my former Worldwide parishioners accused me of no longer taking the Bible seriously, but my conviction was that I was taking it more seriously than ever, and that a close reading revealed it to be a fascinating collection of human voices whose deep trust in God sustained them in all the vagaries and contradictions of life. I saw as well that the collectors and final editors had exhibited not only literary skill but also honesty. This was expressed, for instance, in the inclusion of prophecies not fulfilled, or only partially, along with those that were. It was an honesty that permitted the inclusion of Koheleth (Ecclesiastes) and Job alongside the pious certainties of the Proverbs. The Bible, I came to see, was an anthology that repaid repeated attentive reading.

That points to a second reason why the Reformed Church here in Switzerland felt like home. The first reason, as mentioned, is that it was like a homecoming to return to the church in which my father had been raised. But the second is more important: it is a broad church, which allows me to continue learning and questioning.

I felt relieved that I had finally made a decision. The hardest part was informing John Halford after my return to Europe. He had been nurturing me along with two others—one with a specialty in Old Testament, another in church history—to educate Worldwide's existing and future ministry. I respected and admired John. He was a good friend and I was sorry to disappoint him. He told me he regretted my decision, but understood it, and I believe he did.

I had come full circle, thirty-six years after my first exposure to the *Plain Truth* magazine. My way out of Worldwide was, in a way, a mirror image of my way in: a long, tortuous process. I had not rushed into the church—I was baptized and began attending services five-and-a-half years after beginning to study Worldwide's writings. My decision to continue my ministry outside of Worldwide was the culmination of an even more extended period of reexamination since my first Greek class in October 1991.

The next step in implementing the decision was to see Hans Strub, responsible for the Reformed Church's training and continuing education program. He welcomed me to his office in the *Haus am Rechberg*, an imposing baroque villa on Hirschengraben. I had passed it often as I walked from the theology faculty to the main university building, just before beginning the steep climb up the Künstlergasse (sometimes, for a change, I walked through the ornate garden behind the building instead), never suspecting that the cantonal church had its headquarters there.

The building was imposing but Hans was low-key and reassuring. I told him of my intention to enter the Reformed Church and reviewed with him the steps I'd need to take to enter their ministry.

First, I would need to write to the church board in Dällikon, where we lived, to request admission to the Reformed

Church. My request was approved in February 2000. Then I would need to petition the executive council of the Zurich cantonal church to become a candidate for the ministry. I prepared the required papers—a short resume, a statement of motivation, and confirmation of my membership in the Reformed Church—and submitted them. In due time, an invitation arrived for a formal interview—a colloquium—with Ruedi Reich, the council president, whom I'd already met when he had held a service in Dällikon. After the colloquium, I would be eligible to enter the vicariate, thirteen months of practical training between university and ordination. Three-fourths of the time was spent working in a congregation, mentored by a pastor; there were also ten week-long courses spent cloistered in various seminar campuses.

In the past, at times of a shortage of ministers, the church had been liberal in recognizing the qualifications of ministers of other denominations and allowing them to take over pastorates directly. The experience hadn't always been positive. But now, since the need was not as urgent, Strub recommended that I do a vicariate and outlined the advantages. For one thing, it would mean that my credentials would be accepted not only for the cantonal church that accepted me but in all the churches that belonged to the concordat in Switzerland. It also covered me, in the event of a conflict, from the accusation that I wasn't adequately trained.

Typically, candidates for ministry would have done a school-teaching practicum; Strub agreed to waive this in light of my teaching assignments at the university and the cantor's school.

In preparation for the colloquium with Ruedi Reich, Strub advised me to read the thin volume that accompanied the church's five-volume order of worship and explained the thinking behind the typical Reformed service. In addition, I should study the structure of the Zurich church, with particular attention to its role in the public schools, where religious instruction was still part of the curriculum. Finally, I should study Swiss church history, with a concentration on the Zurich church. He named a long list of writings, beginning with one of Zwingli's works, *Der Hirt* (*The Shepherd*).

The colloquium took place in a conference room in the *Haus am Rechberg* less than a month later; Hans was also present to protocol the discussion. In my preparation, I tried to fill gaps in my knowledge. Heinrich Bullinger, for instance. He was Zwingli's successor in Zurich and for more than four decades exercised influence throughout Europe. Yet I had read little of his writings during my studies, in contrast to the hundreds of pages of Zwingli I'd read. One of Bullinger's central teachings, federal theology, also called covenant theology, not only shaped the way the Swiss church organized itself, but found its way to the British Isles and from there to North America, where its influence was not only important for the Presbyterian-Reformed church tradition but can even be traced in the U. S. Constitution. So, I read up on it and walked into the colloquium ready to share what I'd learned.

I needn't have bothered. The one topic Reich questioned me on was something that would have needed no special preparation, since it was something I'd thought long and hard about throughout my time studying in Zurich, baptism.

Worldwide practiced believer baptism. Reich knew this. One of the most traumatic controversies at the time of the Zurich Reformation five hundred years earlier had been that some of Zwingli's associates had rejected infant baptism, leading them to break with him, ultimately at the cost of their lives. Ever since, there had been individual reservations about the practice, most prominently by Karl Barth, which he expressed in the last volume he finished of his *Church Dogmatics* before his death. Barth conceded, however, the relation between infant baptism and the posture of an established church, a *Volkskirche*. Reich wanted assurance that I wouldn't join forces with those who wanted to change the practice, and I assured him I wouldn't.

This wasn't simply a concession so that I could work for the Reformed Church. Opponents of infant baptism were right, I continued to feel, that the New Testament references to baptism describe the immersion of people who took a personal decision to enter the church. But the record of history was clear. The church had soon begun baptizing infants as well and it wasn't long before it became the usual practice. In a way, it was similar to the change from Sabbath to Sunday: something that could have been decided otherwise at the outset, but had not been. In both cases, to set oneself against these practices now could not help but be divisive.

I had been involved in Worldwide long enough to see that the children of believers do not have the same experience as their parents. A classic conversion experience is rare, since they grew up knowing a way of life and in most cases were receptive to it and by and large had done the right thing.

In my years as a Reformed pastor, I wholeheartedly baptized infants; it was always a joyous occasion. One thing I did not do: I never cited scriptures saying it was for the remission of sins. In common with the early church fathers who had first accepted infant baptism, I believed that one could only speak of sin from the time a young person knows the difference between right and wrong.

Once the Reformed Church accepted me for the vicariate, I sat down again with Hans Strub and he had outlined the goal for the year. For a typical candidate, the program served as an opportunity to learn the role of pastor and gain experience in the basic tasks. Because of the experience I brought, Strub had another goal in mind. I should focus on becoming acquainted with the place of an established church as an institution in society and on the inner workings of its structure. He summed it up in one word: Swissification.

It was time to seek out a mentor to work with during the thirteen-month vicariate.

I was sensitive about my age and long experience and asked some of the Reformed pastors I'd come to know for the names of pastors who might be a good fit for me and soon had a list of six names, none of whom I'd met as yet. I intended to visit a service conducted by each and introduce myself.

I decided to approach Hans Caspers first. He fit my criterium of being older than me, and the town where he pastored, Stadel, was a twenty-minute drive through the countryside from our home.

Edel and I went to services there one Sunday, after which I introduced myself and said that I was visiting congregations to see where I might do my vicariate. He and his wife invited us to their home for coffee. At the end of our visit, I told him that this was just the first of my visits but that based on what I'd heard in services and our discussion, I was ready to put away my list. He said he would also be interested in having me as his vicar.

It turned out to be a good choice. Caspers had trained more than twenty vicars already. In addition, he had served for many years as dean (something like the district superintendent in the old Worldwide structure). He had left that responsibility to serve in the executive council of the Zurich church, the *Kirchenrat*, but soon realized he was not suited for the long meetings and thick dossiers that entailed. He was much happier as an all-around parish pastor.

At the time, I still hoped to complete my dissertation in two years and thought I would begin my vicariate in fall 2000. However, as that date approached, I could see I wouldn't be finished, so I put it off for a half-year, then for another half-year. I finally began in fall 2001. I was thankful for the flexibility of Hans Caspers that permitted me to change this.

The journey into the Reformed Church had been eased by new friendships that my studies brought me. This was important after so many years when my closest relations had been with congregants and fellow Worldwide ministers; the friendship with Peter Folkerts was an exception, and even that arose out of my Worldwide duties. The first of the new friendships were with fellow students, then with faculty, and with time, with men and women already serving as ministers in a Reformed setting. This began with our next-door neighbors, Hans-Ueli and Doris Perels, but expanded beyond this. It wasn't long before some of my new friends began to urge me to enter the Reformed Church and its ministry. One was Sabine Scheuter, who lived in Otelfingen, one train station further from us on the same line, which meant that occasionally we rode to or from Zurich together. She and her husband Ilya, who pastored the Otelfingen congregation, had invited me to take an active part in a service there on July 4, 1999, one month before our family trip to Pasadena. It was my first sermon to a Reformed congregation.

A year later, I received a call from the pastor in another neighboring town, Rümlang. He asked me to cover for him for two weeks in the fall while he went on vacation. I wasn't sure whether I was allowed to do it, since I hadn't done my vicariate; I explained to him that I would check. I called Hans Strub. He informed me that since I'd passed the first level of exams at the university, the propaedeutic, I'd fulfilled the only requirement in the church order for pulpit substitution.

Between saying yes and conducting services there, I had to fill in on short notice in another congregation, Dürnten. This was the first Sunday after the Feast of Tabernacles 2000. On the first day of the Feast in Bonndorf, I had given the sermon (my last ever at the Feast). In Dürnten, the following Sunday was *Erntedank* (Thanksgiving). I spoke on the thanksgiving celebration of ancient Israel, the Feast of Tabernacles, and showed how Jesus, when speaking of taking up a dwelling (John 1; John 14), uses the equivalent Greek term for the Hebrew word translated tabernacles, or booths. Jesus wants to tabernacle in us. It was refreshing to speak of the significance of this statement of Jesus in light of its rich Old Testament background without having to engage in debates over whether we had to observe these days today. It was another indication to me that I could in the future use the familiarity with the teaching of the Old Testament and the customs of ancient Israel as a resource for any potential ministry.

I held services on the next two Sundays in Rümlang and had two funerals during the week in between. After the second Sunday service, I stood and shook hands with congregants who said *Guet's g'si* (a neutral way of saying it was a pleasant service). One woman stopped longer to say she had been so disappointed in services that she was on the point of no longer coming. She decided to give it one more try that day and was glad. The next person in line identified himself as the president of the local church board. The pastor for whom I was subbing was going to leave soon, and they would need a replacement. He asked for my resume. I said I'd be glad to give it to him but that I wasn't eligible, since I still needed to do the vicariate.

The experience was significant, though. One thing holding me back from switching to the Reformed ministry was my uncertainty of whether the way I preached and conducted services was transferable to a Reformed context. This was an external confirmation that it might be.

If I were going to give sermons regularly, I had to reevaluate to deal with the prophets. Worldwide's public thrust was centered on interpretation of prophetic writings. Many other groups spread the belief that we lived in the end times based on the usual day-for-a-year calculations. What set Worldwide apart from others, though, was British Israelism.

I'd given up that teaching because of the lack of evidence, and by the time Worldwide abandoned date-setting, I was at the corner waiting for them. But these two points were just the tip of a collection of teachings based on the prophets, including the later apocalyptic writings such as Daniel and, in the New Testament, Revelation, as well as the general matter of eschatology. To drop an end-time focus affected large portions of scripture.

I became aware of how completely I'd jettisoned British Israelism a few years earlier when a good friend showed me the first booklet Rod Meredith had published after leaving Worldwide forming the Global Church of God. In it, Meredith wrote about how his heart burned to deliver the warning message to "our Israelite brethren." I completed the thought in my own mind: "And the rest of the world can go to hell." Even in the decades I accepted British Israelism, it was to me no more than a key to interpreting history and prophecy. Spiritual salvation, however, was available to all mankind. But I was beginning to see that for some, the British Israelism teaching was simply a veneer over good old-fashioned Anglo-Saxon white supremacy teachings.

My project for Fritz Stolz had immersed me in that thought world and inured me to it. Attending Steck's lectures on Isaiah, I'd come to appreciate how eloquently that book spoke to its time, an insight I was able to carry over to the rest of the prophets. When Jeremiah urged his correspondents to "seek the peace of the city" (Jer. 29:7) to which they'd been carried captive and to pray for it, it was essential to look first at the historical situation of the Jews transported to Babylon and not limit its meaning to the U.S. in the late twentieth century. At the same time, there was an undeniable abiding message in these words, "for in its peace shall ye have peace," although it was one I couldn't recall having heard preached in Worldwide, with its expectation of the imminent downfall of the U.S. and Britain.

Then again, when Micah said: "He hath shown thee, O man, what is good; and what doth the Lord require of thee, but to do justly, and to love mercy, and to walk humbly with thy God?" (Mic. 6:8)—was there ever a time when this did not apply?

Worldwide had taught that one-third of the Bible is prophecy and that ninety percent of that to be fulfilled in our day. Close attention to the proclamation of the early church showed me they would have been surprised with that calculation. From their use of Isaiah, the Psalms, and other writings, it seemed they thought all of scripture was prophecy, and that ninety percent was fulfilled with the coming of the messiah, with the remainder to be fulfilled soon, in their day.

Worldwide also had clear views about the classic topics of eschatology, taking positions that were well-grounded biblically, but out of step with the mainstream of Christian tradition, to say nothing of the vague positive expectations of civil religion, which has democratized heaven to the point that many who don't believe in God nevertheless are confident that their loved ones are in heaven. Instead of being taken to heaven, the saved would be a part of the kingdom of God on earth. And the unsaved dead would not be tormented forever, but would experience an offer of reconciliation. Even then, the penalty for the few who persisted in rejecting God would be annihilation, not eternal suffering.

Immortality was conditional, Worldwide stressed, a gift of God (it was only while researching for my memoirs that I learned this was the official teaching of the denomination I'd been raised in, the Lutheran Church Missouri Synod). This still made sense to me, but how would I preach a funeral sermon? Sensitivity to the needs of mourners gradually led me to see that a funeral was not the place for a lecture on eschatology, no matter what I believed. Again, I recalled Ingolf Dalferth's lectures on the topic. He began the first hour by defining eschatology, the teaching of the last things (or most important things, as *eschaton* can also mean) as the study of what we may hope based on what we have experienced in Christ. This was liberating. What may happen in the future is not something we can be dogmatic about (which would have spared me many heated discussions as a Worldwide pastor).

I no longer believed the prophets should be read as a roadmap to our immediate future. In my last years in Worldwide, I rarely spoke on texts from the prophets. It was one thing to attend Steck's lectures, but a sermon has to relate the text to our day and listeners' lives. I came across a collection of sermons Paul Tillich had given in the last days of World War Two and the immediate aftermath, *The Shaking of the Foundations*. In addition to being the ideal way to bootstrap into Tillich's thought, they were also an example of how to use texts from the prophets in a way that would confront and edify present-day congregations.

Aside from the content of my messages, the opportunity to hold services on a regular basis (at least once a month) brought an encounter with an external issue: the cassock. In Worldwide, the ministers conducted services wearing a suit, dress shirt, and tie. The lack of liturgical vestments was consistent with its lack of belltowers, pews, and organs. In the established churches in Europe, as in the mainstream denominations in the States, it was different. The cassock had a long tradition. When Zwingli rejected the Catholic mass, he also stopped wearing the ornate vestments that priests wore when they celebrated it. In those days, there were rigid guidelines not only for what a pastor wore, but for all trades. There were no "ordinary" clothes. Your attire enabled others to see at a glance what your status in society was. If Zwingli no longer dressed as a priest, there was no other option open to him but to wear, as a cassock, the academic gown he was entitled to wear by virtue of his education. This became the rule for centuries to come.

Coincidentally, as I was beginning to attend Worldwide services and become used to see ministers preach without vestments, the uproar in the late sixties in the Western world also reached the theology faculties and churches in Europe. A banner with the slogan: *unter den Talaren, Muff von tausend Jahren*, was unfurled to greet an academic procession ("under the gowns, the musty odor of a thousand years"). This was a protest against the fact that a generation after the end of World War Two, it seemed as if the structures and thought that helped foster the second and third *Reichs* in Germany was still firmly ensconced in the universities.

Theology students of the time, the same age as I, rejected the cassock as a symbolic way of saying their thinking wasn't hidebound. Relevance and authenticity became leading ideals.

Hans Caspers had been through that time, but opted for the cassock. Before my first service, when I arrived in my suit and tie, he offered to lend me his cassock. I demurred but he urged "at least try it on." I acquiesced, and wore it for every worship service I conducted in Stadel.

Meanwhile, one of the leading members in Worldwide's congregation was a master tailor. He told he'd been commissioned to sew a cassock according to the Lausanne cut (there is a variety of regional styles). He thought it turned out well and said if I decided to wear one, he'd be happy to sew it for me. I didn't intend to take him up on it. But after my vicariate, I took up my duties in an area where the majority of the population were Roman Catholic. One of my first duties was to perform an ecumenical service. I arrived in my suit and tie, then watched as two altar boys helped the priest into his vestments. Later, as we stood side-by-side during the service, I was aware how odd that must look for the congregation.

I also realized how helpful it would be on occasions such as funerals, when people attended who didn't know me, for them to be able to see immediately what my role was. Soon I drove to the tailor's shop and had him measure me.

Despite intensive work through a sweltering summer of 2001, my dissertation still wasn't finished but my assistantship at the university was ending. I had postponed beginning the vicariate twice. A further postponement wasn't possible. It was time to move on, regardless of my fear that I would end up as one of those pastors with an unfinished manuscript in a desk drawer (a fear shared by my doctoral advisor, Jean Zumstein).

I was working at my desk on one of my few remaining days in the office I shared at the university when our IT-support guru pushed a banner to all of our computers. It crawled across my screen and I read the news that an airplane had crashed into one of the two towers of the World Trade Center. No big deal, I thought. I remembered hearing in my childhood that a B-25 bomber had hit the Empire State Building a few years before. The pilot had become disoriented in heavy fog, a few people were killed, but the building stood. Then a new banner several minutes later said that the second tower had been struck, too.

Construction on the towers had begun shortly before I left home to enter university in 1970. Whenever I returned for a visit, you could see them going up. A hilltop not far away offered a good vantage point. By the time I stopped at home after graduating from Ambassador on my way to Europe in 1973, they were open. From then on, the towers dominated the skyline and in the years I served Worldwide's central Jersey congregations, I caught frequent glimpses of them by day and night. My cousin Carl had an office in a nearby building; his window offered a close-up view of the towers. When the towers collapsed, I began to worry about him and others I knew, especially when I heard that other buildings had been destroyed when the towers collapsed. It turned out that neither he nor any other family members or friends were there at the time. One had decided to go in late, another had decided to work from home that day.

Although no one close to me was killed, it was a psychically scarring blow. I was sure that for many people younger than I, 9/11 would be an event similar to what the Kennedy assassination had been for me or Pearl Harbor for my parents' generation. For the rest of their lives, they would remember where they were when they first heard the news, and how.

In the succeeding days, as it became clear that the four airplane hijackings that day had not been the opening salvo of a continuing operation, life slowly settled into new normal. But the next time I flew into Newark Airport and walked the passageway at the international arrival terminal, I turned my eyes to where the towers should have been visible through the plate glass window. I had done it without thinking, and was surprised by the shock with which I registered their absence. I thought of the phantom pain that amputees report.

But what I did not think was that it was a sign of the end of the world.

The other new vicars and I began work in our congregations after the fall vacation in mid-October 2001. It would be a month before we met as a group. My duties included religious instruction to a class of middle school pupils, regular worship services, including a family service and one in a regional senior citizens' home. I attended Hans' confirmation lessons and took a couple of the lessons myself. Hans knew that I played in a band, and he invited us to play at that year's confirmation service.

One evening's confirmation lesson made a particular impression. Not that I remember the topic, it may have been on death and hope for the future. Hans presented a well-prepared lesson that covered the major teachings (some teach this, others teach that). Then a hand went up and one of the youths asked the direct question, "And what do you believe?" I sensed Hans's discomfort and listened as he evaded the question. At the time, I was wondering if he might be covering up his own doubts. With reflection, though, I realized how much of the youth work I'd done with Worldwide had been an attempt at indoctrination, and that Hans bent over backward to avoid doing that. His aim was to encourage reflection so that these young people could begin to form their own opinions.

I did my share of visits, including visiting senior citizens on their birthdays. Stadel still had the traditions of a village. When one had a birthday, one was at home and prepared an open coffee table; anyone could come. This meant I didn't have to arrange these visits in advance.

I was still conscious of being an outsider, an American. When Worldwide had sent me to Switzerland, that was one thing; the entire church was headquartered in the U.S. But the Swiss Reformed Church had its own history and identity, and the Presbyterian- Reformed community as a whole had its roots here. What would it be like for me, an American, to serve here? One of the villagers, whose hobby was local history, took me on a walk through Stadel and pointed out, as we passed each house, that at least one person from the household had emigrated to North America at some point in the twentieth century. Many stayed in contact with their family in Switzerland; there had been frequent visits back and forth. I didn't need to feel like such a stranger.

Each trainee had to develop a congregation project during the year. For mine, I assisted Hans in an adult education series he offered on world religions, with presentations by representatives of each. My project was to use the last two evenings of the series to situate Christianity among world religions. The first evening was the Tuesday after Easter. I traced the critical difference between Christianity and the other religions, the Easter faith. On the second evening, I focused on the difficulties of comparison from the perspective of religious studies.

Stadel had a long tradition as a liberal congregation. This was also ideal for me since I was freeing myself from a fundamentalist background. It was striking to see the number and the quality of those who volunteered in one way or another. My experience had led me to expect that level of commitment only in a stricter group.

Hans Caspers often mused on the difference in our experience. He, son of a pastor in Germany, had come to Zurich primarily to study with Gerhard Ebeling, then had married a Swiss woman and stayed in Switzerland after graduation.

His entire pastoral experience was in Stadel. During the same period, I had lived in Belgium, the U.S., Canada, and for the past fourteen years, Switzerland.

He encouraged critical reflection on the differences and similarities between an established church and a "free" church in our conversations. We agreed that the most considerable continuity between what I'd done before and my present duties was pastoral counseling of members. Whereas visits to Worldwide prospective members centered on answering their questions about the church's teaching and helping them prepare for baptism, visits to those who were already members of Worldwide focused on day-to-day life challenges. Whenever I visited a mourning family to prepare a funeral, I encountered sorrows and hopes not unlike those of families in Stadel in a similar situation.

Caspers also gave me helpful feedback on my preaching. He noted that I spoke to the congregation as if they were educated Bible readers, which might not correspond to the reality of *Volkskirche* in modern terms. In his feedback after my first sermon, he said, "I hear the New Testament scholar, but I don't find my Stadler." In the course of the year, and in dialog with Hans, I was able to situate each sermon better in the life of the congregation. In addition, he helped me experiment with beginning my sermon with creative imagery rather than with the exposition of the sermon text.

I learned that preaching in a way relevant to the congregants' lives did not mean doing what other Worldwide colleagues and I tended to do, of using examples from recent visits. This, I learned from bitter experience, was embarrassing to the people who recognized themselves in the anecdotes, even though I hadn't used their names. In the end, it created distance between pastor and congregant, precisely the opposite of what was intended.

When pastors went on vacation, they arranged for someone to conduct services in their absence and be available for funerals or other things that might come up. This would usually be a neighboring pastor (or retired pastor), sometimes an advanced theology student (as I had been when I filled in for two weeks in Rümlang). It was generally not done to have a vicar fill in, but since I was not a beginner, Caspers felt comfortable in having me cover for him while he was away on vacation for a week. During that time, there were two deaths in the congregation. One was an elderly man, the grandfather of one of the youths in the confirmation group. The other was more unusual. A youth tried to kill his girlfriend (she survived), then killed himself. The church was full, with many more young people than most funerals. I struggled to find words that acknowledged the wrong of what the young man had done and yet express my conviction that he was now in good hands. Caspers felt bad when he returned and learned what had happened, as if he had been negligent in being out of touch, but could comfort himself that I was experienced and hadn't been overwhelmed.

The church's training program, with its balance of work at the side of a pastor and ten week-long courses, was good. The program was well-structured, with courses that were relevant for our future responsibilities. Almost all the instruc-

tors were competent, some were excellent. The majority of
the courses were in one of two seminar campuses (*Bildung-
szentren*) that the Zurich church then maintained. One was
in the old monastery at Kappel, a few hundred yards from
the field where Zwingli fell in battle. When the Reformation
in Zurich began, Heinrich Bullinger, the eldest of five sons of
the parish priest in Bremgarten, taught Latin in the monastery; he smuggled in Zwingli's writings, where he cautiously
shared them with the rest of the community, with the result
that the monks there declared for the Reformation.

To the south, one looked past the town of Zug to an Alpine skyline. When we stayed there, I usually shared a room
across from the library. I often rose early to continue work
on my dissertation.

The other seminar campus was Boldern, built after
World War Two on a hillside above the town of Männedorf.
When we stayed there, I liked to be up early for breakfast and
take a seat facing the picture windows that offered a sweep-
ing panorama to the south of Lake Zurich and the mountains
beyond. It was clear why this side of the lake was called the
Gold Coast.

The first two course weeks were in Boldern, one in the
last week of November, and then, after spending the weekend home, the first week of December. We were a large
group, twenty-seven in all. I knew most of those who had
studied in Zurich, although I hadn't been close to more than
one or two of them. Most of the others had studied in Basel, so it was a first acquaintance. I was conscious of being
the oldest in the group, but there were two nearly my age;

that helped. The youngest, who'd gone straight from high school to university, then finished that in six years, was just a little older than our oldest boy. Some had converted from Roman Catholicism, while another had been a fundamentalist minister, a viewpoint he now rejected. More than one had already completed a doctorate. Thus, it was a diverse group to be a part of.

Nearly half the group was female. This was no surprise since the proportion of students at the theological seminar, as well as the friends I'd made among Reformed ministers, was roughly the same. Worldwide, like many fundamentalist groups, had excluded women from ministry. There are isolated verses ascribed to Paul to justify that stance. Still, I'd come to see those statements as the result of a process, understandable at the time, of reining in the role women had played in the early days of the church as worship moved from private homes to semipublic settings. The views ascribed to Paul (but which I'd come to doubt were his) reflected the general role of women in Roman society and not any God-ordained order. In the modern era, crucial impulses for women's emancipation—as well as ending the slave trade—had come from committed Christians.

One of the hallmarks of our vicariate group was that we made music at every opportunity, from our morning devotions to casual gatherings in the evening. One of our group, Martin, had financed his studies by working as a bar pianist. Another, Nicole, was an excellent vocalist. A third, Adrian, had experience with gospel groups, including as choir director. In addition to exploring the church's hymnal, we also went through two new songbooks Hans Strub gave us: *Rise Up*, designed for youth work, and *Thuma Mina*, an international ecumenical collection with an emphasis on spiritual songs from Africa, Latin America, and Asia. We worked our way through both of these collections.

I found the plenary sessions that week and in subsequent weeks somewhat long-winded, but there were small group sessions as well; this helped to break the ice as we got to know each other. They were also helpful for the more reticent among us, who often stayed quiet during the lively exchanges in the whole group. In small groups, however, and in one-on-one interactions, it was clear they had as much to say as those of us who were more voluble.

While in Boldern, I'd hoped to visit Fritz Stolz, suffering from a brain tumor, but when I called, his wife told me it was too late. It was no longer possible for him to speak to anyone. He died a few days later, so I returned to Männedorf yet again that month for his funeral.

After a weekend at home, we reassembled in Boldern in the first week of December for a course devoted to conducting worship. This was my first exposure to Frieder Furler, pastor of a nearby congregation, who gave some energetic input on dealing creatively with Biblical texts and sermon preparation. Daniel Schmid, a cantor whom I already knew from my courses for church musicians, gave sessions on the basics of working with hymns, and Ralph Kunz presented an introduction to the Reformed liturgy, centered on the various types of prayers in public worship and their role in shaping the worship service as a whole.

I enjoyed the course, but some of the others found it difficult to identify anything they could use in the services they conducted. None had conducted as many services as I had, and some none before beginning the vicariate. It's understandable that they wanted something more basic in helping them get started.

We returned to Boldern for a week and a half devoted to catechetic (religious instruction) right after New Year's. The instructors introduced us to basic elements of didactics, including assignment, planning, and design. To stimulate a variety of method, they led us in practical exercises in story-telling, working with pictures and film, and conducting classroom discussion. There was also reflection on the role of religious instruction in public schools.

This was all more basic than the course on worship, still, the response was varied. This was due, no doubt, to the heterogeneous nature of our group. Some had worked as schoolteachers before studying theology; others had minimal classroom experience. An additional factor, though, was that one instructor, in particular, presented in a lifeless way.

We didn't meet again as an entire group until May when we traveled to Geneva for a week devoted to ecclesiology. About half of the time was spent working on and presenting our projects for the church's future, especially in an increasingly urbanized world (church in the city). More memorable to me, however, were visits to the International Committee of the Red Cross (one of Switzerland's most remarkable contributions to the world) and to the World Council of Churches. This last visit was eye-opening. In common with other evangelical American Christians, Worldwide had looked askance at the ecumenical movement. The WCC seemed to us an embryonic super-church, paving the way for the False Prophet of the book of Revelation.

After years of hearing fundamentalist fears of the ecumenical movement as a sinister megalith, it was amusing to experience the reality. I wasn't the only one surprised to see that the Council occupied one floor of a modest office building that it shared with the Reformed World Council. Anything less like a super church was hard to imagine. Nor was there anything in the words Konrad Raiser, a German theologian nearing the end of his ten-year term as secretary-general, spoke to us that would nourish such speculation.

I especially profited from two courses aimed to equip us for counseling. For both of these, we met in half-groups; given the subject matter, the smaller group size was helpful. One of the courses, which met in Kappel, was an introduction to solution-focused brief therapy (SFBT). This had been developed in the U.S. and Verena Meier, our course leader, had introduced the method in Switzerland.

Traditional Worldwide counseling often centered on the minister, as counselor, defining problems and providing the answers. Over time, the limits of this approach became apparent, and some ministers pursued outside degrees in counseling to become trained in other models. One that was especially popular was the client-centered approach of Carl Rogers. However, few of us had any supervised clinical training in this or other methods; we learned by reading, by short courses, and trial-and-error.

The Rogers approach, based on non-directive, reflective listening and building rapport with the person counseled, was in many ways the opposite of Worldwide's traditional approach. I, like others, practiced an ad-hoc mixture of the two. Given our strict moral stance and focus on God's law, it was hard for us to consistently practice one of Rogers's central tenets, non-judgmental listening, to allow time to deeply explore issues.

In SFBT, the pendulum swings back to the counselor, who uses a fixed repertoire of questions to help the client identify difficulties they may be facing and picture positive outcomes. The focus is on the present and the future. The past interests the counselor only to the extent he or she must understand the client's concern accurately and express empathy.

A large part of our week was devoted to role-playing exercises, in which we would alternate roles of client and counselor. Meier filmed the exchanges so that we could discuss them as a group. Sometimes she took the role of counselor. In this role, she did an exercise with me that helped me make peace with myself. I lamented my inability to focus, to concentrate for long periods. My contact with scholars at the university (some of whom I suspected of suffering from attention-surfeit disorder) had made me more aware of this than I had been before. At this point, Meier introduced the technique of re-framing and asked me to picture a setting in which that trait could be beneficial. I immediately thought of a typical day in the pastorate. For example, on consecutive visits, I might go from the home of a grieving family to discuss the funeral to the home of a young family who wanted to have their newborn baptized. I'd also experienced back-to-back telephone calls from a couple planning to get married and a couple on the brink of divorce. Looked at in this way, the fact that it was easy to tear my attention from one thing to another was a plus.

The second course was a basic introduction to clinical psychology and its relation to pastoral counseling, which Franz Kronberger, an Austrian psychoanalyst, taught. It took place in Sornetan, in the Jura Mountains. In advance, we were asked to submit a write-up of an encounter that we'd found surprising or problematic. He used these as points of departure for leading us in discussions that explored our role in the counseling situation and our resources. As the week developed, in addition to working with concrete cases, we received helpful input on depression, religious mania, and the similarities and differences of pastoral counseling and psychotherapy.

Our group profited so much from his course that we petitioned A+W, the continuing education program, to book him for a course the following year that most of us then signed up for (Swiss ministers benefited from five to ten days of continuing education each year, in the first five years after ordination, an additional five days).

Another week we spent in Basel, lodged at Mission 21, just a few hundred yards from the *Spittler-Haus* where I had conducted services for ten years, which afforded me the chance to reflect on the proximity of the two buildings in contrast with the long internal journey that led from one to the other. The topic of that week, appropriately enough, was worldwide mission.

As the thirteen-month program neared its close, Hans Strub took each year's group to experience church in another nation and in other circumstances. This was often to visit churches in the Balkans, but there were four of us in our group with a connection to Prague. Two were Czech, another had spent a year at the theological faculty there as an exchange student, and I had participated in a conference the previous November at the Charles University. Prague offered a diverse church landscape. In addition to the majority Roman Catholic Church, there were two main Protestant groups, one of which traced its roots back to Jan Hus (one of my memories from the Prague conference was the celebration of the Lord's Supper we'd held in the church where Hus had preached). Still palpable were the tensions over processing the role of the church (and the theology faculty at the university) during the communist years, when some had accommodated and others supported the opposition. My recollection was vivid of Jan Palach, a student the same age as I who had set himself on fire in Wenceslas Square in 1969 to protest the crushing of the brief, hopeful Prague Spring by Warsaw Pact armies. One of the professors who welcomed us had performed Palach's funeral, with negative consequences for his own career.

So when Prague was suggested as our destination, I enthusiastically supported the idea, and became part of the group to plan the trip.

But my own participation was not to be. A few weeks earlier, we'd had a course week in Hasliberg, in the *Berner Oberland*. The course was devoted to cybernetics with presentations from Eva Renate Schmidt, a leading German expert on applying insights from management and conflict resolution to church and other non-profit contexts. On the afternoon of the second day, we had a presentation from a different perspective, a Swiss exponent of applying American models of church growth, such as those used by Rick Warren and Bill Hybels. For some of us, this was an unwelcome confrontation with a way of thinking we were putting behind us. The day ended with a presentation of the new assessment program for ministerial candidates, one that raised more questions in our minds than answers. I had been working hard and came to the course in need of a rest. That evening, I sat on a terrace in the Alpine summer evening with a glass of wine and my guitar, playing some favorite songs for colleagues. I couldn't remember the last time I'd felt so relaxed.

The following day, however, I woke up feeling shaky. My heart was racing. Like other times when I had experienced this, I'd shaken it off as a possible touch of the flu. At breakfast, though, one of the colleagues looked carefully at me and asked how I was doing. She said she didn't like how I looked and called over another colleague, who had training as a medical technician. He asked me some questions and advised I should be taken to the nearest hospital, in Interlaken. I tried to tough it out but grew worse during the day and finally conceded. It was evening by the time I arrived at the hospital. As I was wheeled in on a stretcher, I thought to myself, I know that I am mortal and will at some point die, but I don't think it will be here, and it won't be now.

I spent the next hours hooked up to a machine to record my heartbeat. The chief doctor became enthusiastic when he studied the first readout and called over an intern. "You have to see this," he said. "You can practice for many years and not get a clear graph of what this looks like." "This" was supra-ventricular tachycardia—a second, rapid heartbeat caused by blood re-entering the heart. After I stabilized, I was moved to a room, but the night was long. The patient in the bed next to mine was having a bad night, which reflected itself audibly and loudly. I felt sorry for him but also wished for peace and quiet. The following day I discovered that I had a lovely view of the Reichenbach waterfall across the valley in Meiringen, where Sherlock Holmes plunged to his death. Sometimes being wide-read and sensitive to literary allusions isn't helpful.

A carload of colleagues came to visit. I learned something that I could apply later in doing my own pastoral hospital rounds: I was delighted when they arrived but even happier when they left.

Someone called my wife, and she took the train to come to see me. Hans arranged for Martin, my roommate, to switch to another room so that Edel could stay in my room. I was released from the hospital the morning after. I visited the group to update them on my condition before Edel accompanied me home on the train.

I had to go for further testing to the cardiac section of the university hospital in Zurich, where the initial diagnosis was confirmed. I was told there was nothing that needed to be done immediately, but I could expect more frequent attacks as I grew older. But I was advised to rest for the next couple of weeks and avoid stress. That meant forgoing our group trip to Prague. I felt bad about that, but while the group was there, Eastern Europe experienced massive flooding. An adventure for the group, but precisely the kind of excitement I was to avoid in my recuperation.

I've only had one more severe episode since then, coincidentally, just before a trip to Eastern Europe. In the congregation I served after my vicariate, my colleague took each year's newly-confirmed young people to Hungary. Our departure was set for a Friday evening at the close of an intense week. Just down the hill from our church, a man had killed his wife and children, then taken his own life. The other children in the neighborhood were traumatized and I offered any parents who wanted to come meet me and a pastoral assistant from the Catholic congregation. I went directly from that meeting to catch the night train to Budapest. I was looking forward to this experience, but my heart began racing as soon as I took my seat. My colleague called her husband, who picked me up at the next station and took me home.

As the training period drew to a close, we had exams. One was the evaluation of a worship service. I was given three texts to choose from and had to submit a complete order of worship, including sermon, with theoretical reflection. An expert from the concordat commission attended the service and discussed it with me afterward.

The catechetical exam was similar. I had to submit a plan

for a series of five lessons, with a detailed plan of execution of the lesson that would be visited, together with methodological reflection. The class I was teaching was thirteen-year-olds. They were pupils who would end their obligatory schooling at sixteen and enter an apprenticeship in a manual trade. It was a heterogeneous group prone to mobbing; in general, an unruly group, but I was able to handle it. In the last lesson before my exam, I told them that experts would be in the next lesson, but they would be there to examine me, not them. They could behave normally. Instead, they were so well-behaved that it was difficult to coax anything out of them for the class discussion. Thankfully, the expert recognized what was happening and accounted for it.

The third exam during the year was a book report with reflection. We could choose a recent work from any of the four fundamental fields of pastoral activity; both vicariate mentor and vicar were to read it, then the vicar had to write a paper within three days of receiving four questions about it from the examiner. The essay should reflect on my experience based on the book. I chose Gerd Theissen's *Zeichensprache des Glaubens*, a book in the field of homiletics. Hans Caspers and I both placed emphasis on our preaching, but our two styles differed markedly. It was fruitful to explore our approaches in light of Theissen's book.

By the midway point in the year, one of the discussion topics during the breaks and at meal-times was the question of which congregation each of us would serve in. I was surprised how many had already applied for positions and had even accepted firm offers, so I began to send out my resume as well, roughly thirty in all. In most cases, I heard back quickly that I was not being considered. It is never enjoyable to be rejected, but I took it in stride, realizing that I had three strikes against me: I was an American, I had long experience in a fundamentalist church that many considered a sect (not unreasonably), and I had already celebrated my 54th birthday. When I received my letter and resume back from one congregation, my birth year was underlined in red. In the U.S., one doesn't divulge the year as a small measure against age discrimination, but this information was expected in Switzerland. To underline it in this way before sending it back, though, wasn't done, so I felt this gave me an excuse to telephone the church board president. He explained that the congregation had many young people, and they wanted a younger minister for the youth work. I considered whether it was my place to point out how mistaken that was but decided not. As it turned out, the congregation that I eventually served also had many young people (in most years, we confirmed between fifty and sixty youths), and I felt I did the best youth work of my career. There are inevitable mistakes when starting out in working with young people (or anyone else), and you learn as you go along. In addition, I was much too old to play at being a contemporary. In fact, by now, I was closer in age to their grandparents than their parents. The feedback I got from many parents was that their young people felt *gut aufgehoben* ("well-taken care of").

One of the other trainees in the group, Martin, with whom I often roomed during the course weeks, and who was a driving force in the music we made during our courses, was serving as vicar in Zurich's main church, the *Grossmünster*. One of the two pastors there was due to retire, freeing up a fifty per cent position, and the pastoral search committee found it hard to get a successor. They approached many pastors but had been refused. Martin suggested it might be a good fit for me since the retiring pastor had maintained close relations with the theology faculty (housed in a building on the church's southeast wall) and nurtured a cultural-historical tradition appropriate for the church. Martin suggested I look into it. I discussed it with Hans Caspers; he knew well the other colleague there, Käthi LaRoche, and urged me to speak to her. I made an appointment and went to see her in mid-March. At the time, they wanted someone who would fit the same profile as the pastor who was retiring, a scholar-pastor.

Käthi LaRoche expected there would not be many candidates. The church board didn't want someone starting out, whereas older pastors were concerned about what effect a fifty per cent position late in their career would have on their retirement plans. She said that others had already been to see her, to whom she had said, you're welcome to apply, but I'm not going to do anything for you. In my case, though, she felt there was a reasonable hope that I would fit the profile. When we next spoke, she told me that the search committee, having failed to find a suitable candidate, had asked her for a recommendation. At the end of our conversation, she said she could picture working with me. When she informed the church board, however, they decided to launch a new search.

Part of the self-understanding of the congregation was that it was the local parish of the old, established Zurich families. The idea of a non-Swiss interloper didn't appeal to them.

It all worked out for the best. The pastor who came to the *Grossmünster* instead reimagined the position in a good way, emphasizing the social role that the congregation could and should play in the new twenty-first century.

In fall 2002, the vicariate approached its end, and we began preparing for our ordination service. I was uneasy. The feeling grew in me throughout my time in Stadel that what I would be doing in the coming years was a continuation of the work I had done for the past twenty-five years since my ordination in Montreal in 1977.

I approached Hans Strub with my concerns, stressing that I didn't want to cause a commotion and would without question participate in the ceremony with the others. Still, I felt it would be wrong to accept a second ordination. I had stressed to Hans that I wasn't asking the Reformed Church to make a blanket decision recognizing all Worldwide ordinations. Its education standards and training weren't on the same level, to say nothing about its history of heterodox teachings and its past sectarian attitude toward other Christian fellowships. I asked only that a decision be made in my case, based on their knowledge of me.

Hans took the matter to Ruedi Reich, president of the Zurich church's executive council. He was reluctant to make an exception, but Hans reminded Ruedi of his efforts to promote ecumenism. Together, they hit on a solution. I would take my place in the service, at the beginning of which Reich announced that fourteen candidates were being ordained, another was having his ordination renewed and confirmed. I was delighted with the formulation, for that was precisely how I felt.

I also informed Joe Tkach, Jr., of the step I was taking but that I was not resigning from the ministry of Worldwide. He put the matter to Worldwide's board. Despite some strong opposition—apparently, no one had ever done that before— my request was approved, and I became dual-credentialed.

On Friday, November 15, we had our final colloquia at the church hall in Wollishofen, followed by a worship service in which we received our certificate of eligibility from the concordat, and finished with a meal, together with our partners, at the church hall.

Two days later, on Sunday, the ordination service for those of us whose home church was in the canton of Zurich took place in Effretikon. Thirteen of us—half the group— would be ordained along with two others whose credentials were accepted in a separate procedure. The other half of the group would be ordained in their respective cantonal churches, nine in all.

In planning the service, the group assigned roles to enable many of us to have a direct part, such as a scriptural reading or announcing the offering. The role they assigned me was celebratory and appropriate, given the significant role music had played whenever we were together. During the processional, we would walk in singing a song we'd learned from the *Thuma Mina* collection, "Siyahamb' ekukhanyen Kwen Khos," a Zulu song that means "come, let us walk in the light of God." The group asked me to lead the procession with my guitar. At many times in the past years, it had felt I was walking in darkness; but now, indeed, it was a moment of walking in the light. Whatever twists and turns life still had in store for me, this was a moment to savor—not only as the culmination of thirteen months of training, but of all the years as a child of God, walking along the road.

Coda

The ordination service marked the end of our vicariate. With only one exception, all those who sought a pastorate had found one. I was the exception, despite sending out thirty applications. Two congregations expressed interest, but in the end decided on someone else. I understood it; I was over fifty, not Swiss, and I had previously worked for a little-known church that many considered a sect. Yet could it be something more—a nudge to work full-time on finishing my dissertation? I decided it was. I made good progress, so when a congregation needed someone part-time to substitute for a sick colleague, I was happy to say yes. Coincidentally, this was in Effretikon, where our ordination service had been.

Before long, I also received a solid job offer. It was in Muri, across the Reuss river in the canton of Aargau. I would begin just after Easter, and work for fifty percent for the first two months, then full-time after we moved there. Just before beginning there, I submitted my dissertation and then successfully defended it on a sweltering Friday afternoon at the end of June; the same weekend, we moved from Dällikon to the parsonage in Muri.

It was the first defense under the new promotion regulations, therefore, the first open to the public. My wife noticed that one or two of my examiners seemed surprised at the turn-out. There were friends from the university, some Worldwide members, and some we'd already gotten to know in Muri, including the pastoral assistant of the Catholic congregation there. The mix reflected the complicated journey of my life.

The examination was a draining experience. When it was over, Jean Zumstein congratulated me by saying, "You are now a doctor of the church. The church has expectations."

It's satisfying to complete a dissertation and have it accepted. The down side is that, as soon as the first printed copies arrive from the publisher, one becomes painfully aware of how it could have been better. However, one does the best one can in the time available, publishes, and in this way contributes to an ongoing conversation.

It is now twenty-five years since I cut myself from the Worldwide payroll, more than twenty years after my last sermon at a Feast of Tabernacles. It has been a time during which I felt fully at home as a member and minister of the Reformed Church in Switzerland, yet there is a part of me nostalgic for what once was.

I'm not alone in this. I think anyone who was ever deeply involved with Worldwide finds that one never totally leaves the experience behind. For some, this is traumatic, either because of abuse they experienced or the self-reproach they now feel for having bought into it. Others persist in believing Worldwide was right, and have continued their allegiance in split-offs that claim to hold to Worldwide's traditional teachings. Some of my good friends have aligned with messianic Judaism.

While not fully free of the questions of how I could become hooked or why I maintained my commitment for more than twenty-five years in the face of repeated disconfirmation, I also maintain positive memories. Chief among them was life as part of a close-knit community of believers. Our shared insider experience—Sabbath, holy days, even the Dwight Armstrong hymns we sang—meant that we swam against the mainstream. As a result, our experience was similar to that of the first communities of Jesus-followers in the first and second century. Many brethren were the proverbial salt of the earth and we retain friendship with good people around the world to this day.

A question that some have is whether, after the death of Herbert Armstrong, Worldwide could have reformed its teachings and engaged in dialogue with the mainstream— similar to the way the Seventh Day Adventists and the Church of God, Seventh Day have done—while maintaining distinctive practices such Sabbath and Holy Day observance.

As attractive as the idea is, I don't think that the authoritarian culture of the church would have permitted it. Of course, we'll never know, since that is not the path that was taken. Perhaps it would have been possible, and perhaps it would have meant that many more than did could have continued to feel that Worldwide was their spiritual home.

Certainly Joe Tkach, Sr., did not have the temperament or the intellect to lead such a process. His son, Joe, Jr., was more qualified for the job, both on the basis of his skill set and the way he had supplemented his Imperial/Ambassador education by grad school and work experience off the payroll of Worldwide. One trait of his was both an asset and a flaw: He had a big heart and genuinely cared for others.

But many weren't ready to accord him even the modicum of respect they had shown his father. He and three other leaders—Mike Feazell, who had spent his adolescence in the Tkach home, Greg Albrecht, and Bernie Schnippert—were characterized by some opponents of the changes the Gang of Four. This phrase, one that Mao had popularized during China's Cultural Revolution, was not meant as a compliment, and knowing these men as I did, I felt it deeply unfair.

Worldwide needed to change both its teachings and the way it treated the members. Could it have achieved a more tolerant atmosphere with such a radical change in its teachings? I don't know. United started out trying to do that, but many of the pastors who switched their allegiance to it carried over the old Worldwide way of treating the members.

Classic Worldwide had been ahead of the curve in questioning the Lutheran interpretation of Paul's word that Christ was the "end" of the law, typically understood to mean "abolish". The Greek work *telos* can more naturally be taken to mean that Christ is the goal toward which the Torah pointed. Sadly, this still suggests a supercession (the teaching that the church has replaced Israel as the people of God), which is problematic enough, but at least doesn't portray the Torah as something destructive that needed to be done away with.

Despite the fragmented and diminished legacy of Herbert Armstrong and the Worldwide Church of God, it remains true that through it, many became Bible-literate and developed a relation with God. One cannot truly know the heart of another, but I remain convinced that many experienced a genuine conversion through the proclamation of Worldwide and continue to have a deep relationship with God. I treasure the years my time was scheduled around the pattern of weekly Sabbath and annual holy days. Doing is learning, and I developed a deeper understanding of the Jewish matrix in which the Christian movement arose than I would have had I not practiced these things.

My own mixed feelings about Herbert Armstrong are just one response out of many of those who lives were touched by him and his message. For some, he was an evil monster; they are sorry they ever heard his voice. In others, he inspires a reverence that, in some cases, seems to be fanatical worship, thirty-five years after his death.

These strong reactions correspond to the exalted claims he made for himself. He frequently quoted passages from Paul in which that apostle defends his authority and applied them to himself. Like Paul, this claim to apostleship included the demand that his followers imitate, submit to, and obey him (1 Cor. 11:1). Paul lived long ago, there is no way for us to assess whether such total surrender was an appropriate response. When Paul called for his converts to follow him, he added, "as I follow Christ." That is perhaps a helpful measure to assess Herbert Armstrong as well.

He was a not a theologian. Many of the core teachings that convinced me that Worldwide was the true church were teachings he'd found in the writings of others, particularly G. G. Rupert, who died in 1922. Instead, he was a popularizer, a gifted communicator. He was also an entrepreneur who created a three-pronged enterprise (church, college, media) out of nothing. At times, he seemed to have no resources other than the force of his personality and his limitless trust in God. Yet in other areas of his life, he fell far short of following Christ. Dealing with his legacy means also factoring in a treatment of his family that cannot be characterized as Christ-like. And the contrast between Paul's refusal to burden his converts by taking their financial support and Armstrong's own financial stewardship makes it seem to border on the cynical that he should invoke Paul as the template for his own ministry.

Herbert Armstrong preached quality and lived extravagance, thereby giving quality a bad name and leading his successors to accept shabbiness. He preached loyalty to the Bible and an uncompromising willingness to accept its message, but loved contention and sensation, leading his successors to practice fuzzy thinking about the Bible and theological issues.

If Armstrong had claimed a less-exalted status for himself, the standard by which we would be invited to judge him would be more humane, since all of us fall short of the glory of God. For my part, I readily acknowledge that his mistaken notion that one could "prove" the existence of God brought me back to a faith in God's existence that has deepened over fifty years into a living relationship. His controversialist pitch of Bible teachings at variance with common assumptions provoked me to begin reading for myself this collection of ancient texts that continues to fascinate me and reveal untold riches. His insistence of a lifestyle out of step with the broad mainstream at first led me to simply to transfer my conformist traits to another way of life, but eventually—slowly and painfully—gave me the strength to stand on my own convictions.

In sum, he was one of the most impressive characters I've known. Although I reject much of what he taught, his influence will remain part of me.

What was left of the Worldwide Church of God, now rebranded as Grace Communion International, seems to have stabilized to a viable denomination in the U. S., Canada, Great Britain, and some other areas. It has found its new home in the broader evangelical movement. I was not at home there.

When baptized by immersion, I was conscious of being called by God and having become part of a collective of believers, the body of Christ. At the time, I equated this with the Worldwide Church of God. An automobile accident less than a week later, which I survived through what seemed divine protection, was a strong confirmation of this.

When I was ordained, eight years later, it meant a further step of commitment. The need to honor a commitment had been drummed into me by my dad, who, like Issachar, one of the twelve sons of Jacob, crouched down between burdens. As I learned more of our family history, I realized that one reason this was important to him was the shame of his father's bankruptcy. Several generations earlier, in the seventeenth century, our direct ancestor was the bailiff in town. Among other things, he was responsible for the wooded areas. Like the fields the villagers worked, these belonged to the local nobility. Once, the nobleman learned that the trees had been cleared and summoned my ancestor to explain. The story as I had heard it growing up is that he had defended himself by saying that marauding Swedes had burned the village and the farmers had taken the lumber to rebuild their houses. He was nursing his wife, who was sick with the plague, and was unable to stop them.

These things may have happened, but when I read a chronicle of our village, I found an alternate account. At the time, Dutch merchants were expanding their reach and ravenous for wood to build the ships they needed to ply the seas. In addition, Amsterdam was rapidly growing. It was the financial center of the world, like London would become in the nineteenth century or New York in the twentieth. Houses in the newer neighborhoods needed wooden pilings driven into the swampy land. It seems my ancestor had made a quick buck, but was removed from the office of bailiff. This didn't affect him alone, for this duty was typically passed from generation to generation; now it was in the hands of another family. The lesson for us: it takes several generations to build trust, but only one sharp deal to destroy it.

The last treasurer of the Confederacy was a Clark from Georgia, appointed in the closing days of the war. He accompanied Jefferson Davis in his flight, carrying the treasury, in the form of gold, with him. When apprehended, not an ounce of it had gone missing. He wasn't close kin, but since we could only trace our Clark line as far back as when central Georgia was first taken from the Cherokees and settled by whites in the 1820s, it was impossible to say he was no kin. Nevertheless, I felt a kinship to this man who faithfully executed the trust placed in him, even in the service of a losing cause.

So, it's not surprising that, when Larry Salyer asked whether I couldn't see that Worldwide was falling apart I answered that if they needed someone to turn out the light after everyone had left, I'd be willing to do that, too.

But that's not how it turned out. It happened differently because I learned that the church—the body of Christ—to which I was committed was larger than Worldwide. Instead, it was worldwide in another sense. But commitment takes concrete form locally. The intervening years had brought me to the point where I saw that I could continue my service by working as a pastor for the Reformed church and stay true to my commitment.

Anyone who claims to have no regrets might be kidding himself. I made choices that, knowing what I do now, I would not make again. But it was making them and experiencing the consequences that formed what I know now. It's probably best not to try to get to the bottom of that conundrum. But I can say that it has been an interesting life.

In the aftermath of laying myself off, I felt as if I were groping toward understanding, made necessary by the changes in Worldwide's teaching and the related question of what I would do in the coming years. In those years, I was guided by a strong mental image: More than once, whether in Canada, New Jersey, or Europe, I'd come home late at night after my last visit for the day, and a heavy fog had gathered. Visibility was low, so poor that all I could do was limit my speed to always see the next white post with reflectors on the side of the road. It took concentration, and there was always a struggle to stay awake, but time after time, I'd experienced that sooner or later, I'd find myself in my driveway, in front of the garage door. That's what these years were like. I felt as if God hadn't revealed where I would end up. In fact, no more than the next white post at the side of the road. But that was enough to keep me going.

Postlude

I began to write the first volume of this trilogy, *Fooled into Thinking*, in 2013, when a grandchild was born. I imagined him at some point wondering why his Opa was once in a sect that lived in imminent expectation of the end of the world. And what if I were no longer around to explain? I wrote to make it plausible.

What in 2013 seemed absurd—that someone could believe in the end of the world—soon became once again plausible. Within a few years, words such as "apocalyptic" turned up in the headlines of serious newspapers.

A friend, Hans Strub, asked to see the manuscript of that book; his reaction was emphatic: I shouldn't just keep it for my family, but should publish it. It's above all due to his encouragement that I not only published that book, but have now written two more.

In addition to Hans, other first readers were my wife, Edel, and daughters, Kathryn, Sarah, and Deborah.

As with the previous books, I was gratified that so many

of those whom I contacted responded to my offer to see what I'd written about them. They include Dave Albert, Greg Albrecht, Michael Baumann, Jörg Büchli, Jeff Calkins, Emidio Campi, Olivier Carion, Hans Caspers, Carn Catherwood, Wayne and Doris Cole, Ingolf Dalferth, Randal Dick, Mike Feazell, Wade Fransson, Dexter Faulkner, Konrad Haldimann, John Karlson, John Kossey, Ralph Kunz, Tom Lapacka, Alois Mair, Hans-Ulrich and Doris Perels, Daria Pezzoli-Olgiati, Bill Rabey, Beat Schaefer, Peter Schwagmeier, Kyriakos Stavrinides, Wolfgang and Linda Thomsen, Joe Tkach, Hans Weder, Colin Wilkins, and Jean Zumstein.

Knowing all of these has enriched my life and words only inadequately express the gratitude I feel. A special word of thanks to a life-long friend, Michael Johnson, who performed the service of a perspicacious book editor.

Of course, neither he nor any of the others mentioned are responsible in the least for any remaining inaccuracies or infelicities of expression.

All scripture quotations, unless otherwise noted, are from the King James Version.

CPSIA information can be obtained
at www.ICGtesting.com
Printed in the USA
LVHW051756220322
714085LV00004B/645

9 783952 522738